JOHN KIRBY'S SUFFOLK:
HIS MAPS AND ROADBOOKS

Oil portrait of John Kirby by Thomas Gainsborough

JOHN KIRBY'S SUFFOLK: HIS MAPS AND ROADBOOKS

Introduced by
JOHN BLATCHLY
with contributions by JENNY JAMES

General Editor
DAVID DYMOND

The Boydell Press

Suffolk Records Society
VOLUME XLVII

A Suffolk Records Society publication
First published 2004
The Boydell Press, Woodbridge

ISBN 1 84383 051 5

Issued to subscribing members for the year 2003–2004

The Boydell Press is an imprint of Boydell & Brewer Ltd
PO Box 9, Woodbridge, Suffolk IP12 3DF, UK
and of Boydell & Brewer Inc.
668 Mt Hope Avenue, Rochester, NY 14620, USA
website: www.boydellandbrewer.com

A catalogue record for this book is available
from the British Library

This publication is printed on acid-free paper

Printed in Great Britain by
St Edmundsbury Press Ltd, Bury St Edmunds, Suffolk

Contents

Contents of the packet of maps

1–4   Suffolk, 1736, engraved by Richard Collins, black and white, originally one-inch to the mile, reduced to 56 per cent linear scale. Printed by John Bagnall for John Kirby.
By kind permission of the Syndics of Cambridge University Library.

5.   Suffolk, 1737, engraved by Isaac Basire, hand-coloured, originally half-inch to the mile, reduced to 51 per cent linear scale. Printed for and sold by I. [John] Shave, Bookseller, Ipswich [*c*.1766].
By kind permission of Mrs Charles Abel Smith.

6.   Suffolk, 1764, engraved by Andrew Baldrey, hand-coloured, originally quarter-inch to the mile, reduced to 84 per cent linear scale. Printed for John Shave and issued as the frontispiece to the second edition of *The Suffolk Traveller*.
By kind permission of A.T. Copsey, Esq.

7 and 8.   Four road maps, 1764, engraved by Andrew Baldrey, reproduced at original size. Printed for John Shave for insertion in the second edition of *The Suffolk Traveller*.
From the editor's collection.

9–12.   Suffolk, 1766, engraved by John Ryland, hand-coloured, originally one-inch to the mile, reduced to 45 per cent linear scale. This was printed from the original plates and hand coloured for sale by Stephen Piper of Ipswich in 1825.
From the editor's collection.

Illustrations and Tables

Frontispiece Oil portrait of John Kirby by Thomas Gainsborough.
By kind permission of the Fitzwilliam Museum, Cambridge.

Figures

Tables

Preface

The Society is publishing *John Kirby's Suffolk* to make more widely available four rare and little-known early large-scale maps of the county and four road maps. A facsimile of the scarce 1735 edition of *The Suffolk Traveller* is included because this is believed to be the first single county roadbook, and although later editions are better organised and more informative, there are many rewards from an adequately sceptical reading of this somewhat quaint piece of topography. Drawing on the arms, families and houses shown on the maps and named in the roadbooks, it has been possible to make select alphabetical lists of the great and the good of the county in the mid-1730s and 1760s in Appendices A and B respectively. John Kirby's claims to accuracy have been examined in some detail, and his other known surveys and those of his partners have been listed in Appendix F.

Jenny James has combed the maps for the features which are tabulated or listed with some explanation in Appendix D. Hers are the comments on changes to selected areas in east Suffolk since Kirby and the notes on Naunton Hall Farm in Appendix F. Hugh Moffat describes the ships shown sailing off the coast of Suffolk on all four maps in Appendix E. David Dymond has, as usual, been a meticulous general editor, bringing order and consistency where this was lacking. Dr Pat Murrell kindly lent transcripts of several illuminating newspaper advertisements and Edward Martin helped distinguish some of the antiquities which Kirby lumped under 'castles' and 'hills'. Raymond Frostick, a Norfolk enthusiast for early maps, helped with Norwich newspaper evidence, and John Millburn identified surveying instruments. Our President Norman Scarfe elucidated the strange 'Benhall Sr Roberts' at Friston and was, as always, enormously encouraging. Joan Corder and her dictionaries were the sources of heraldic information, and others are thanked by name in the map and illustration credits.
J.M.B.

Abbreviations

BL   British Library
CUL   Cambridge University Library
DNB   *Dictionary of National Biography*, in 2004 the *Oxford DNB*
NRO   Norfolk Record Office
SROB   Suffolk Record Office, Bury St Edmunds
SROI   Suffolk Record Office, Ipswich
SROL   Suffolk Record Office, Lowestoft

Glossary

chain	a measure of 22 yards, a tenth of a furlong *and* the device for measuring this distance which had one hundred links, each of 7.92 inches
compass rose	a circular design which indicates the cardinal points on a map
furlong	220 yards, an eighth of a mile
perambulator	a wheel of known diameter on a handle, with a device which counts the revolutions
surveyor's level	spirit level on a stand which is the base for a theodolite
theodolite	an instrument with optical sights and a scale so that the angle between two distant objects can be measured
triangulation	the method of using bearings and distances from three vantage points to check accuracy, and adding further triangles as necessary

Introduction

The earliest large-scale maps of Suffolk were the result of a survey of the whole county carried out by John Kirby and Nathaniel Bacon between 1732 and 1734. Though it is easy to point out inaccuracies, they are highly decorative and correct many of the errors common on earlier Suffolk maps in county atlases. They are also informative about the owners and occupiers of the larger estates at two dates thirty years apart. The one-inch maps were published in association with two editions of The Suffolk Traveller, *the first of which has often been described as the earliest single-county roadbook; indeed those who subscribed for the 1736 map received the 1735* Traveller *gratis.*

In 1972, for Volume XV of the Suffolk Records Society, our present co-ordinating editor David Dymond prepared an edition of Joseph Hodskinson's Map of the County of Suffolk, engraved and first published by William Faden in August 1783. Rare and valuable in the original, this map at a scale of one inch to a mile has always proved a most useful work of reference for those studying the county in the century before directories became fully informative. The 1972 facsimile was reduced to approximately three-quarters of an inch to a mile.[1]

   Hodskinson, however, was not the first in field, for John Kirby (1690–1753) spent the years 1732 to 1734 surveying the county for a map, also at one inch to a mile, which appeared in 1736, with a half-inch map following the next year. Before this flurry of activity, county maps for atlases had been copied more or less blatantly from those of Christopher Saxton, the last man to attempt anything like full surveys of individual counties.

The challenge to action from a Norfolk rival

It is likely that Kirby was spurred into action by the activities of James Corbridge, originally from Northumberland, who as early as December 1727 advertised his intention to survey the counties of Norfolk and Suffolk,[2] and in 1730 published a map of Norfolk.[3] In October 1731, Corbridge and his then partner Francis Emerton of Gillingham announced that they were surveying Suffolk in order to make 'a compleat map of the 2 counties together',[4] though, long before the Suffolk map was ready in December 1735, Emerton had for some reason decided to transfer his loyalty to Kirby. Corbridge claimed, without justification, that his maps were the result of new surveys, but the merest glance shows that they perpetuate the errors of earlier

---

[1]   Hodskinson's Map was republished by the Larks Press in 2003. The A4 map sections are at the original scale and Dr Dymond's introduction is slightly abbreviated.
[2]   *Norwich Mercury*, 2 Dec. 1727.
[3]   There is a copy of Corbridge's Norfolk map of 1730 in a later reprint (*c.*1785) at CUL Maps d.77.78.1. The NRO has some twenty surveys by Corbridge with dates between 1720 and the early 1730s. He was appointed assessor to an estate in 1738 (see Colman catalogue).
[4]   *Norwich Gazette*, 2 Oct. 1731.

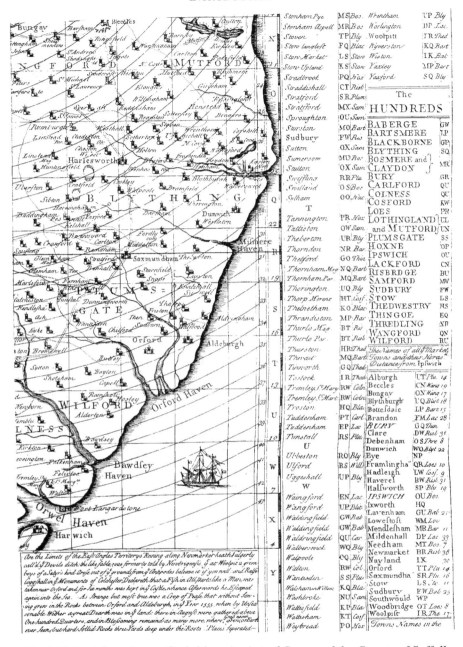

Fig. 1. Extract from James Corbridge: *An Actual Survey of the County of Suffolk, to which is added great part of the County of Norfolk*, 1735 (59% linear).

smaller-scale maps. The coastline of the Suffolk map is copied from Saxton and Speed, and many parishes are strangely named and oddly placed.[5] The clarity and decorative quality of the Corbridge maps is not improved by two sets of concentric circles drawn at three-mile intervals radiating from Bury St Edmunds and Norwich and by wide borders crammed with tables of place-names and the symbols needed to locate them.[6]

Kirby lost no time in responding to Corbridge's declared intention to survey Suffolk. In November 1731 the first of his many advertisements in the county newspapers promised his own survey of the county, and more followed the next year. At this stage Kirby was as anxious to recruit Norfolk subscribers in opposition to Corbridge as to arouse interest in Suffolk. He announced that he would be assisted by Nathaniel Bacon junior, little known apart from a handful of Suffolk estate maps dated between 1736 and 1744. The price was fixed at the outset and never varied. Progress on the map was slow, lasting from late 1731 to 1736, but, to keep his supporters enthusiastic, successive advertisements skilfully reveal new information piecemeal about the contents of the map and details of the survey methods to be employed.

[*Ipswich Journal* No. 587, 13 Nov. 1731 and *Norwich Mercury*, 22 Jan. 1732]
Proposals for surveying the county of Suffolk, by Nathaniel Bacon, jun. and John Kirby. In which map shall be described all the rivers (and where navigable) brooks, bridges, locks, &c., roads (and the true distance from town to town), the ground plots of all market and other considerable towns, parish churches, castles, demolished in whole or in part, monasteries, and other religious houses, and what order they formerly were of, the names of their founders, when founded, with their ancient revenues, division of hundreds, antient kings' seats, and fields of battle, the seats and parks of all the nobility and gentry residing in the said county, with their arms on the sides of the map, latitude and longitude,[7] with whatever else remarkable that may offer itself to view in surveying the same.

This map shall be protracted from a scale of one mile to an inch, and is proposed by subscription at ten shillings a map; the one half paid in hand, the other on delivery; they who subscribe for six shall have a seventh gratis.

[*Ipswich Journal* No. 598, 29 Jan. 1732; *cf. Norwich Mercury* 19, 26 Feb., 4 Mar. 1732]
Whereas Nathaniel Bacon, jun., and John Kirby did lately publicly advertise their design of taking an actual survey of the county of Suffolk; these are therefore to certify, that the said surveyors do design to begin the said survey . . . as soon as the roads are fit for perambulation to travel in, which will be March or April next at longest.

The authors plan to begin at Ipswich, and first to take a true and actual survey

---

[5] Craven Ord's copy of the Suffolk map is bound into Vol. 20 of his 24-volume 'Collections for the History of Suffolk' (SROI HD1538/20).

[6] As on all Suffolk maps before Kirby's, Corbridge showed Aldringham on the coast and Thorpe[ness] inland, but only he named where Seckford Hall stood 'Beckford', and sited a second Buxhall near Woolverstone. His Witnesham is Wittlesom, Bucklesham is Buckleston and Chelmondiston is Chatsham a/s Chelmodiston. The hundred 'Bartsmere' is his worst gaffe.

[7] This promise was hardly kept: just 'Latitude of' and 'Ipswich 52d. 14m.' is found at the extreme edges of the map. Reasonably accurate latitude and longitude could have been taken from Morden's map of the county. Basire did add them to his half-inch map of 1737 but the longitude was based on Ipswich.

of the said town, and from thence to proceed in a trigonometrical method to find the true bearings and distances of every parish church in the said county from the said town of Ipswich; the bearings and distances in the roads shall be taken with a perambulator; and in the said map shall be inserted the true distances not only between market towns, but all other towns of any traffic in the said county. The Rivers and Brooks shall be traced up to their Fountains Head, and the Coast from Harwich to Yarmouth; all woods that are remarkable shall be taken notice of; as also all Monasteries, Religious Houses, Gentlemen's Seats and Parks, antient Kings' Seats, &c. as before proposed. And the whole work shall be performed with that care and industry as shall render it useful, pleasing and intelligible, and so as to stand the Test of a Mathematical Demonstration.
[The *Norwich Mercury* version ends:]

Subscriptions are taken in and receipts given in Norwich by Mr William Chase; in Suffolk by the Revd Mr Christopher Eachard in Cransford, by Mr Hugh Wright in Ipswich, by Mr John Calver in Woodbridge, by Mr Henry Warner in Wickham-Market, by Mr Thomas Crispe in Saxmundham, by Mr Nicholas Newson in Framlingham, by Mr William Roberts in Aldeburgh, by Mr John Scoulding in Orford, by Mr Henry Searles in Yoxford, by Mr William Soans in Halesworth, by Mr Abraham Todd in Beccles, by Mr James Percivall in Bungay, by Mr Robert Money in Harleston, by Mr Benjamin Shuckforth in Diss, by Mr Daniel Meadows in Redgrave, by Mr William Butler in Buddesdale, by Mr Michael Barnes in Rickingale, by Mr John Mason in Euston, by Mr Hannibal Hall and Mr Thomas Baily in Bury St Edmund's, and by the Authors in their progress through the county.

Kirby had a network of innkeepers (where an inn is named), parsons and booksellers in the two counties acting as his agents while he and Bacon were peripatetic around the county.

A brief life of John Kirby[8]

John Kirby's origins are elusive. According to his grandson William the well-known entomologist, he was descended from a north-country Royalist who, his circumstances reduced by his loyalty, brought his family to Halesworth. The reference supports William Kirby's belief that his father William used the arms of the Lancashire Kirkbys of Kirby, a family with royalist leanings, mentioned in heraldic visitations.[9] The only John Kirby in the Halesworth registers was born to a local shoemaker, Stephen, in 1682 and died in 1736.

Apparently, John Kirby at first kept a school at Orford, but was certainly 'of Erwarton' occupying 'a small overshot mill at the bottom of the park [of the Hall]' when he married Alice Brown at St Nicholas church, Ipswich, on 10 October 1714. Moving to Wickham Market where John kept a mill, probably Glevering watermill,[10] Alice bore him five sons and six daughters all christened at Wickham Market or at

---

8 See also his entry in *Oxford DNB*, 2004.
9 F.R. Raines (ed.), *Visitation of Lancashire 1664–65*, Chetham Society 1872, ii, 169.
10 The watermill at Wickham Market appears on none of the Kirby maps whereas the one at Glevering is marked on all of them, nor is the former mentioned in either edition of *The Suffolk Traveller*. It may not have been built in Kirby's time. Mention in advertisements of his house in Wickham Market is puzzling, but from a distance Wickham Market would be a better postal address than Glevering.

Hacheston.[11] The best known are three of the four eldest: John (1715–50 s.p.), Under Treasurer at the Middle Temple; Joshua, artist and friend of Gainsborough (to whom John and Alice sat for separate portraits[12]); and William, attorney of Witnesham Hall. Family letters published by William's grand-daughter Sarah Trimmer demonstrate that John Kirby brought up the family to be devoutly God-fearing.

By 1725 Kirby was land surveying to support a growing family, and plans exist of estates in more than twenty east Suffolk parishes (and one west) with dates between then and 1745,[13] when he was also selling books at Wickham.[14] From the tower of the church there, those of 'very near, if not altogether 50 parish churches'[15] were visible, giving Kirby a head start in one part of his survey.

John Kirby is best known as author of the slim duodecimo roadbook *The Suffolk Traveller* of 1735. His careful manuscript draft of part of the work is at Ipswich.[16] John Tanner, vicar of Lowestoft from 1708 to his death in 1759 was the 'reverend gentleman' thanked for the forty-page table of parishes, patrons and impropriations at the end of book. However, it is Kirby's large-scale map of the county which ought to be celebrated, because when the book was ready in August 1735, at which time the plates of the map were 'very near engraved', an advertisement in the *Norwich Gazette* offered the book free to existing and new subscribers for the map.[17]

By 1751, the Kirbys had moved to Ipswich; John died on 13 December 1753 of 'a mortification of the leg which came on very suddenly' at William's Ipswich house, and was buried three days later in St Mary-le-Tower churchyard. His wife Alice survived until she was laid beside him on 30 October 1766, aged 80. Their table tomb has not survived churchyard reorganisation.

Changing loyalties

Returning to the autumn of 1733, between Kirby's August and October announcements, Nathaniel Bacon's name is significantly dropped, and the local agents listed have changed a good deal; there are many more innkeepers, perhaps recruited after lodging with them on the survey. In Corbridge's absence in Devon surveying an estate of the Hobart family there, 'that curious Surveyor Francis Emerton at Gillingham', near Beccles, deserted him for Kirby. Emerton gave up working on Corbridge's Suffolk map and, what is worse, gave Kirby the names and subscriptions of those who had ordered it from him. These subscribers would instead receive Kirby's map on payment of the difference between the two sums. It seems likely that, judging Kirby's work superior, he preferred to give his clients better value for money.

[*Ipswich Journal* No. 625, 5 Aug. 1732]
Whereas Nathaniel Bacon, jun. and John Kirby have formerly advertised their designs of taking a true and actual survey of the county of Suffolk, the proposals for doing thereof, and in what manner they proposed to do the same, need not be here mentioned, as being before made public in taverns and other public places.

[11] Registers of Wickham Market for 1733 and Hacheston 1715–29.
[12] Gainsborough's portraits of John and Alice Kirby are in the Fitzwilliam Museum at Cambridge.
[13] See Appendix F.
[14] The imprint in *The Psalm-Singers Devout Exercises*, London 1741, includes Kirby at Wickham Market as a stockist.
[15] *Suffolk Traveller*, 1735, 18.
[16] SROI HD376/1.
[17] *Norwich Gazette*, 30 Aug. 1735.

This is therefore to give notice, that the said surveyors have begun the said survey, and made a considerable progress in the same, having now surveyed the coast from Dunwich to Harwich, and up into the country, so as the Hundreds of Colneis, Wilford, Loes, Plomesgate and Carlford, are very nearly finished, with part of some other Hundreds, in respect of the true bearings and distances of the parish churches situate in the said Hundreds. The beginning of the said survey was on Tunstall-heath, by taking (on a plain parcel of land) a measured distance of fifty chains, or five furlongs, by help of which the true distance was found between Tunstall church and Wantisden church; and likewise between the said churches and that of Wickham-market, having thus completed a triangle by gaining all its sides and angles (which upon proof was true, according to the rules of geometry, having its three angles equal to 180 degrees), from thence the calculations have been carried on hitherto (and it may be said without boasting) with great exactness,[18] for as it is undeniably true that, if two or three lines concur in one point, the work cannot be erroneous, so in the perambulation that has been taken, the object for proof was Stoke wind-mill in Ipswich (being all that could be discerned of Ipswich town from off Rushmere steeple); then taking another perambulation from Baudsey through the Hundred of Wilford, Colnes and part of Samford, at Woolverston the angle was taken from Nacton to the said wind-mill at Stoke in Ipswich; also again at Freston another observation was made of the quantity of the angle from Nacton to the said wind-mill at Stoke in Ipswich; and by drawing two lines from Woolverston and Freston (according to the quantity of their respective angles observed from Nacton), they concurred in the point before assigned for the said wind-mill, so that, although we dare not say that it is mathematically true (for if so it must not vary the thousandth part of an inch), yet we dare take the liberty to say, it will stand the test of a mathematical demonstration, and be useful, pleasing, and intelligible. And as such an undertaking is too great and too expensive to be undertaken by private persons, without encouragement, it is hoped that, as several gentlemen have already subscribed, others will follow their examples, for the promoting so useful an undertaking. There shall be no more printed than are subscribed for, nor sold for any other or lower price.

[*Suffolk Mercury*, 29 Oct. 1733]
Proposals for surveying the county of Suffolk: By John Kirby [*only*]. [*Description and prices as in the advertisement of 1731.*] The author gives this publick notice, that such gentlemen as think fit to subscribe for their arms, may do it to the persons undernamed; the author defers the engraving of the plate for that reason, till the first day of next March.

Subscriptions with arms are taken in and receipts given, in Ipswich by Mr William Craighton, bookseller; in Bury St Edmunds by Mrs Mary Watson, bookseller; in Yarmouth by Mr Holliday, bookseller; in Lowestoft by Mr John Stannard at the Queen's Head; in Southwold by Mr Turner at the Swan; in Halesworth by Mr Palgrave at the Angel; at Harleston by Mrs Money at the Pye; in Bungay by Mr Percivall at the Tuns; at Scole-Inn by [*the proprietor*] Mr Harwin Martin;[19] in Sudbury by Mr Samuell Lawsell at the Crown; in

---

[18] Detailed comments on Kirby's accuracy appear below, page 231.
[19] Harwin Martin at Scole Inn commissioned from Joshua Kirby two drawings of his premises, giving prominence to the elaborate sign which stretched across the road. They were engraved by Joseph Wood. But see *Suffolk Traveller*, 1735, 53.

Lavenham by Mr Thomas Paulson; in Beccles by Mr Abraham Todd at the King's Head; by that curious surveyor Mr Francis Emerton of Gillingham (who has declined to the survey of the county of Suffolk and a delivered a list of his subscribers to me, with a valuable consideration for their subscription money), and by the author in his progress through the county, and at his house in Wickham Market.

The author does hereby oblige himself to deduct out of his subscription money the money that have been subscribed to Mr Francis Emerton. Dated from Haverhill, 22 Sept. 1733.

[*Ipswich Journal* No. 645, 23 Dec. 1733]
The survey of the county of Suffolk, as before proposed to be undertaken by Nathaniel Bacon and John Kirby, has been, and now is, attended on by the said John Kirby; the coast now being truly surveyed from Harwich to Yarmouth, and the river Waveney from Yarmouth to Diss in Norfolk. The authors hope it will not be unacceptable to the readers to give an account of the true horizontal distances of the several towns under-named, from the market cross of the town of Ipswich, viz. from the market cross in Ipswich the horizontal distance to Diss, 17m. 5f.; Eye, 15m. 3f.; Debenham, 10m. 6f.; Harleston, 22m. 1f.; Yarmouth, 43m. 7f.; Halesworth, 22m. 1f.; Framlingham, 13m. 1f.; Lowestoft, 38m. 2f.; Southwold, 27m. 2f.; Wickham-market, 10m. 3f.; Woodbridge, 7m.; Aldeburgh, 18m. 6f.; Orford, 15m. 4f.; Harwich, 9m. 3f.

Corbridge must have been devastated at Emerton's defection, but toiled on for two more years until in December 1735 he could announce that the maps of Norfolk and Suffolk were printed and ready to be delivered to subscribers at Norwich. He also promised a four-sheet map of Cambridgeshire which seems never to have material-ised.[20] Kirby, however, needed even longer to produce his map. Ever hopeful of solic-iting a few more subscriptions particularly from the gentry, he was prepared to set new deadlines for the receipt of gentlemen's arms.

[*Ipswich Gazette*, 12 and 19 Oct. 1734]
The survey of the county of Suffolk being now compleated by John Kirby, and a great Part thereof engraved by Mr Collins at Bury St Edmunds who proposes to have the plates compleated in January next. The county of Suffolk contains in circumference 196 miles, its greatest length from east to west is from Southwold to the county river in the fen country of Mildenhall and is 52 Miles; its greatest breadth south and north is from Landguard Fort to Harleston, and contains 28 miles; containing 1196 miles square, and 748160 acres. [*Prices and terms unchanged.*]

Subscriptions are taken in by Mr Craighton, bookseller, and Mr Bagnall, printer; in Bury St-Edmund's by Mr Collins, engraver, and Mr Watson, book-seller, and by the author in Wickham Market. Such gentlemen as please to have their arms, are desired to send them to any of the abovesaid persons truly blazon'd by the end of November next, otherwise they cannot be inserted.

[*Suffolk Mercury*, 14 Oct. 1734]
The survey of the county of Suffolk being now compleated by John Kirby, and engraving at Bury St Edmunds, will be ready for the press by February next.

---

[20] *Daily Gazetter*, 3 Dec. 1735.

[*County dimensions repeated, terms unchanged and final invitations to Gentlemen to have their Arms inserted.*]

In just under a year, the book's publication was announced in Ipswich and Norwich in late August, with yet another appeal for new subscribers to the four-sheet map. The book was offered gratis to all those who had ordered the map, and to those who now put their names down. There seems to have been no separate offer of the book for sale on its own. It was also too late to have one's arms engraved.

[*Ipswich Journal*, 23 Aug. 1735; *Norwich Gazette*, 30 Aug. 1735]
This day is publish'd in 8vo. *The Suffolk Traveller*: or, a journey through Suffolk. [*The descriptive material which follows is familiar.*]
     The books will be delivered to such gentlemen as have already subscribed to the map with all speed, and such other gentlemen as please to become subscribers may have these books sending their names and subscription money (which is 5s. down, and 5s. on delivery of the map) at the following places, Mr William Creighton bookseller, Mr Stephen Kirby at the Gryffin, both in Ipswich, Mr Watson bookseller, and Mr Richard Collins, ingraver, both in Bury, Mr John Gudgeon in Eye, Mr Hall in Debenham, Mr Francis Emerton at Gillingham, near Beccles, the printer J. Bagnall in Ipswich, and the author at his house in Wickham-Market.
N.B. The plates of the map are very near engraved, which when finished, shall be printed off without loss of time, and published with all expedition.

The first maps and roadbook published

When in 1736 the decorative and well-printed map eventually appeared it was worth the long wait. Kirby dedicated it to Charles Fitzroy, 2nd duke of Grafton, placing a full achievement of his impressive arms at its head. For this there will have been no charge, but more than one hundred members of the nobility, clergy and gentry paid the premium to see their arms engraved also. The engraver Richard Collins of Bury St Edmunds had used four copper plates 750 by 600mm. In 1747 he engraved Thomas Warren's plan of Bury, beautifully embellished with elevations of the principal buildings and arms of local worthies.[21] Complete copies of Kirby's maps are rare; of the one dated 1736 copies have been located only in the Map Rooms of the British Library and Cambridge University Library, both uncoloured save for washes along hundred boundaries.[22] The map is singularly free of explanations of the conventional signs, but mills, churches, houses, parks, woods and castles are easily recognised without them. Watermills appear as pierced and rayed black circles. There is a compass rose, and a delightfully decorative cartouche with John Kirby's name, the date, the engraver's name, 'According to Act of Parliament' and a scale of miles. Winged putti are busy with measuring instruments and a large globe. Otherwise the following notes suffice:

N.B. *This Character* [a church inverted] *denotes a Church or Chapel to be in ruins. This* [a house] *a Steeple in ruins. The Roads Survey'd are mark'd thus,* .... *Cross Roads not Survey'd thus,* ======

---

[21] A framed copy hangs on the staircase at SROB; BL Maps 5250(I).
[22] Suffolk 1736 by John Kirby: BL Maps K.Top 39.4, 11YAB and CUL bb.17.G.62.

Taken together, Kirby's map and book provide a selective directory of the nobility, gentry and clergy of the county. Much of the detailed information Kirby promised on the 1736 map had to be consigned to the book which has become rare, so that it is here reproduced in facsimile and, for the first time, given an index and tables of mills and other features of interest.

In 1737 a cheaper edition of the map appeared at half the scale; the heraldry, names of property owners and much other detail was omitted, and the engraver was Isaac Basire whose characteristic rococo shell cartouche contains all the titling and descriptive matter. The earliest copy of this map so far located was printed in the 1760s by John Shave, the Ipswich publisher of the second edition of the *Suffolk Traveller* in 1764, who added his imprint in the lower margin of the impressions he took for sale then.[23] Perhaps as a response to the Corbridge maps, which fit together in a way which makes some journeys between the counties plain, Basire's map has Norwich at the extreme northern edge and roads join that city to Thetford, Bury St Edmunds, Botesdale, Scole and Ipswich, Bungay, Beccles and Yarmouth.

Further plans unrealised

It is not generally realised that John Kirby began to plan a new edition of the *Traveller* as early as 1739. Indeed, according to his July advertisement that year, it should have appeared early in 1740. Failing that, there is no known reason why he did not complete the project before his death in 1753.

[*Ipswich Journal*, 14 July 1739]
John Kirby, the author of the map of Suffolk and *Suffolk Traveller*, published in the Year 1736, is obliged in gratitude to acknowledge the encouragement he received from the subscribers to that undertaking: which has emboldened him to publish a second edition of his *Suffolk Traveller*, with considerable additions and corrections. The book is designed to be put to the press before Christmas next; and it will be acknowledged as a great favour, if any gentleman will be pleased to give the author notice of any errors or omissions that they have observed in the first Impression, by letters directed to him at Wickham Market; which he desires may be left with Mr William Craighton, bookseller in Ipswich; or Mr Samuel Watson, bookseller in Bury St Edmunds.

[*Ipswich Journal*, 22 Sept. 1739]
[*As last with this additional note*:] *NB* His last map of Suffolk, (Price 2s) is sold by S. Watson at Bury, and W. Craighton at Ipswich.[24]

As well as advertising for improvements, John Kirby called on two expert antiquaries, Thomas Martin of Palgrave (d.1771) and the Revd John Tanner of Lowestoft (d.1759) to suggest amendments and additions to the first edition. It was during Kirby's lifetime that at least some of the material was added to an interleaved copy of the first edition,[25] but as it was not until the early 1760s that the Revd Richard Canning of

---

[23] Suffolk 1737 by John Kirby, republished in 1760s by John Shave of the Butter-Market, Ipswich: SROI MC4/14.

[24] It is the 1737 half-inch map which is offered for two shillings; by March 1750 the price was further reduced to 1s 6d.

[25] The annotated copy is now Bodley, Gough Adds Suff. 8vo 31. John Tanner's own interleaved copy containing most of the additions and corrections he contributed is in SROI HD1538/66. In just a year after

Ipswich began to incorporate them in the second edition of 1764, discussion of their nature will be found in the section after next.

[*Ipswich Journal*, 31 March 1750]
[*This advertisement offers the Basire half-inch map of 1737 cheaply.*]
Whereas there are a quantity of the lesser sort of maps of the county of Suffolk, taken from an accurate survey made by the Author John Kirby, undisposed of: Notice is hereby given, that the publick may be supplied with them by Joshua Kirby, painter in Ipswich, and Mr Tinney, print seller, in Fleetstreet, London at 1s 6d each, till all are sold.
NB. No more will be printed, unless by subscription.

Joshua and William Kirby continue their late father's work

Just as the first maps were preceded by the 1735 edition of *The Suffolk Traveller*, so the later ones came out shortly after the 1764 edition. In 1763, Joshua and William Kirby (John's second and third sons) advertised an octavo *Traveller*, with frontispiece map (4 miles to the inch) and four detailed road maps all prepared for the engraver by Andrew Baldrey, Joshua Kirby's partner in business as domestic and heraldic painters. The Kirbys made a special point of giving pride of place to their late father's name on the prospectus and title-page of the new edition, perhaps because in his lifetime he carried out more of the work of revision than is yet known. The first page of the bifolium prospectus[26] is reproduced in Fig. 2. That the Revd Richard Canning was the editor of the improved *Traveller* is only revealed in the account given of his life and work in John Nichols' *Illustrations of Literary History of the Eighteenth Century*. The subtitle of the section is 'The Editor of the second Edition of the Suffolk Traveller', and there is no reason to doubt Nichols' authority since Canning chose anonymity in five other publications, only putting his name to two sermons, and the *Traveller* was his last.[27] The book was published on 15 September 1764, price 5 shillings sewn in paper wrappers and 6 shillings bound. A plan of Ipswich, reduced from Ogilby (1674) and maps of separate hundreds which Baldrey had drawn for the new book exist only as originals in private possession. Useful additions to this edition were the lists of borough and county Members of Parliament and High Sheriffs. Shave offered copies of John Ogilby's nine-sheet map of Ipswich at the same time for just 4s 6d.[28]

Revisions between the first and second editions

The process of amending and supplementing the information in the 1735 edition probably began as soon as the first readers answered John Kirby's invitation in his preface. The appeal was repeated in the *Ipswich Journal* of July 1739, about which time John Kirby sent an interleaved copy of the book to his two principal helpers, John Tanner and Thomas Martin. Tanner, the natural administrator, gave accurate and precise information; Martin's style was more anecdotal.

---

his death it passed from Browne Willis to William Cole, both of whom added notes which do not appear in the 1764 edition. The book went from Cole, Ord and Phillipps to Lord Iveagh.
26 The only known copy was collected by Richard Gough in Bodley, Gough Gen. Top. 364 at fol. 750.
27 Nichols VI, 538–45 (1831) and see his entry in *Oxford DNB*, 2004.
28 Surveyed in 1674, published in 1698.

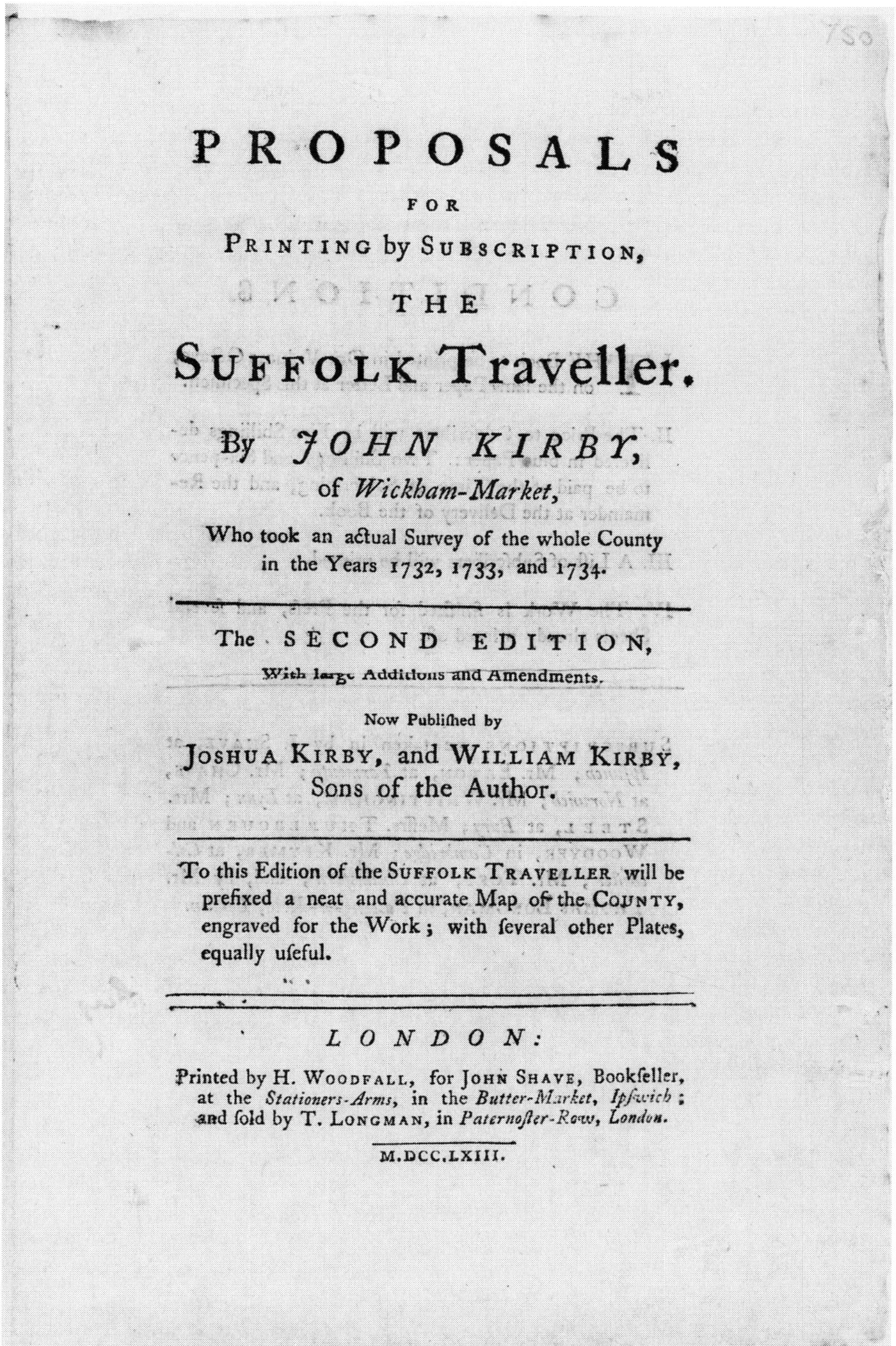

PROPOSALS

FOR

PRINTING by SUBSCRIPTION,

THE

SUFFOLK Traveller.

By *JOHN KIRBY*,

of *Wickham-Market*,

Who took an actual Survey of the whole County
in the Years 1732, 1733, and 1734.

The SECOND EDITION,

With large Additions and Amendments.

Now Published by

JOSHUA KIRBY, and WILLIAM KIRBY,

Sons of the Author.

To this Edition of the SUFFOLK TRAVELLER will be
prefixed a neat and accurate Map of the COUNTY,
engraved for the Work; with several other Plates,
equally useful.

LONDON:

Printed by H. WOODFALL, for JOHN SHAVE, Bookseller,
at the *Stationers-Arms*, in the *Butter-Market*, *Ipswich*;
and sold by T. LONGMAN, in *Paternoster-Row*, *London*.

M.DCC.LXIII.

Fig. 2. Prospectus for the second edition of *The Suffolk Traveller*, London, 1763.

John Kirby's frequent 'To whom it was granted at the Dissolution of that priory we find not', was just not good enough. Bishop Thomas Tanner's *Notitia Monastica*, first published in 1696, contained information of which Kirby was unaware. John Tanner, the bishop's younger brother made sure that all the monastic foundations in the county were correctly described (as abbey, priory or college) and that the date of their dissolution and names of new, mainly lay, proprietors were given. Tanner was also the first to quote Dugdale's *Monasticon*. Both antiquaries gave dates at which disused churches ceased to hold services. Tanner enthusiastically combed wills (most of them 'in the Beccles office') for bequests to church buildings, towers and porches, etc., and these details he gave at, for example, Woodbridge and Framlingham. He corrected an error of some twenty years in the date of the arrest of Thomas Bilney while preaching in St George's chapel, Ipswich (not in Mary's, but in her father's reign).

Tom Martin and John Kirby debated the non-existent silver crown of Mendlesham in time to take it out of the second edition. On page 31, Kirby gave 'In this Age some Persons in digging here, found an Antient Silver Crown weighing about 60 Ounces, which is thought to have belonged to Redwald, or some other King of the East Angles.' Thomas Martin corrected him: 'I think this was found at Rendlesham, not here' but Kirby only confused matters by adding his 'Answer: That was a Piece of Money according to this Author, not a Crown.' It was of course Bishop Gibson who, in his 1695 edition of Camden's *Britannia*, reported the find at Rendlesham in the 1660s; it was unfortunately sold and melted down before it was recorded. This is the story repeated in the second *Traveller* at page 105. If Kirby had used Camden, he misread the placename. It was also left to his helpers to add information from John Weever's *Antient Funerall Monuments*, 1631.

Both Martin and Tanner did much to improve the account of Bury St Edmunds, and the places near which they lived and worked: Botesdale, Bungay and Beccles, Lowestoft and the whole north-eastern part of the county. Kirby had taken very little trouble over Lothingland and Mutford. Tanner understood what was caught by the fishing vessels of the coastal towns, correcting 'herring' at Aldeburgh to 'sprats, soles and lobsters'. Unlike Kirby, Tanner and Martin had the status to penetrate the private chapels of large houses, such as Tendryng Hall. They also eliminated much of the faint praise which Kirby had lavished on such places as Haverhill, and, surprisingly, Wickham Market. On the other hand, they felt that Kirby praised some 'Houses of good Entertainment' too highly, particularly those at Botesdale, Halesworth and Scole.[29] Tanner pointed out that East Bergholt's church tower was unfinished rather than in ruins. No one spotted the error 'Barham' for Baron Pretyman at Bacton on page 109. Tanner wanted Covehithe called Northales, and improved such names as Ash-boken. Kirby, no stranger to the Shotley road, should have known Freston Tower, but did not mention it, leaving Martin to suggest that 'Freston is remarkable for a Sumptuous high tower near the River.' Tanner noted that the 'steeples of Alderton and Bawdsey made very good sea marks, but both greatly decayed'. Both men tried to demonstrate that Hartismere hundred had the best record for longevity of its inhabitants, citing a man dying at ninety-five, whose wife had borne him a daughter in her fifty-eighth year. Under the parish of Cotton the new edition has two similar stories. It was, however, Martin who provided the last and best anecdote about the Revd Richard Lovekin, for fifty-seven years rector of Ufford, said to have been 111 years old when he died in 1678, having preached the Sunday before his death.

---

29 The manuscript addition on page 53 contradicting 'Scole-Inn is a good House . . .' with 'a damned Lye' is in the hand of Charles Stisted, the Ipswich attorney who first owned the copy used to make the facsimile.

'This gentlemen was plundered in the grand Rebellion, and lost all his Goods except one Silver Spoon, which he hid in his Sleeve.' The 1764 edition, better organised and about half as long again as the first, has this story on page 116.

John Kirby acknowledged the help he found in Browne Willis's *Parochiale* when compiling the final table of parishes, church dedications, patrons and impropriations. Tanner stated the obvious when he urged Kirby to revise it completely for it was thirty years out of date. The new edition uses the table, stripped of Hundreds, Deaneries and Religious Houses to which livings belonged (two-hundred-year-old information), to provide an index of parishes and hamlets. Canning certainly accepted all the suggestions made by Tanner and Martin, as well he might. It was he, however, who quoted Dowsing's Journal in his edition, from the manuscript version of one of his St Lawrence parishioners, Edward Duck, brasier.[30] No printer is named on the second edition title-page, but as Henry Woodfall printed the prospectus, he probably took on the whole volume.

The one-inch map of 1766

[*Ipswich Journal*, 20 Oct. 1764]
The editors of the second edition of the large map of the county of Suffolk, request the favour of those gentlemen who have subscribed for their arms, and have not yet sent them to the agents of the editors, that they would send them truly blazon'd, within one month from the date of this paper, to Mr Shave, bookseller, in Ipswich, or the same cannot be inserted on the map.

Having published the new *Traveller*, Joshua and William Kirby, mainly as underwriters, turned their attention to a new edition of the one-inch map. The brothers still owned the original plate for the half-inch map and could reprint it without alteration. But the larger map presented two problems, one trivial and the other insurmountable. At some stage, to provide an armorial bookplate for one of the viscounts Hereford, a piece of copper measuring 3½ by 3 inches was cut from the north-east plate.[31] A fragment of the upper swirl on the 'V' of Viscount which appears below the motto scroll on the bookplate demonstrates its origin. None of the other arms have been found in similar use, so that four large copper plates were ruined by one thoughtless piece of cannibalism. A more serious problem for the Kirbys was that the copper plates had passed from Craighton to a rogue printer and bookseller, called Thomas Page, who enters the story twelve years later.

Meanwhile, a complete re-engraving of the map was essential and John Ryland was chosen to do this. Like their father, the brothers had to coax subscribers to order in advance and to pay extra for their arms to be displayed. There is no evidence that the second edition *Traveller* was offered free of charge to map subscribers. The new plates had all things decorative in the latest fashion. First of all, however, since no fresh survey was carried out and the accuracy of the 1736 map was accepted, Ryland pasted sheets of the first map on to the face of his copper plates so that he could score through the outline of the county, its rivers and roads without further trouble. Fresh titling was then added, and the names of the owners of arms and estates were revised. The 'Explanation' at bottom left makes explicit for the first time the symbols used on

---

[30] Trevor Cooper (ed.), *The Journal of William Dowsing*, Woodbridge 2001, 142–3.
[31] Price, 9th viscount, succeeded 1700, sold Christchurch at Ipswich in 1735, and died in 1740. Price, 10th viscount, died in 1748 and with the death in 1760 of Edward, 11th, the line ended.

Fig. 3. Armorial bookplate for Viscount Hereford, printed
from a copper cut from the Kirby map of 1736.

the earlier map, adding a black letter B for Boroughs and M and T in ligature for
Market Towns. The measured distance between two places is expressed by a figure in
a circle placed across the linking road. The example given was for Ipswich and Woodbridge: 7-5 in a circle indicating 7 miles and 5 furlongs.

The title of the map in the cartouche at top right reads:

1766 A New Map of the County of Suffolk;
Taken from the Original Map published by Mr John Kirby in 1736.
Who took an Actual & Accurate Survey of the whole County;
Now republish'd (with Corrections, & Additions) by Joshua & William
Kirby, sons of the Author, 1766;
And Engrav'd by Jno. Ryland.

Again, contemporary impressions of the new plates are exceedingly rare; just one
copy at the British Library is known.[32] There is approximately the same number of
coats of arms as on the first edition, but the landowners are those of a generation later,
and room was made for twelve views of antiquities, seven owing something to the
engravings of the brothers Buck (with a B below), and five others (K below) from
Joshua Kirby's own pen.

Suffolk antiquities depicted on the 1766 map
B Burgh Castle	K Butley Priory
B Mettingham Castle	B Wingfield Castle
B Framlingham Castle	K Covehith [*sic*] Church

[32] BL Maps K.Top.XXXIX.5 or Maps C.24.e.26; SROI S1/2/300/5.

B Orford Castle
K Bungay Castle
B Leiston Abbey

B The Gateway to Bury Abbey
K Blithburgh Priory
K St James's Church at Dunwich

These twelve views of antiquities in the county are reproduced on the jacket of this volume. The 1764 *Traveller*, its subscribers' list and the 1766 map provide the select directory to the county in the 1760s in Appendix B.

Joshua and William Kirby called 'Pirates'

Ten years after the new one-inch map was published, Thomas Page (born 1710), a ruthless operator on the fringes of the Ipswich book trade, advertised copies of the 1736 and 1737 Suffolk maps for sale. He began as journeyman to William Craighton who in 1738 bought John Bagnall's business, selling the bookbinding side to Page, on condition that he did not trade in books. Page did not keep to his side of the bargain, and in late 1750 he and Craighton conducted an acrimonious correspondence in the pages of the *Ipswich Journal*, of which the latter was the publisher. At some stage before 1776, Page either bought, was given, or misappropriated not only a considerable stock of the earlier maps, but also the original copper plates of the large-scale one. He could now, with some justification, refer to the Kirbys' 1766 map as 'a pirated or pretended survey'. After all, he was selling the original fruits of John Kirby's three-year survey.

[*Ipswich Journal*, 2 Mar. 1776]
The large set of maps of Kirby's actual and real survey of the county of Suffolk, printed off upon four sheets of imperial paper, from the finely engraved copper-plates, thereof, are sold by Tho. Page, bookseller and stationer in Ipswich.
The beauty and correctness, as well as the very small price of the above map, being only 10s a set, it is presumed will recommend it to the public in opposition to any pirated or pretended survey.
NB. Any bookseller or other persons in Suffolk, Essex, or Norfolk, desirous of vending the above map, may be supplied with sets, with proper allowance for their trouble, by applying to the said Thomas Page.
Also the above plates are to be disposed of.
Enquire further of the said Tho. Page.

One week later the Kirbys, through Shave, expressed their disapproval in dignified terms, stating that Basire's and Baldrey's maps were to be 'sold wholesale and retail by J. SHAVE, bookseller, and *by no other person in Ipswich*'. It is odd that they were not offering the 1766 map, for, even if they had exhausted the first printing, they presumably still had the plates. Perhaps they saw an advantage in offering maps at a fraction of the cost of Page's.

[*Ipswich Journal*, 7 Mar. 1776]
Mr Kirby's map of the county of Suffolk, taken from an actual survey, on one large sheet of imperial paper, and coloured, is sold wholesale and retail by J. Shave, bookseller, and by no other person in Ipswich, pr. 1s 6d and may be had of all the vendors of this paper; likewise the smaller map, price 6d only.[33]

---

[33] The maps here offered are Basire's engraving of 1737 for 1s 6d and Baldrey's frontispiece map to the second *Traveller* for 6d.

Of whom may be had, Mr Kirby's last edition of *The Suffolk Traveller*, price bound 6s a book, found truly useful for every person who is desirous of acquiring the knowledge of the history of this county; giving a large and full account of Ipswich, with its suburbs; the hundreds contained in the county, in their several orders, viz. Babergh, Blackbourn etc. . .; and from the above every village is taken in alphabetical order, and some account given of each. To render this work of general utility, to this edition is added four engraved plates, by which the traveller is directed by Plate I. from Stratford upon Stour to Yarmouth. Plate II. The road from Yarmouth thro' Beccles, Bungay &c. to Newmarket. Plate III. From Ipswich to Thetford, and from thence to Newmarket. Plate IV From Ipswich to Scole, and from Bury through Melford, Sudbury, Boxford and Hadleigh to Ipswich; with directions at large for travelling all the cross roads in the county. It likewise contains lists of the members of parliament. . . Alphabetical lists of the parishes in the county, and the patron of the livings, with their valuation, as they stand in the King's book.

Stephen Piper reprints the 1766 map in 1825

The hand-colouring of most extant copies of the 1766 map, including the one reproduced for this edition, was added in 1825, when Stephen Piper of Ipswich, claiming to have revised the plates, merely amended the fifth line of the title. He erased the words 'Joshua & William Kirby, sons of the Author, 1766' and substituted 'S Piper, Bookseller &c., Ipswich'. Piper was unconcerned that, by 1825, most of the owners of properties named on the map were long dead. Piper had obtained the 1766 plates from the estate of a fellow 'Yellow', Henry Seekamp, Whig leader of Ipswich in the early nineteenth century. Piper was completely open, however, about what he had done in the following advertisement. Prices had inflated a good deal since the map originally appeared, especially for the more elaborate.

[*Ipswich Journal*, 12 Nov. 1825]
This day Stephen Piper advertises this late impression from the 1766 plates which were until his death penes Henry Seekamp. Few impressions had been taken earlier. The whole map measures five by four feet, and includes 124 coats of arms and twelve views of antiquities in the county. Plain uncoloured sheets 15s.; coloured sheets 20s.; On rollers and canvas 30s.; ditto coloured 35s.; views and arms coloured £4; highly finished £6 6s. 0d.

Later editions of the Traveller

Two contemporary editions of *The Suffolk Traveller* claiming to be more up-to-date were printed at Woodbridge and sold by Smith and Jarrold, *c*.1817, and John Munro in 1829; the second is the more useful. Augustine Page's *Supplement to the Suffolk Traveller* (Ipswich 1844) has much information not found in earlier editions.

THE
SUFFOLK
TRAVELLER:
O R,
A Journey through *Suffolk*.

In which is inferted the true Diftance in the Roads, from *Ipfwich* to every
Market Town in *Suffolk*, and the fame
from *Bury St. Edmund's*. Likewife the
Diftance in the Roads from one Village
to another; with Notes of Direction for
Travellers, as what Churches and Gentlemen's Seats are paffed by, and on which
fide of the Road, and the diftance they
are at from either of the faid Towns.

With a Short Hiftorical Account of the Antiquities of every Market Town, Monafteries, Caftles, &c. that were in former
Times.

By JOHN KIRBY,
*Who took an Actual Survey of the whole County
in the Years* 1732, 1733 *and* 1734.

IPSWICH:
Printed by JOHN BAGNALL, M.DCC XXXV.

TO
The Right Honourable the
NOBILITY,
The Worſhipful
GENTRY,
And the Reverend
CLERGY
Of the County of *SUFFOLK*.

Right Honourable, Worſhipful and Reverend,

BY your Encouragement I have been enabled to make an *Actual Survey* of the County of *Suffolk*. At firſt I only propos'd to my ſelf (having taken the Horizontal Diſtances of the Pariſh Churches and other remarkable Places) to Survey the Roads of the moſt conſiderable Traffic iſſuing from *Ipſwich*, *Bury St. Edmund*'s and other conſideable Towns in the County, and to inſert the Diſtances in my MAP; with an Account of the Civil Government of each Town, the Fairs, Markets &c. But in my Travels many venerable Pieces of Antiquity offering themſelves to View, I thought

it

it would not be unacceptable to give a fhort Hiftorical Account of the Monafteries and Caftles that have been in the County, whofe Ruins ftill befpeak their former Grandeur. To all which I have added a fhort Account of your Seats, and from whom they defcended to you, according to the beft Accounts I could get. What Errors I may have committed in this or any other Matters, (which at the firft Effay were almoft unavoidable) I fhall be very ready to acknoweldge and correct in another Edition which I defign to make in a little Time, upon better Information; and I fhall acknowledge it as a great Favour, if any Gentleman will be pleafed to give me Notice of fuch Errors, and how they fhould be corrected, by Letters directed to me at *Wickham-Market*.

AND here I muft thankfully acknowledge, that being deftitute of that Learning that might qualify me for fuch a Work, I have been favoured by feveral Reverend and Learned Gentlemen, with fuch Materials as I could not my felf have found, befides the correcting my incoherent Copy; particularly to one Reverend Gentleman for the Alphabetical Table at the end of this Treatife; but I forbear to Name them, without leave, for fear of giving Offence.

Wickham-Market.
June 26. 1735.

I am, My Good Lords,
and Worthy Gentlemen,
Your moft obliged and obedient
Humble Servant,

JOHN KIRBY.

THE

S U F F O L K

Traveller, &c.

S UFFOLK is a Saxon Appellation, figni. fying the Southernfolk, with refpect to Norfolk, or theNorthernfolk. It is a Maritime County, being bounded on the Eaft with the Ocean, on the Weft with Cambridgefhire, on the South with the River Stour, dividing it from Effex; and on the North with the Little-Oufe, and Waveny, dividing it from Norfolk. Its length from Eaft to Weft is 52 Miles, its breath from South to North is 28 Miles; making the Circumference 196 Miles; containing therein 1169 Miles Square, or 748,160 Acres; being divided into 22 Hundreds, in which are 28 Market-Towns, the whole Number of Parifhes is 523, befides Hamlets, of which more at the End of this Treatife.

T H I S County is naturally divided into the Sandlands, the Woodlands, and the Fielding.

The Sandlands is that Tract which extends itfelf by the Sea Coaft, from Landguard-Fort to Yarmourh, and contains moft (if not all) of the Hundred of Colnes, part of the Hundreds of Carlford, Wilford, Lo:s, Plomet-

B gate

gate, Blything, Mutford, and Lothingland. This Part
may also be subdivided into the Marsh, Arable, and
Heathlands. The Marsh-land is naturally Fruithful,
fatting great Numbers of Oxen and Sheep; and some-
times when ploughed, affords the greatest Crops of Corn
of any other Land in this Country. That Part which
is Arable, is in some Places naturally good for Tillage,
and produces excellent Crops of all sorts of Corn; and
where it is in a manner Barren, it is found fit for Im-
provement by Chalk Rubbish, Clay, and a late dif-
covered Cragg, or Shell, thought (where it can be found)
preferable to the other two, and also Cheaper to come
at. So that many Hundreds of Acres of that Land which
formerly was counted of little Value, now produce good
Crops, to the no small Profit of the industrious Huf-
bandman.

The Heathy Part may contain about one-third of
the Sandlands, and is used for Sheep-walks.

The Woodland Part extends itself from the North-
East Corner of the Hundred of Blything, to the South-
West Corner of the County at Haverill; and includes
Part of the Hundreds of Carlford, Wilford, Loes, Plomefgate, Blything, Blackbourne, Thedwestry, and Thing-
goe; all the Hundreds of Risbridge, Babergh, Cosford,
Samford, Stow, Bosmere and Cleydon, Hartfmere,
Hoxne, Thredling, and Wangford. This Part is generally very Dirty and Fruitful. In this Part is made
the Suffolk Butter, so managed by the Neat Dairy-
Wife, that it is justly esteemed the pleasantest and best
in England. The Cheese, if right made, none much
better, and if not so, none can be worse.

The Fielding Part contains all the Hundred of
Lackford, and the remaining Parts of the Hundreds of
Blackbourne, Thedwestry, and Thingoe; and is most of
it Sheep-Walks, yet affords good Corn in divers Parts.

The Ecclesiastical Government is under the
Bishop of Norwich, it being Part of that See; for the
more convenient Government whereof, it is divided into
two Archdeaconarics, viz. Suffolk containing the Eastern
Parts of this County, and Sudbury including the Weft-
ern Parts. These two Archdeaconries are subdivided into

22 Deanaries. The Deanaries in the Archdeaconry of Suffolk are, Bofmere, Cleydon, Hoxne, Lothingland, Wilford, Loes, Carlford, Samford, Wangford, Dunwich, Orford, Southelmham, Gipwic, and Colnes. The Deanaries in the Archdeaconary of Sudbury are, Sudbury, Stow, Thingoe, Clare, Fordham, Hartfmere, Blackbourne and Thedweftry. The Towns and Parifhes in each Deanary, appear in the Table of the Names of the Towns and Villages at the End of this Treatife. There are moreover in the Archdeaconary of Sudbury 12 Parifhes in Cambridgefhire, whofe Names appear in the Map, viz. Afhly, Silverley, the Burwells, Cheevely, Chippenham, Fordham, Kirtling, Kennet, Snailwell, Soham, Woodditton, and New-Market-All-Saints, a Hamlet of Woodditton, they are Part of the Deanary of Fordham.

THE CIVIL Government of this County, is in the High Sheriff, for the Time being. The divifion of this County, in refpeēt of its Civil Government, was formerly divided into the Geldable, and the Liberties of St. Edmund, St. Etheldred, and St. Audry ; but the prefent Divifion, is into the Geldable and the Franchife or Liberty of St. Edmund, each of them furnifhes a diftinēt Grand Jury at the Affizes. What Part is in each Liberty appears at the End of this Treatife. Suffolk and Norfolk were formerly under the Government of one High-Sheriff, till the 17th Year of Queen Elizabeth, when Suffolk had a High Sheriff of its own, diftinēt from Norfolk, which was Robert Afhfield of Netherhall, Efq;

TOWARDS the MILITARY Defence of the Kingdom, this County furnifhes, as its Quota to the Militia, 4 Regiments of Foot, the White, the Red, the Yellow, and the Blew, each confifting of 6 Companies. The White is raifed in the South Part, the Red in the North about Hoxne Hundred, the Blue in the Eaft about Beccles, and the Yellow in the Weft about Clare. There is one Regiment of Horfe of four Troops, each feverally carrying the Colours of the Foot Regiments, and belonging to them, being raifed in the fame Parts of the Coun-

try

try. The Militia is under the Command of the Lord Lieutenant of the County, the Moſt Noble CHARLES Duke of GRAFTON, being the preſent Lord Lieutenant.

As to this Survey, the Author in making it firſt took the true Horizontal Diſtances of the Pariſh Churches, and other remarkable Places, at 250 Stations, from the tops of Steeples, the Country being Woody, or the Pariſh Churches moſtly ſituated in Vallies, which made the Task more tedious; having taken the Horizontal Diſtances of Places, his next Task was to take an Actual Survey of the Roads; which being effected, in the Map is inſerted the neareſt Diſtance that can be found between any two Places, and alſo the Travelling Diſtance; as for Example, from Ipſwich to Saxmundham, the true Horizontal Diſtance is 16 Miles and 4 Furlongs; the Travelling Diſtance exactly 20 Miles, and 10 of the reſt.

The Journal that was taken in the Survey of the Roads informs the Traveller of the Diſtances in the Roads, not only from one Market Town to another, but likewiſe from one Village to another, the Turnings to be avoided to the Right and Left, with other Notes of Direction, as what Churches and Gentlemens Seats are paſſed by, and on which ſide of the Road they are ſituate, with other Remarks touching the Ancient Eſtate of all Monaſteries, Caſtles, and other Pieces of Antiquity.

THE Roads do not follow in an Alphabetical Order; but Ipſwich is made the firſt Centre, and Bury St. Edmund's the next, and then other Towns as they follow; and the Roads are treated of, as they iſſue therefrom.

I KNOW of no Miſtakes, in either the Horizontal or Travelling Diſtances; but as nothing of this nature was ever yet performed with that Accuracy, but that ſome ſmall Slips might be obſerved by the Curious, this perhaps may be my Caſe; yet if the Map, and this ſmall Treatiſe be judged of with as much Candour and Impartiality, as the Author uſed Induſtry and Care, in compleating them, he doubts not but both will meet with Acceptance.

IPSWICH,

IPSWICH, formerly called GIPPESWIC, is a very large Town, and the Chief Town in the County. It lies on the North side of the River Orwell, which rises chiefly from two Springs, one in Rattlesden, and the other in Wetherden, though there are some other Springs which run into it, the most observable of which are described in the Map.

THIS Town was pillaged twice by the Danes in the space of 11 Years; and before that Time it had been a Corporation and Half-Hundred, and had divers Hamlets and eight Parishes, viz. Trinity, St. Mary, St Michael, St. Botolph, St Laurence, St. Peter, St. Stephen, the eighth by some mistake is omitted in the Book of Records from whence this Account is taken, but it may be supposed to be Osterbolt; for in the 21st of Edward the IIId. I find mention of a Tenement abutting on St. Clement's-street on the East, and upon the Empty Place call'd Shire House-Hill, and the Church-Yard of the antiquated Church of Osterbolt on the West; and in the 3d Year of the same King there is mention made of a Tenement in the Key Parish, which had Shire-House Hill on the North, and the Salt Water on the South; from whence may be collected that Shire-House-Hill was on the North of the Angel-Inn at the Key, and Osterbolt's Church-Yard above that. The Town had 48 Acres of Demesn, and paid 15 l. per Annum Fee-Farm Rent to the King. It was encompassed with a Rampart and Ditch, which the Danes demolished in the Year 991; but King John in the 5th Year of his Reign, ordered them to be re-built by the Aid of the Country, and of the County of Cambridge. When the Normans got Possession of this Kingdom, the Conqueror, to keep the People in Awe, built many Castles, and among them one at Ipswich, which Hugh Bigod, Earl of Norfolk, maintained against King Stephen, but was obliged to Surrender it. This Castle is so entirely demolished, that not the least Rubbish of it is to be found. It is by many supposed to have stood in or nigh Westerfield, but by others more probably on the North-west side of the Town, between Brook's-Hall and

and Dale-Hall, in a Place now commonly called Broom-Hills; but in the Memory of some now living, it was commonly called Caftle-Hills. There is frequent mention of Caftle-Hill in the Archives of the Town, in particular in the 21ft of Elizabeth, of a Difference with Mr. Withipol about nine Acres of Ground at Caftle-Hill.

IT is a very neat and well built Town, much larger than many Cities, and well filled with Gentry and other Inhabitants. It was formerly Famous for the Manufactures of Broad-Cloth, and the beft Canvas for Sail-Cloth, called Ipfwich Double; it has had feveral Companies of Traders incorporated by Charters, as Clothiers, Merchant-Taylors, Merchant-Adventurers, &c. It has a very Spacious Market Place, in the midft of which is a fair Crofs, in which is the Corn Market: Adjoyning to this is the Shambles or Butchery, which is very Commodious, commonly fuppofed to have been built by Cardinal Wolfey; but this I find to be a Miftake, for that it was built long fince, that is, towards the End of the Reign of Queen Elizabeth, for in her 40th Year, Nov. 16, there is an Order of Court for a Committee to build the Butchery, and to cut down and carry Timber for it from the Copyhold Eftate at Ulverftone. Behind this is the Herb Market. There is alfo a large Market for Butter, Poultry, and other Country Provifions, in a fpacious Street a little diftant from this; and another for Fifh, with which the Town is ferved in great Plenty. It has five Market Days Weekly, viz. Tuefdays and Thurfdays for fmall Meat, Wednefdays and Fridays for Fifh, and Saturday is the general Market Day for all forts of Provifions. It has five Fairs Yearly, one on St George's Day, April 23. one on St. James's Day, July 25. and one on Holy-Rood Day, Sept. 14. which is a very confiderable Fair for Butter and Cheefe, whither the whole Country round come to furnifh themfelves with Winter Stores, and many alfo of the London Traders in thofe Commodities, who are not fuffered to buy till the firft three Days are paft. The other two Fairs are for Cattle, the one on the 7th and 8th of May, the other on the 11th and 12th of Auguft. Thefe two Fairs were granted by the laft Charter of King Charles II.

IT

IT drives a confiderable Maritime Trade, but not fo great as formerly, it having been reduced in its Shipping by Shipwrecks and other Misfortunes, particularly by the lofs of the Cloth Trade, of which vaft quantities were fhipped off here for Foreign Parts. There have been fix Yards conftantly in ufe, where were built near 20 Ships every Year, and there have been feen in the Winter near 200 Sail of Ships belonging to the Town, many of them of 300 Tons, and none under 80.

THERE are at prefent in this Town but 12 Parifh Churches, St Mary Tower, St. Margaret, St. Laurence, St. Stephen, St. Nicholas, St. Peter, St. Mary Key, St. Clement, St. Helen, St. Mary-Stoke, St. Mary at Elms, and St. Matthew ; but there are evident Memoirs of four others, St Mildred, St. Auftin, St. George and St. Edmund Pountney; the former was where the Town-Hall now is, and is frequently mentitioned in the Records of the Town, and it was a Church fo lately as Speed's Survey. And that it was a Parifh Church appears from a Record in the 6th Year of Edward III. where there is mention of a Tenement in St. Mildred's Parifh, between a Tenement on the Weft and the Apple Market on the Eaft, one Head abutting on St. Mildred's Church on the South, and the Corn-hill on the North.

IN the Rolls of Court Pleas, 5th of Edward II. mention is made of a Tenement between Lofegate-way and St. Auftin's Church on the one Part, and the Salt Water on the other.

IN the 3d of Edward II. Electors were chofen out of the feveral Parifhes to choofe Portmen, viz. out of St. Margaret's 4. Tower 4. St. Matthew's and St. George's 3. St. Mary-Elms and St. Nicholas's 4; St. Peter's and St. Auftin's 4. Key and St. Clement's 4; St. Stephen's and Laurence's 4. St. Helen's being left out in this Election.

AND in the 4th of Richard II. there is a Roll of the lawful Men of full Age in the feveral Parifhes, where I find the Hamlet of Stoke was united to St. Auftin's ; for there we have in St. Margaret's 214. St. Hellen's 29. St. Clement's 137 Key 45. St. Peters's 103. Brooks Hamlet 7. Wicks-Bifhop 15 St George's 26. St. Auftin cum Stoke

Stoke 26. St. Nicholas's 136. St. Mary-Elms 56. St. Mary
Tower 147. St. Laurence 127. St. Matthew's 89. St.
Stephen's 31.

St. Auſtin's Church ſtood near St. Auſtin's Green, on
the other ſide of the River ; it is now a Barn or Stable,
at the Corner of the Road leading from the Bridge,
where it meets with that leading from the Dock, formerly called Loſegate way, in the Way to Bourn-Bridge.
This has been called Trinity Chapel ; but I cannot
find the leaſt mention of ſuch a Chapel, or any
marks of a Church elſewhere.

St. George's is ſtill almoſt entire in St. George's-Lane
in St. Matthew's Pariſh, to which it is now united, and
was a Chapel in Uſe in Queen Mary's Time, mentioned in Fox's Acts and Monuments. See his Account
of Bilney

St. Edmund-Pountney was lately almoſt entire, in a
Yard in Brook-ſtreet on the ſide of Roſemary-lane. I
find, in the 6th of Richard II, mention of a Tenement
between Brook-ſtreet on one ſide, and the Way under
the Friers Preachers Wall leading to the Key [now
called Foundation ſtreet] on the other, abutting South
on Robard's Tenement, and North on the Church-Yard
of St. Edmund-Pountney ; but I believe this was never
a Pariſh Church, becauſe I find, in the 26th of Edward I,
mention of John de Bergham Parſon of St. Edmund's Chapel in Ipſwich. I find likewiſe mention, in the 12th Year
of Edward III, of All-Saints Church and Hoſpital, which
Church, I ſuppoſe, is what in the 8th of Edward II is
called All-Saints Chapel, and indeed is ſaid to be in St.
Matthew's Pariſh.

But there are now two others in the Liberties of the
Corporation, Weſterfield and St. Thomas at Whitton,
now called Whitton-Chapel. Beſides theſe there were
ſeveral other Chapels, which are entirely demoliſhed,
as St. James's, ſome remains of which were lately to be
ſeen near the lower End of St. Clement's-ſtreet, between
the two Roads leading to the Heath ; St. Mary-Cald-
well, over-againſt Caldwell-Hall, now Cold-Hall, Famous for a Conſecrated Spring But the moſt celebrated
of all was that of our Lady of Grace, where was a
Shrine of the Bleſſed Virgin, Famous for the Miracles
performed

performed there, and on that Account vifited by Pil-
grims from all Countries ; it is mentioned in one of
the Homilies of our Church (againft the Peril of Ido-
latry, Part 3.) by the Name of our Lady of Ipfwich.
This ftood at the Northweft corner of Lady Lane, near
St. Matthew's Gate, over againft the George Inn. There
was alfo a miraculous Rood in Stoke Parifh, near the
Place now called Golden Rood Lane. Here were alfo
many other Religious Houfes, filled with Monks, and
Friers viz.

I. THE Priory of theHoly Trinity replete with black
Canons Auguftins, founded by Norman Gaftrode, the
Son of Edfiot, and John de Oxenford Bifhop of Norwich, in the Reign of Henry II. King John, in the
5th Year of his Reign, confirmed to them this Houfe,
with the feveral Lands, Churches, and other Poffeffions
given them by many Benefactors, and granted them a
Fair to laft for three Days, beginning on Holy Rood
Day, Sept. 14. But this Fair was fince granted to the
Town by the firft Charter of King Charles II, to be
held in fuch Place as they fhall appoint. This Houfe
was valued at its Diffolution at 88 l. 6 s. 9 d per Ann.
in the Kings Books. It was fince granted to Edmund
Withipol, Efq; by the Intereft of Philip Barnard, Efq;
of Rice Hall in Akenham, Efcheater to the King, a
Man of a vaft Eftate, faid to have been owner of moft
of the Lands between Woodbridge and Stow-Market,
whofe Daughter Mr. Withipol married, and built a
handfome Seat here, called Chrift-Church. It continued in the Family of the Withipols till the laft of
them, whofe Daughter was married to Leicefter Lord Vifcount Hereford, who left his Honour and Eftate to two
Sons by a fecond Wife, Leicefter and Edward, fucceffive-
ly. After them his Daughter, who married a private
Gentleman, enjoy'd the Eftate. This delightful Seat
has been lately purchafed by CLAUDE FONNEREAU, Efq;

II. THE Priory of St. Peter and St. Paul, a
Priory likewife of Black Canons, near St. Peter's
Church This Houfe was granted to Cardinal Wolfey ;
and here he built and plentifully endowed a College, as a Nurfery to his College at Oxford, then
called Cardinal Colledge ; but after it was feized by

C   the

the King it was called, as it is now, Chrift-Church College. The Gateway leading into this College at Ipfwich, is now ftanding entire with the King's Arms over it in the fame Manner as over White-Hall-Gate, which was likewife built by him. This is now a Gateway to a private Houfe built where the College ftood.

III. The White Friers Carmelites, founded by Lord Bardefly, Jeoffery Hadleigh, and Robert Norton Knt. This ftood where the County Goal lately was and the Seffions Houfe, which was a part of the old Building ; but that, and almoft all the reft, is now pulled down.

IV. The Grey Friers Minors, or Francifcans, founded by Lord Tiptoth. This was in the Parifh of St. Nicholas, near the Church by the fide of the Frefh River. Confiderable remains of it are yet to be feen

V. The Black Friers Preachers, founded by Henry de Manesby, Henry Redred, and Henry de Londham, was at its fuppreffion granted to Mr. John Southwell, the King's Chirurgeon, of whom the Town purchafed the greateft Part, where now Chrift's Hofpital, the Free-School and Library are ; and the Executors of Mr. Henry Tooly puichafed the reft, where now his Foundation for the Poor is, of which anon.

There is alfo mention in the 19th Year of Edward III of the Friers of St. James and St. Mary Magdalene, and of an Eftate that belonged to them.

There was befides thefe the Houfe of St. John Baptift, where now the Crofs-Keys Inn is. Likewife the Hofpital of St. Mary Magdalene over againft St. Helen's Church, frequently mentioned in the Records of the Town with that of St. James's. And in the firft Year of King John St. James's Fair was granted to the fick Houfe of St. Mary Magdalene.

There are remains of many other antient Buildings to be feen, but what they were is unknown. There is alfo frequent mention of St. Leonard's Hofpital, particularly in the 25th Year of Queen Elizabeth; and in her 41ft Year Mr. William Smart by his Will left a Benefaction to the Sick and Lazar Houfes of St. Leonard in Ipfwich and St. Thomas Apountney. I find alfo a

mention

mention of the Church of St. Petronilla, on the Heath towards Bixley.

Among the Persons of Note born, or inhabiting in this Town, Cardinal Wolsey must have the first Place; who was (according to common Tradition) a Butcher's Son of this Town. His most trusty Servant, who always attented him, even to the Hour of his Death, who wrote his Life, and must be supposed to have had as exact a knowledge of him as any Body, says, ' Truth it ' is, Cardinal Wolsey was an honest poor Man's Son of ' Ipswich in the County of Suffolk.' He rose to the highest Pitch of Honour and Grandeur, that it was possible for a Subject to attain to, and was suddenly stripped of all, being arrested for High Treason at his Archiepiscopal Palace at Cawood in Yorkshire, (he being Archbishop of that Province) and as he was carrying to London, he died at Leicester Abby, and was buried in St. Mary's Chapel belonging to the same : Thus fell the greatest Clergyman that ever England bred.

CHARLES BRANDON, Duke of Suffolk, who married the Queen Dowager of France, Sister to King Henry VIII, had a Mansion House here, now the Coach-House in Brooks-street. The Mansion-House of Sir Humphry Wingfield, Knight of the Garter, is in Tankard-street. There is still a beautiful Room, with a very fine Chimny-Piece, and a Ceiling wrought something after the manner of that in King Henry VII Chappel at Westminster, finely painted and gilded, and adorned with a great Number of Coats of Arms. This was a Popish Chapel, in King James IId's Time, when Sir Christopher Milton, one of the Judges, lived here ; it has been for some Years a Dancing-School. The Mansion sometime of Lord Curson, and after him of divers Knights of that Name, now commonly known by the Name of the King's Hospital, because in the Time of the Holland Wars, it was an Hospital for sick and wounded Seamen, since known by the Name of the Elephant-and-Castle, is remarkable for its stately Porch. It now belongs to the Bishop of Norwich, and is Lett upon Lease. The Archdeacon of Suffolk has also a very good House in Brook-street near St. Margaret's Gate,

built

built by Wm. Pekenham, Archdeacon, in the Time of
Henry VII. It is now Lett upon Leafe for three Lives.
Bifhop Wren had alfo a Manfion Houfe here, over-
againft the Sea-Horfe in St. Peter's ftreet. There are
many other good Houfes in this Town, of which the
moft confiderable are Chrift-Church abovementioned.
There is another good old Houfe belonging to Sir
John Barker, Bart. with others of private Gentlemen and Tradefmen. Here is a fair Town-Hall, with
a fpacious Council-Chamber, and large Rooms under
them, with Chimnies, Dreffers &c. fit for Cookery,
Paftry &c. on any publick Occafion. A Shire-Hall,
where the County Seffions are held for the Divifion
of Ipfwich. A large publick Library, where is a
good Collection of the Fathers, Schoolmen, Commen-
tators &c. This is adjoyning to a noble Hofpital
founded by the Town, and confirmed by a particular Charter of Queen Elizabeth, by the Name of
Chrift's Hofpital; the Governors of which are enabled
to hold any Lands and Tenements that fhall be given
them by any Benefactor to the Value of 200 l. per
Annum, any thing in the Statute of Mortmain to the
contrary notwithftanding. This is for the Maintenance of poor Children, old Perfons, thofe that are
diftracted; alfo Rogues, Vagabonds, and fturdy Beg-
gars, are to be kept to hard Labour here. Adjoyning
to this is alfo the Free School, confirmed alfo by
another particular Charter of Queen Elizabeth, with
a Sallary for the Mafter and Ufher, paid out of the
Fee-Farm Rents belonging to the Crown. Likewife
the noble Foundation of Mr. Henry Tooly, for poor
old Men and Women, confirmed alfo by another particular Charter of Queen-Mary, Anno Dom. 1556.

Ipswich was a Borough by Prefcription before
the Norman Conqueft. In the time of Edward the
Confeffor, it had 800 Burgeffes that paid Cuftom.
King William the Conqueror, to whom they paid
a Fee-Farm Rent of 37 l. per Annum, granted them
Free Markets upon their own Demefns, Cart Wm. 1.
c. 61. In the Time of Henry I it was fo much decay'd,
that in the Doomfday Book in the Exchequer, it is
related that there were but 110 Burgeffes, that bare
S cot

Scot and Lot, befides 100 of the poorer Sort, that were not able to give more than 1 d. to the King; and yet the Farm to the King was raifed again to 36 l. per Annum. This King granted to Allain of Britanny out of the Hamlet of Wicks 13 s. 4 d. to be paid by the Bailiffs of Ipfwich, which fhews that the Town was Governed by Bailiffs at that Time. In the Time of Henry II, there was no Market between this Town and Orford; but the Prior and Canons of Woodbridge moving for a Market, a Suit was commenced before the King, and on the 9th of October 1161 in the 8th Year of his Reign, it was Decreed that the Burgeffes of Ipfwich fhould have one Moiety of the faid Market, and that they fhould have their Servants in the faid Market, together with thofe of the Priory and Canons of Woodbridge to receive Toll, &c. and a Piece of Ground was granted to them in the faid Market 30 Foot long and 20 broad, to build a Houfe on for their Ufe, for which they were to pay 4 d. at St. Michael. Witnefs William Prior of Trimly, Thomas de Otley, Osbert de Baudrefey, Knt. Giles Ruffo, Arnulph Ruffo, John de Bennys, Jeofferey de Bennys, Bailiffs of Ipfwich. Many other Privileges were granted the Town in this Reign, which I muft pafs over. In fhort, their Power extends to all fuch Caufes, and Pleas within themfelves, as any Court in Hundred or County could take any Cognizance of Richard I confirmed the Liberties of this Town, but it coft them 6 Marks, befides 100 s. increafe in the Fee Farm Rents; towards the latter end of his Reign, he gave the Hamlet of Wicks to John Bifhop of Norwich, he paying to the Town 10 l. fo that ftill it remained Part of the Fee Farm.

THIS Town was new modelled by a Charter of King John, with larger Privileges, in the firft Year of his Reign, and it has had from feveral other Princes 17 Charters fince that; one from Henry III, one from Edward I, one from Edward II, one from Edward III, two from Richard II, one from Henry IV, one from Edward IV, one from Henry VII, two from Henry VIII, one from Edward VI, one from Queen Elizabeth, one

from

from James I, one from Charles I, reciting at large and confirming all the former, and two from Charles II.

It is now a Town Corporate, governed by two Bailiffs, a Recorder, 12 Portmen, whereof 4, besides the Bailiffs, are Justices of the Peace, two Coroners, 24 Common Council Men, who are also High-Constables, and 12 of them Headboroughs; and 15 Petty-Constables, one for each Parish, and the other 3 for the Hamlets of Brooks, Wicks-Ufford, and Wicks-Bishop.

This Town has many peculiar Customs and Privileges; I shall mention a few of each.

1. All Tenements in the Town are by a Gavelkind equally partable between the Heirs Male and Female, if not foreclosed by the Gift of their Ancestors.

2. The first Wife of any Peer or Commoner shall at her Husband Death have his chief Messuage in the said Town, to hold the same in Frank Bank, while she remains a Widow, without Waste or Alienation, in disheritance of her Husband's Heir; and besides shall be endowed with half the remainder. If her Husband had but one Messuage, she shall have that; but her Husband's Children must in that case be lodged with her.

3. Such Women as are not entituled to this Free Bank, shall remain in the chief Messuage 40 Days after the Death of their Husbands, in which Time their reasonable Dower shall be assigned them by their Husband's Heir, viz the half of all the Tenements and Rents in the Town.

4. The Widow of any Freeman shall be Free after her Husband's Death.

5. Any Minor, Male or Female, that can reckon an Accompt, (which is commonly done by measuring some Yards of Cloth, or telling 20 s.) may pass away an Estate at the Age of 14 Years. And they have many other peculiar Customs.

As to their Privileges: They send 2 Members to Parliament. The Bailiffs pass Fines and Recoveries, hear and determine Criminal Causes and Causes of Debt &c. arising in the Town, preferably to any of
his

his Majefty's Courts at Weftminfter, and to all other
Courts whatfoever, though they be Caufes that may
concern the Crown; and they fhall be allowed, fhew-
ing their Charter. They appoint the Affize of Bread,
Wine, Beer and other Provifions, by Weight and Mea-
fure. No Freeman can be obliged to ferve on Juries
out of the Town, nor to bear any Offices for the King,
without his Confent; yet many of them have been
made Sheriffs for the County. Nor are they obliged
to pay any Tolls or Duties in any other Parts of
the Kingdom. They have Caft the City of London
in a Tryal at Law, for Duties demanded by the
City of Freemen's Ships in the River Thames. They
are entituled to all Waifs and Strays, Goods of Felons,
Outlaws and Fugitives, and other Deodands, within
their Liberties; to all Flotfons and Jetfons, or Goods
loft at Sea and fwimming or caft on Shore within their
Admiralty Jurifdiction, which reaches to allPlaces where
the Sea flows, or in time to come fhall flow, from the
Town to the fartheft Point of Langarthfton, at a Place
called Lepoiles,Pollefhened, or Pollifhed in Alto Mari,
and to allPlaces within that, on the Coaft of Effex beyond
Harwich, and on the Suffolk Coaft on either fide; and
the Bailiffs hold their Admiralty Court on the faid
Point of Langarthfton, beyond Landguard Fort, fum-
moning a Jury or Inqueft of the Inhabitants on both fides.
And their Water Bailiff receives Money of all Ships for
Anchorage or taking up Ballaft within thefe Limits.
This Town is honoured in giving the Title of a
Vifcount, to his Grace CHARLES Duke of GRAFTON.

THUS much for Ipfwich, from whence we will
now fet out upon our Survey of the County.

THE Road from the Market Crofs in Ipfwich to
Yarmouth Bridge.

AT 5½ f. leave Ipfwich Town at St. Helen's Pound.
At 1 m. 3 f. the left goes into Ipfwich being the Coach
Road. At 2 m. 2 f. the left turns acute forward through
the Beacon Lane to Martlefham Lion; leaving the
Gallows a little on the right, and Rufhmer Church
about 2 f. on the left. At 3 m. 4 f. is Kefgrave Church
clofe

clofe on the right; here the right turns to Brightwell, the left to Playford. At 5 m. 6 f. the right turns acute backward to Landguard Fort by a Direction Poft, of which hereafter. Paffing along down a Hill paft Martlefham Lion, where the Beacon Lane comes in on the left, the right leades to Newbourn. At 6 m. is Martlefham-Bridge; keep the left hand way, paffing by Sackford Park leaving it and the Hall on the left. At 6 m. 6 f. Beggers Green, the left leads to Bealing mag. the left acute forward goes into Woodbridge by the Alms houfes. At 7 m. 3 f. enter Woodbridge Street at the Cherry Tree Inn. At 7 m. 5 f. is Woodbridge Crown Tavern.

WOODBRIDGE, a confiderable large Market Town, extending itfelf on the Road from North to South fomething above half a Mile, and near as much from Eaft to Weft. It is fituate near 11 m. from the Sea on the Weft fide of the River Deben, which is Navigable to the Town, where Ships of confiderable burthen come up to the Key to lade and unlade their Goods. It drives a confiderable Maritime Trade, having feveral Veffels imploy'd in the Newcaftle, Holland and London Trades; there are one, or more Paffage-Hoys that Weekly fet out for London on Thurf-days; and others return from thence Weekly. The Church and Steeple are noble Buildings, founded by John Lord Segrave, dedicated to the Bleffed Virgin Mary. On the South fide of the Church ftood the Priory, founded by Sir Hugh Roufe or Rufus, to which one Hanfard was a confiderable Benefactor, but of what Order I am not informed. It was valued at its Diffolution 50 l. 3 s. 5 d. ½. per Ann. It is a good old Seat, now the Eftate of Thomas Carthew of Benacre in this County, Efq; This Town has formerly traded confiderably in Sackcloth; and now is imploy'd in refining Salt. It has a tolerable Market weekly on Wednefdays, whither the Farmers in the Neighbourhood refort to fell their Corn, Cheefe, Butter &c. It has two Fairs yearly, the one on the 25th day of March, very confiderable for young Cattle, the other on the 21ft day of September. In the midft of the Market Place is a Handfome Pile of
Building

Building ferving for a Shire-Hall, where the Quarter Seffions are held for that Part of the County, under which is the Corn-Crofs. The Street called the Stone-ftreet is well built and paved; the Thorouhghfare is toleraly well built, but the Streets are dirty. The Market Place is well built and indifferently clean; the other Parts of the Town are meanly built The Keys and Warehoufes are very commodious. Here is a Grammar-Sehool, an Alms Houfe well endowed, and divers reputable Inns of good Entertainment.

HAVING given this fhort Account of Woodbridge, proceed we now on our Journey towards Yarmouth from the Crown Tavern in Woodbridge.

AT 3 f. is the end of Woodbridge-ftreet. At 1 m. 1 f. Melton Goal, the left turns acute backward to Grundisborow. At 1 m. 2 ½ f. Melton Village, the right leads over Wilfordbridge, of which hereafter. At 1 m. 4 f. the left acute forward goes to Bredfield. At 2 m. 1 f. the right leads to Ufford Church. At 2 m. 3 f. the right leads to Ufford Church, the left to Bredfield. At 2 m. 6 f. is Ufford Crown Inn on the right. At 2 m. 7 f. the right leads to Ufford Church, the left to Dallinghoe ; paffing along thro' Ufford Village up a Hill avoiding the firft left hand way leading to Petiftree Church, at 4 m. ½ f. is Jay's Corner, the right goes to Campfey Abby, the left to Dallinghoe. At 4 m. 6 f. is Wickham Crown Inn ; the left leads to Eye, of which hereafter.

WICKHAM-MARKET, fo called to diftinguifh it from the other two Wickhams in this County, viz. Wickham-Brook and Wickham-Skyth, is a Thoroughfare Town, extending itfelf on the Road about half a Mile. It has been a Market Town, but now not fo. The Quarter Seffions were held here, having had a Shire-Hall for that purpofe, and fome now living remember its being removed by the Lord of the Mannor, and a Farm Houfe built therewith at Letheringham, now called the Old-Hall. The Church and Spire Steeple are fituate on a Hill ; the top of the Steeple (tho' but 23 Yards high) affords the beft Profpect of any in the Country, in a clear Day there may be eafily

D   difcerned

difcerned from it very near (if not altogether) 50
Parifh Churches. It is now a Village of indifferent
Trade ; and Weekly on Saturdays there ftill appears
fome Foot-fteps of a Market. The Generals and Spiritual Courts are held here. Here are feveral Inns of
good Entertainment.

HAVING given this Account of Wickham, proceed
we now on our Journey towards Yarmouth.

FROM the Crown Inn in Wickham; At 2 ½ f. the
left turns to Eafton. At 4 ½ f. is Wickham Bridge, a
little further a Blackfmith's Shop clofe on the left, the
right leads to Campfey-Afh. At 5 ¾ f. the left to
Framlingham, of which hereafter ; here turn on the
right. At 1 m. is the 5 Crofs-ways, the right to Campfey-Afh, the right acute forwad to Aldeburgh (of which
hereafter) the left to Eafton. At 1 m. 3 f. the left
acute forward to Glemham mag. At 1 m. 7 f. a Blackfmith's Shop clofe on the right ; the right goes to Orford, the left to Framlingham ; paffing from hence over
the River Ore at Dymers Bridge, at 3 m. is Glemham
parva Village ; paffing from hence leaving the Park
and Mr North's fine Seat on the right, at 3 m. 5 ½ f
is the North View of the Hall. At 4 m. 6 f. Strat-.
ford St. Andrew's Church a little on the left, the left
to Glemham mag. here turn to the right over the
Bridge through Farnham Village. At 5 m. 1 f. the
left road forward ; goes to Sweffling ; here turn on the
right. At 5 m. 4 f. is Benhall Stockhoufe clofe on the
left, the left acute backwards leads to Sweffling. At
5 m. 5 f. the right to Aldeburgh. At 6 m. the
right acute backward to Langham-Bridge, here
turn to the left paft Benhall Dial Poft on the left, and
Benhall Green on the right. At 7 m. 5 f. is Saxmundham, a Blackfmith's Shop clofe on the right, the right
leads to Aldeburgh, of which hereafter.

SAXMUNDHAM, is a Thoroughfare Town, extending itfelf on the Road fomething more than 3 f.
It is indifferently built, but dirty, by reafon the Streets
are not paved. Its Church ftands a little Eaft of the
Town, and is not very beautiful. Here is a fmall Market

ket Weekly on Thurfdays, and a Fair Yearly on Af-
cenfion-Day. Here is a Seat which is now the Manfion Houfe of Charles Long, Efq.

LEAVING Saxmundham Blackfmith's Shop, at 2 f.
is the end of the Street; the left turns in at a Gate
towards Rendham. At 6 f. is the white Crofs, the right
goes to Knodifhall, the left to Carlton. At 1 m. 2 f.
Kelfale Village, the right goes to Middleton ; paffing
from hence leaving the Church a little on the right,
at 1 m. 5 ½ f. the left turns towards Sibton ; here turn
to the right. At 2 m. 6 f. Kelfale Lodge, the Seat of
Capt. Hobart, about 2 f. on the left. At 3 m. 6 f. the
left acute forward to Yoxford Church. At 3 m. 7 f. is
Yoxford Blackfmith's Shop clofe on the right.

YOXFORD, is a thoroughfare Village, the Road
lying through it from Saxmundham to Halefworth On
the North-fide of this Village is Cockfield-Hall, pleafantly fituate in a Valley by the fide of a Brook ; it
is now the Seat of Sir Charles Blois, Bart. Here are
feveral other good Houfes belonging to private Gentlemen and Tradefmen. In this Village are two good
Inns of Entertainment.

LEAVING the Blackfmith's Shop above-mentioned,
avoid going right forward to Middleton, but turning to the left over the Brook, come to a Direction
Poft ; here the Road right forward goes to Dunwich,
therefore turn on the left. At 1 m. 2 f. the right to
Darfham. At 3 m. is Thorington-Hall, a little on the
left ; the left here goes to Bramfield. At 3 m. 7 f.
the left turns to Wenhafton. At 4 m. 1 f. the right
goes to Dunwich, the left to Halefworth. At 5 m. 1 f,
the left goes acute backward to Wenhafton. At 5 m.
3 f. is Blithburgh Church clofe on the left. At 5 m.
4 ½ f. Blithburgh White-Hart Inn.

BLITHBURGH, is a Place of great Antiquity,
of which the Word Burgh, which fignifies a walled
Town or Caftle, is an Evidence ; but there are other
Things that confirm it, viz. That not many Years ago
there were Roman Urns dug up here among fome old
Buildings ; and that in the Saxon Times it was of Note,

D 2   appears

appears by its having the Gaol there for the Divifion of Beccles Befides it is Memorable for being the Burying Place of Anna King of the Eaft Angles, and Firminus his eldeft Son, flain in a pitched Battle near this Place, by Penda King of Mercia. It was alfo Memorable for a College of Black Canons, called Præ·monftratenfes, founded by King Henry I, which that Prince granted as a Cell to the Canons of St. Ofyth in Effex. Richard Beauvais, Bifhop of London, and after him King Richard I, were great Benefactors to this College. It was valued at its Diffolution at 48 l. 8 s 10 d. per Annum ; confiderable remains of this College now appear a little North-Eaft of the Church. Blithburgh Church is juftly efteemed a noble old Build-ing, and confidering its Bulk, the number of its Glafs Windows, and the fmall number of the Inhabitants, it is very commendable that it is in fo good Repair.

B L I T H B U R G H has been an ancient Market Town ; for we find that John de Clavering in the 17th Year of King John's Reign, obtained that King's Char-ter, for a Market Weekly on Mondays, to be held at this Town (being then his Manour) and two Fairs Yearly, the one on the Annunciation of the Bleffed Virgin Mary, March 25, and the other on the Eve and Day of her Nativity, Sept. 8. How long this Market and laft Fair have been difufed it not known ; the former only is now held in this Town. It is now a mean Village ; yet the Generals and Ecclefiaftical Courts are held here. Here are two Inns of good Entertainment. Thus much for Blithburgh.

F R O M the White-Hart Inn laft mentioned, paffing over the River Blith, at 3 ½ f is Bulchamp, a Hamlet of Blithburgh ; here the right goes to Wangford, of which hereafter. At 6 f. the left goes to Halef-worth, the right to Southwould, paffing by Henham-Park. At 1 m. 6 f. is a View of Henham Hall, leav-ing it on the right 2 f. At 2 m. 5 f. the right leads to Southwould, the left to Halfeworth. Paffing by Sotherton Crofs-bow, at 2 m. 6 f. crofs the River Wang. At 2 m. 7 f. the right leads to Uggefhail Hills, leaving a Blackfmith's Ship clofe on the left, and a little fur-ther a Windmill on the right. At 4 m. 1 ½ f. is Bramp-

ton

ton Church clofe on the right. Here the right forward goes thro' Wefthall to Halfeworth, of which hereafter. Here turn to the right; at 4 m. 4 ½ f. the right
to Stoven. At 5 m. 1 ½ f. the right acute backward to
Stoven. At 5 m. 4 ½ f. is Shaddingfield Church, clofe on
the right. At 6 m. 3 f. is Shaddingfield Blackfmith's
Shop, clofe on the right, and a Stone Dial clofe on the left.
At 7 m. 3 f. the white Bench and Mr. Leman's Manfion a
little on the left. At 7 m. 5 f. Wefton Church a little
on the right. The right here goes towards Henftead.
Leaving Wefton Houfe clofe on the left. At 8 m. 5 f.
the left turns acute backward to Halfeworth. At
9 m. 4 ½ f. enter Beccles Street. At 9 m. 6 f. is Beccles
Church.

BECCLES, is a large well built Town, fituate on
the Eaft fide of the River Waveny, which is Navigable for Barges from Yarmouth beyond this Town to
Bungay. The Streets are generally well paved, and
kept very clean. The Church, and the Steeple which
ftands at fome diftance from the South-eaft corner of
the Chancel, are noble Buildings, and are great Ornaments to the Town. The Ruins of Ingate Church
appear on the South-eaft Parts of the Town, and was
formerly Parochial to the greateft Part of the Town,
but is now in a manner (if not altogether) fwallowed up in the Name of Beccles.

IN this Town is a large Common upwards of 1000
Acres incorporated, for the ufe and benefit of the Inhabitants, governed by a Portreeve, Twelve and
Twenty-four, who are his Affiftants. The Portreeve
is yearly chofen out of the Twelve.

IT has a plentiful Market weekly on Saturdays, and
three Fairs yearly, the firft on Afcenfion Day, the fecond on the 29th Day of June, and the third on the
21ft Day of September.

THE Quarter Seffions of the Peace, are held here
for this Part of the County. Here is a Grammar and
Englifh School well endowed.

THREE Forelongs from Beccles Church is Beccles
Bridge, where enter Norfolk. At 1 m. 1 f Gilling-
ham Village, the left forward goes thro' Loddon to
Norwich

Norwich; take the right hand way at 1 m. 3 $\frac{1}{2}$ f. Gill-ingham Hall clofe on the right. Here the left turns acute backward to Earfham Park. At 1 m. 5. the left leades to Raveningham. At 2 m. 3 f. the right goes to Aldeby; here turn on the left over a Common. At 3 m. 4 f. the right goes to Whitacre, the left to Lod-don. At 3 m. 7 f. a Pound clofe on the left. Pafs along from hence and avoid feveral turnings to the right and left. At 5 m. 1 f. Hadfcoe Church clofe on the left. At 5 m. 5 f. enter Hadfcoe Village, the left turns towards Norwich; now paffing over Had-fcoe Damm, at 7 m. 2 $\frac{1}{2}$ f. re-enter Suffolk at St. Olaves (commonly called St. Tooley's) Bridge. A little fur-ther on the left the Ruins of St. Olaves offer them-felves to our View. This was a Religious Houfe of Canons Regular of St. Auftin, dedicated to the Honour of St. Ol-ave, founded by Robert Fitz Osbert, valued at its Dif-folution at 49 l. 11 s. 7 d. per Annum, and is now the Eftate of Sir Edmund Bacon, Bart.

PASSING from hence over a Brook, leave the Decoys on the right, at 8 m. the right goes to Hering-fleet, the left to Belton. At 8 m. 2 f. the right forward goes to Fritton Church, therefore turn on the left in at a Gate. At 10 m. the right leads to Loweftoft, the left to Belton. At 10 m. 4 f. the left turns to Belton Church, leaving it on the left near 3 f. At 11 m. the right turns to Somerleiton. At 11 m. 2 f. Bradwell Windmill, clofe on the left. At 11 m. 7 $\frac{1}{2}$ f. the right goes crofs the Fields into Gorlefton Street. At 12 m. 4 $\frac{1}{2}$ f. the left turns acute backward to Burgh-Caftle, which let us go out of our Way to take a View of,

BURGH-CASTLE, or Cnobersburge, lies about three Miles Weft of Gorlefton, and was a Place of con-fiderable Account in the Time of the Romans, as may be conjectured by the Roman Coins often found with-in the Walls. The Walls are now ftanding on the Eaft-North and South Sides. It was in the Form of a Parallelogram, the length of the Walls on the Eaft-fide is 220 Paces, its breadth 120; the Entrance was on the Eaft-fide. It is probable it was never Walled on the Weft-fide, the River being a fufficient Defence. The

The Walls are now ftanding pretty entire; a little North of the Caftle appear the Ruins of a Monaftery built by Furfeus a Scotchman in the Time of King Sigebert, about the Year 636; the faid King himfelf for fometime led a Monaftick Life here, till being perfwaded to fhew himfelf at the Head of his Army, he unwillingly comply'd, but Marching to engage, Penda the Mercian, was cut off. The Rectory Houfe now ftands where this Monaftery was.

THUS much for Burgh-Caftle. Return we now to the laft mentioned Turning. Paffing through fome Part of Gorlefton Street, at 13 m. 1 f. the right turns acute backward through Gorlefton to Loeweftoft, of which anon. Paffing along by the fide of the River at 14 m. 3 f. come to Yarmouth Bridge.

From Ipfwich to Woodbridge ————	7 m.	5 f.
From Woodbridge to Wickham Market	4 m.	6 f.
From Wickham to Saxmundham ———	7 m.	5 f.
From Saxmundham to Yoxford ————	3 m.	7 f.
From Yoxford to Blithburgh ————	5 m.	4 ½ f.
From Blithburgh to Beccles ————	9 m.	6 f.
From Beccles to Yarmouth ————	14 m.	3 f.
From Ipfwich to Yarmouth ———	53 m.	4 ½ f.

YARMOUTH, is a Town in Norfolk, built upon a little Tongue or flip of Land between the River and the Sea. The River Yare wafhes the Weft-fide thereof, making the beft Key in England. It is a very neat well built Town, and well filled with Gentry and other Inhabitants. It drives a confiderable Maritime Trade to divers Parts. It is ufual to fee in the Winter Seafon 200 Sail of Ships unrigged and laid up in the River, the chief Part of which belong to the Town. There is in this Town but one Parifh Church, but that a noble Structure, and is a good Ornament to the Town. It was built by Herbert Bifhop of Norwich. But here is a Chapel of Eafe to the Parifh Church, a curious Piece of Architecture, lately built. This Town drives alfo a confiderable Trade in exporting Herrings, Malt &c. It is a Town Corporate; governed by a Mayor, Recorder, and Steward. The

Mayor

Mayor is yearly elected out of 18 Aldermen, on the the 29th of Auguſt, by an Inqueſt of 12 Perſons, who are choſen out of 36 Common-Council-Men, they are ſhut up cloſe in a Room without either Meat, Drink, Fire or Candle, till there be a Majority. It enjoys divers Privilege, ſends two Members to Parliament; and was Honoured in giving the Title of an Earl to the Right Honourable WILLIAM PASTON Earl of Yarmouth, now Extinct. It has a conſiderable Market weekly on Saturdays, well ſerved with all manner of Proviſions; here is but one Fair in the Year, and that is held on the Friday after Good-Friday.

THUS much fot Yarmouth. Proceed we now in our Return to Melton Village by Way of Loweſtoft, Southwould, Blithburgh &c.

THE Road from Yarmouth Bridge, to Loweſtoft Queen's Head Inn, viz. Returning back by the River ſide, at 1 m. 2 ¼ f. the right turns acute forward to Beccles, being the Road laſt treated of; here keep the ſtrait way through Gorleſton-ſtreet. At 2 m. the right turns to Beccles, the left goes to the Havens Mouth.

GORLESTON, is a tolerable well built Village about 4 f. in length, in which is nothing obſervable, but the Ruins of an old Building, ſuppoſed by Mr. Camden to be the remains of ſome Religious Houſe.

PASSING along from hence about 3 f. beyond Gorleſton, we obſerved a Stone Croſs in the Road. The Road now leads over Commons; paſſing through a Hamlet of Hopton called Brotherton a little beyond this at 4 m. 5 f. is Hopton White Hart Inn. Here the Road right forward goes to Mutford Bridge, of which hereafter; therefore turn to the left, at 4 m. 7 ½ f. is Hopton Church cloſe on the left. At 6 m. 2 f is Corton Church cloſe on the left; the right goes to Lound. At 6 m. 5 f. the left turns backward to Gorleſton by the Shore ſide. Paſſing from hence leaving Gunton Church about 3 f. on the right, avoiding the right hand Way leading to Loweſtoft Church. At 8 m. 6 f. enter Loweſtoft-ſtreet, and at 8 m. 7 ½ f. come to Loweſtoft Queen's Head Inn.

LOWESTOFT

LOWESTOFT, is a confiderable large Town, ftanding fo near the Sea, that it feems to hang over it. It is indifferently well built, and the Streets well paved. The Church which is fituate near a Mile on the Weft-fide of the Town, is a good Building; but for the Eafe of its Inhabitants, there is a Chapel in the Town, wherein Divine Service is celebrated. The Cliff on which this Town is built, is the moft Eaftern Point in Great-Britain. Its chiefeft Trade, is Fifhing for Mackerel, and Herrings in their Seafons. It has a confiderable Market weekly on Wednefdays; and two Fairs yearly, the one on the firft Day of May, and the other on the 29th Day of September. Here are feveral Inns of good Entertainment.

LEAVING the Queen's-Head Inn at Loweftoft, and paffing out at the South-end of the Town, between the Shore and the Lake Lothing, at 1 m. 4 f. the right acute backward goes to Mutford-Bridge. At 1 m. 5 f. is Kirkely Church (in Ruins) clofe on the right. Pafs through Peakfield, a tolerable large built Village, whofe Inhabitants imploy themfelves in Fifh- ing. At 2 m. 2 f. the right forward goes to Beccles. Here turn on the left, paffing over a Common, at 4 m. 4 f. is a Blackfmith's Shop clofe on the left, and alfo Keffingland Church on the fame hand about 4 f. At 4 m. 7 f. the right goes to Beccles. At 5 m. 4 f. is Latimer-Bridge. Paffing over the Dam, at 6 m. 2 ½ f. is Benacre Walnut-Tree Inn. The right turns to Henftead; therefore take the left. At 6 m. 3 f. the left forward goes to Benacre Church, therefore turn to the right. At 7 m. is a View of Benacre-Hall, leaving it on the left near 2 f. At 7 m. 5 f. is Wren- tham Spread-Eagle Inn, paffing through Wrentham- Street, at the entering on the Common, the right turns to Wrentham Church, the Road right forward goes to Wangford; here take the Way on the left fide of the Common. At 8 m. 5 f. is South Cove Church clofe on the left; a little further the right goes to Froftendon. Here turn on the left; at 9 m. 6 f. is Potters-Bridge. At 10 m. 7 ¼ f. the right turns to Wangford, of which anon. Here turn on the left

E

over

over Southwould-Bridge. At 11 m. 4 f. is Southwould
Swan Inn.

SOUTHWOULD, a Town pleasantly situate on
a Hill, being almost surrounded with the Sea and
the River Blyth, over which it hath a Bridge for entrance into the Town. The Bay, called corruptly
Sowl-Bay, is a commodious Place for Anchorage, and
makes the Town much resorted to by Mariners,
which adds exceedingly to its Trade and Commerce.
It is also Famous for the Rendezvous of the Royal
Navy, and near it the English and Dutch have dif-
puted the Dominion of the Ocean with Powder and
Ball, especially in that memorable Sea-Fight, Anno
Dom. 1672. in which the English remained Conque-
rors.

IT is a Town Corporate, governed by two Bailiffs
and other Sub-Officers, but sends no Members to Parliament. It has a tolerable Market weekly on Thurfdays, indifferently well serv'd with Provisions; and
two Fairs yearly, the one on the Monday after Trinity Sunday, and the other on the Feast of St. Bartholomew. It drives a considerable Trade in Salt and
old Beer, having excellent Springs of good Water,
which may be the greatest Reason their Beer is so much
esteemed.

THUS much for Southwould. Returning back
over the Bridge, at 4¾ f. the right as aforesaid goes
over Potters Bridge to Lowestoft. At 5 f. the left leads
over Wolsey-Bridge to Halesworth. At 1 m. 4 f. the
right turns to Frostendon. At 1 m. 5½ f. is Raydon
Church close on the right. At 2 m. 2½ f. the right
goes to Frostendon. At 3 m. 2½ f. is Wangford Village, where the right turns to Henstead, of which
hereafter. Here turn on the left.

WANGFORD, is of Note for a Priory or Cell
of Cluniac Monks, dedicated to the Blessed Virgin
Mary, founded by one Dodo, or Ado Ansered, the
King's Purveyer, a Frenchman, valued at the Suppression in the 32 Henry VIII at 30 l. 9 s. 5 d. Considerable

fiderable remains of it adjoyning to the Church appear at this Day.

At 3 m. 4 f. crofs the River Wang ; pafs along avoiding the firft turning to the right leading to Uggerfhall, and leaving Henham Park clofe on the right, at 5 m. 1 f. the right leads to Halefworth, the left over Wolfey-Bridge, to Southwould. At 5 m. 4¼ f. is the Beecles Road through Bulchamp Hamlet. At 6 m. ¼ f. is Blithburgh White-Hart Inn.

Continuing our Journey from Blithburgh White Hart Inn to Melton Village, we pafs along from thence, avoiding the firft turning to the right leading to Yoxford, and keeping the Road right forward. At 2 f. the left leads to Weftwood Lodge. At 5½ f. is a Windmill clofe on the right, the right goes to Wenhafton, the left to Walderfwick. At 1 m. 6 f. the firft right hand Road leads to Halefworth, the fecond to Darfham, the left to Walderfwick. At 3 m. 3 f. the right goes to Darfham. At 3 m. 6 f. the right leads to Weftleton, the left to Dunwich, leaving it on the left about 2 Miles.

DUNWICH, is a very ancient Town, and Roman Coins are often found here, from whence it may reafonably be inferred that it was formerly a Roman Station. In the Reign of William the Conqueror, we are told in Doomfday Book, what a confiderable Place it was, viz. That in it were 130 Burgeffes, and 100 Poor ; and that it was valued to that King at 50 l. and 60000 Herrings. In King Henry IId's Time we are told it was a famous Village well ftored with Riches of all Sorts. It was then fortified with a Ramport, on purpofe to awe that Arch-Rebel, Robert Earl of Leicefter, who infulted and over run all thefe Parts ; fome remains of which now appear.

It was made a Bifhop's See, in the Reign of King Sigibert, Anno Dom. 630. Felix, being conftituted the firft Bifhop ; who governed this See 17 Years. After him fucceeded Thomas his Deacon, who governed here 5 Years. The next was Bergilfus who governed 17 Years ; and after him fucceeded Bifus, who being Old and Infirm, divided the Bifhoprick into

E 2

two Parts, of which one he appointed for the Jurrifdi-
ction of a Bifhop, that fhould have his See at Elmham ; in the other he continued himfelf. There were
10 Bifhops of Elmham, and 11 (after Bifus) at Dunwich. But by reafon of great Troubles in thofe Times,
thefe Sees ftood void almoft 100 Years. In the Year
955, in the Time of Edwy King of the Eaft Angles,
one Athulfus was ordained Bifhop at Canterbury, and
had his Palace at Elmham ; and after him 11 others
had alfo their Refidence at the fame Place, till the
Time of William the Conqueror, who fubftituting his
Chaplain Arfaftus in the Place of the laft of thefe,
by his Advice tranflated the See from Elmham to
Thetford. William Herbert fucceeded him in Thetford, having purchafed it of William Rufus for 1900 l.
To fatisfy for which Simony, Pope Pafchal enjoyned
him by way of Penance to build certain Churches and
Monafteries at his own Charge, which he did, and a-
mongft them the Cathedral Church at Norwich, lay-
ing the firft Stone of the Foundation with his own
Hands, with this Infcription, HUNC PRIMNM HUJUS
TEMPLI LAPIDEM, DOMINUS HEREBERTUS POSUIT
IN NOMINE PATRIS ET FILII ET SPIRITUS SANCTI,
AMEN. He dedicated this Church to the Bleffed
Trinity. And tranflated the Epifcopal See from Thet-
ford thither.

THERE were feveral Religious Houfes in Dunwich ;
1ft. The Friers Minors, who had a very fair Church,
and their Houfe, which was encompaffed round with
a Wall, was a good Building, as was alfo, 2d. That
of the Dominicans or Black Friers. The former was
founded by Richard Fitz-John, the latter by Sir Roger Holifhe. 3d. St. James's Hofpital, which had a
large Church, and divers Tenements, Houfes and
Lands belonging to it, which were appropriated to
the Ufe and Suftenance of Sick, Poor, and impotent
Perfons.

Maifon Dieu, another Hofpital dedicated to the
Holy Trinity, now wholly in Ruins. The Temple
of our Lady, was a very old Church, or Religious
Houfe : It was a Place of great Note for Pardons and
Indulgences, and had divers Tenements, Houfes and
Lands

Lands not only in Dunwich; but also in Dingle, Westleton, &c. and there was a Court commonly kept in it, called Dunwich Temple Court, on November 2.

WE have a certain account of 6 Parish Churches and three Chapels in this Town, besides the Religious Houses before mentioned; St. John's, St. Leonard's, St. Martin's, and St. Nicholas's, these four Churches, and St. Anthony's, St. Francis's and St. Catharine's Chapels have been long devoured by the merciless Ocean. There were two Parish Churches standing in this Age; but one of them also is now swallowed up by the Ocean, there being now only one Church standing.

AND now this once beautiful and flourishing City is reduced to a small Village, made up of mean Cottages; yet it retains its Privileges of a Corporation, being governed by two Bailiffs and other Sub-Officers; and sends two Members to Parliament. It has a very mean Market weekly on Saturdays, if yet it be worthy the Name of a Market, and a Fair yearly on July the 25th.

THUS much for Dunwich. Return we now to the Road leading from Blithburgh to Melton.

AT 4 m. 1 f. the right goes to Westleton, the left to Dunwich; passing along and leaving a Windmill a little on the right, at 5 m. 4½ f. is East-Bridge. Passing along from hence past the Inn, at 6 m. 7 f. the right turns backward to Yoxford; here leaving the Abby a little on the right, at 8 m. is Leiston White-Horse Inn.

LEISTON, is remarkable for a Priory of Black Monks, called Premonstratenses, which was first founded by Ranulph de Glanvil, in the Time of King Henry II, about the Year of our Lord 1183, who endowed it with a Manour and with certain Churches which he had before given to the Priory of Butley, who resigned them to the Canons of this Place.

THIS Priory being much decay'd, was repaired, and almost new built, by Robert de Ufford Earl of Suffolk in the Year 1363, and was by him dedicated to the Blessed Virgin Mary the Mother of Jesus.

There

There are confiderable remains of it now ftanding; it was valued at its Diffolution at 18 l. 17 s. 1½d. per Ann. and is now in the Hands of two Perfons: That now called the Abby, and the Manour of this Town, is now the Eftate of the Lady Anne Harvey. The other Part called Lady's old Abby, was the Eftate of Edward Spencer, Efq; and now remains to his Family. There remain the Ruins of a Chapel on the South of Mifmer-Haven, which doubtlefs was part of this Priory.

THUS much for Leifton Priory. Return we now to Leifton White-Horfe Inn, to purfue our Journey to Melton.

GOING from the White-Horfe Inn aforefaid avoid the left hand Way, which goes to Aldeburgh, and the right that leads to Saxmundham, and take the Way right forward. At 1 m. ½ f. is Coldfair-Green, where there is a Fair kept yearly on the Feaft of St. Andrew and the Day following. At 1 m. 4½ f. the right goes to Knodifhall, the left to Aldeburgh, leaving a Windmill a little on the right. At 2 m. 3½ f. the right goes to Saxmundham, the left to Aldeburgh. At 2 m. 5¼ f. is Polsborough-Gate; the left goes to Aldeburgh, the right to Benhall; leaving Frifton Decoy a little on the left, at 3 m. 3¼ f. a View to Frifton-Hall. At 4 m. the left acute backward, over Snape Race-Ground, goes to Aldeburgh. At 4 m. 3 f. is Snape Crown Inn.

SNAPE, was formerly of remark for a Monaftery of Black Monks founded in the Year 1099 by William Martell and Albreda his Wife, and Jeffrey Martell their Son and Heir, and by them dedicated to the Bleffed Virgin Mary. The Original Deed of the Foundation of this Monaftery (faith my Author) is in the Tally-Court of the Exchequer. It is faid, all Wreck of the Sea, from Thorp (or near that Place) to Orford-Nefs, belonged to this Monaftery. And doubtlefs the Manours of Aldeburgh, Snape, Haflewood, and Beding belonged alfo to the Monks of this Houfe. Anno 1155 this was granted as a Cell to the Abby at Colchefter, but was no further in Subjection
thereto,

thereto, than the Payment of half a Mark as a Penfion of Acknowledgement; and that the Abbot of Colcheſter might Viſit them twice a Year, and abide there with 12 Horſes four Days. It was valued at its Diſſolution at 99 l. 1 s. 11 ½ d. per Ann. It is now the Eſtate of the Right Hon. the Earl of Strafford; very little now remains of this Monaſtery. In this Pariſh is a very conſiderable Fair yearly for Horſes, now called Dunnifer-Fair, beginning the 11th of Auguſt, and laſting 4 Days; to which the London Jockeys reſort.

THUS much for Snape Monaſtery &c. Paſſing from the Crown Inn aforeſaid over Snape-Bridge, leaving the Abby a little on the right, avoid the firſt left hand Way leading to Orford, taking the right hand Road. At 5 m. 1 f. is Dunningworth Hall cloſe on the right; avoid the right hand Way that leads to Wickham-Market, (of which anon) and leaving the Ruins of Dunningworth Chapel a little on the right, go ſtrait forward for Tunſtall Church, avoiding divers turnings to the right and left. At 7 m. 2 f. is Tunſtall Village, the left turns to Orford. Here turn on the right, at 7 m. 3 f. is Tunſtall Inn; the right turns to Blaxhall, the Road right forward goes in at a Gate to Campſey-Aſh, therefore turn to the left. At 8 m. 2 f. the right goes to Campſey-Aſh, the left to Butley. At 8 m. 6 f. is a View of Rendleſham-Houſe.

RENDLESHAM, or as Bede calls it, RENDILISHAM, i. e. as he Interprets it, the Houſe or Manſion of Rendilus. Here it was that Redwald King of the Eaſt-Angles kept his Court. He was the firſt of that People that was Baptized and became a Chriſtian, but afterwards being ſeduced by his Wife, he had (as Bede expreſſes it) in the ſelf ſame Church, one Altar for the Chriſtian Religion, and a little one for Sacrifices to Devils. The Palace where he then kept his Court, ſtood in the ſame Place, where Rendleſham-Houſe now ſtands, which was the Seat of Edward Spencer, Eſq; and now remains to Madam Anne Spencer his Daughter. Here it was that Suidhelmus

helmus King of the East-Angles was Baptized by Bishop Cedda.

Thus much for Rendlesham. Pursuing our Journey, at 9 m. 4 ½ f. the right goes to Wickham-Market, the left to Hollesly ; a little further the right goes to Rendlesham-Green ; passing by Rendlesham-Church on the right, at 10 m. 1 f. the right turns backward to Campsey-Ash, avoiding divers turnings to the right and left, at 10 m. 5 f. is Eyke-Castle Inn. Pass by the Church on the left, where the right leads to Ufford, the left to Orford. At 11 m. 1 f. are two Gates, the right goes to Ufford, the left to Sutton, leaving Bromeswell Church about 2 f. on the right, at 11 m. 7 f. come to a Sand-Pit on the right ; here the Road turns backward from Woodbridge to Orford, of which hereafter ; passing over a Brook, at 12 m. 5 ¼ f. the Road turns backward to Baudsey ; of which anon. At 12 m. 6 f. is Wilford-Bridge. At 13 m. 2 ¾ f. is Melton Village.

From Blithburgh White-Hart Inn to Melton Village by Way of Snape is —	21 m. 2 ¾ f.
From Blithburgh White-Hart Inn, to Melton Village, by Way of Saxmundham is	20 m. 4 f.
So that it is the nearest Way by Saxmundham, by the Distance of —	00 m. 6 ¼ f.

Thus having finished the Road from Ipswich to Yarmouth, and its return to Melton Village, come we now to treat of three other Branches issuing out of the Yarmouth Road at Melton Village, to Baudsey, Orford, and Aldeburgh.

And first of the Road to Baudsey-Ferry.

Returning back in the last described Road over Wilford-Bridge, at 5 ½ f. take the right hand Way up Wilford Hills ; at 1 m. 3 f. leave the right which goes to Sutton Church, passing over Heathy Land, leaving the one Bough Oak about half a Mile on the left, and Sutton Holly Bush a little on the right. At 2 m. 4 f. the right goes to Sutton Church

(in

(it being on the right 4 f.) the left goes to Eyke; now avoiding divers turnings to the right and left, leave Shottisham Church a little on the right. At 4 m. 6 f. is Shottisham Cross, the right goes to Shottisham, the left to Hollesly. At 6 m. 6 f. the right turns to Ramsholt, here turn on the left, leaving Alderton Church a little on the right. At 6 m. 6 ¾ f. is Alderton Village; here turn on the right, leaving the left hand Way leading to Hollesly. At 7 m. 7 f. is Baudsey Church close on the right; at 9 m. 6 ¾ f. is Baudsey-Ferry, the Ferry-House on the Colnes side of the Water.

From Woodbridge to Melton Village is 1 m. 2 ½ f.
From Melton Village to Baudsey-Ferry is 9 m. 6 ¼ f.

From Woodbridge to Baudsey-Ferry is 11 m. 1 ¼ f.

BAUDSEY, Written in ancient Records BAW-DRESEY, was anciently a Market Town (but is not at present so) for we find that Robert de Ufford, after he had been twice Justice of Ireland, obtained a Licence of King Edward I, in the 11th Year of his Reign, to hold a Market weekly on Fridays, and a Fair yearly upon the Eve Day and Morrow of the Nativity of our Blessed Virgin, September 8, at his Manour of Bawdresey. How long this Market and Fair has been disused we know not.

RETURN we now to Melton Village, and from thence to Orford.

RETURNING from Melton Village in the Blithburgh Road, at 5 m. 3 ¾ f. coming at the Sand-Pit before mentioned, avoid the left forward leading to Eyke, and the right leading to Sutton, take the middle Way, avoiding divers turnings to the right and left. At 3 m. the right leads to Hollesly; the left to Eyke, enter in at a Gate, passing through Sprats-Street. At 4 m. 3 f. Stavender-Park on the left. At 5 m. 2 f. leave it. At 5 m. 5 f. is Butley-Oyster on the right, the right on this side the Oyster goes to Capell; the right on the other side to Butley-Abby.

F   BUTLEY,

BUTLEY, was of Note for a Priory of Canons Regular there founded by Ranulph de Glanvill, and dedicated to the Bleſſed Virgin Mary, about the Year of our Lord 1171, (after he had founded his Priory at Leiſton.) The Revenues and Poſſeſſions of this Priory were very large, for beſides the Endowments of its Founder and other Benefactors, we find King Henry VII, in the 24th of his Reign, granted to Robert Brommer, Prior of this Monaſtery of Butley, and the Convent of the ſame, the Priory of the Virgin Mary at Snape, in this County, with all the Rents &c. to be annexed to the ſaid Priory at Butley. In was valued at its Diſſolution at 318 l. 17 s. 2¾ d. per Ann. It is now the Eſtate of ___ Wright, Eſq. In the Church of this Priory was interred the Body of Michael de la Pole, the 3d Lord Wingfield and Earl of Suffolk, who was Slain at the Battle of Agincourt in France, with Edward Plantagenet Duke of York.

THUS much for Butley-Abby. Purſue we now our Journey to Orford. Turning on the left at Butley-Oyſter, paſs over the River; at 5 m. 7 f. the left goes to Wantiſden, therefore turn on the right, paſsing over Puddle-Water. At 7 m. is Chilleſford Church a little on the left. At 7 m. 2 f. the right turns acute backward to Chilleſford Mill, the left goes to Tunſtall. At 7 m. 3 f. is Chilleſford Froize Inn, paſsing from thence by the ſide of Sudbourn Park, at 9 m. ½ f. the left goes to Saxmundham; here turn on the right. At 10 m. 2 f. is Orford Market Croſs.

From Woodbridge to Orford is ——— 11 m. 4½ f.

OREFORD, now commonly called ORFORD, is ſituate on the North-Weſt Side of the River Ore, and ſo took its Name of Oreford. Moſt of our Hiſtorians ſay it is ſituate on the River Ore, where it empties it ſelf into the River Ald, which is notoriouſly Falſe; for the Conjunction of thoſe Rivers are about a Mile South-Eaſt of Glemham Parva Church, and therefore could never be where Orford now is. It was anciently

ciently a Town of good Account, having a ſtrong Caſtle for its Defence, which formerly belonged to the Valoinies, afterwards to the de Uffords, and now to the Hon. Pryce D'Evereux, Eſq; Son and Heir Apparent to the Right Hon. the Lord Viſcount Hereford. Other Towns on this Coaſt complain of the Incurſions of the Sea upon them; but this Town has more reaſon to complain of the Seas unkindneſs, which with drawing it ſelf ſeems to envy it the advantage of an Harbour. At preſent it is but a mean Town, yet it is a Town Corporate, governed by a Mayor, 8 Portmen, and 12 Chief Burgeſſes, and ſends two Members to Parliament. It has a mean Market on Mondays, and a Fair yearly on Midſummer-Day.

THERE appears in this Town, towards the Key, the Ruins of a Benedictine Nunnery founded by Ralph de Albineio ; but the Time of its Foundation, or its Revenues doe not appear. There are conſiderable remains now ſtanding of the Caſtle and Nunnery.

RETURN we now once more to Melton Village, to take a Survey of the Road leading from thence to Aldeburgh.

PASSING along from Melton Village over Wilford-Bridge, through Eyke, Tunſtall and Snape, to Polsborough-Gate; it being thither, (as is mentioned in the Road from Blithburgh to Melton) 10 m. 5 $\frac{1}{2}$ f. here take the right hand Way, leading through a Lane called Ruſhmer-Street, over Haſlewood Common, at 3 m. 1 $\frac{1}{4}$ f. from the ſaid Gate, is Aldeburgh Market Croſs.

From Woodbridge to Aldeburgh is — 15 m. 1 $\frac{3}{4}$ f.

ALDEBURGH, is a Town pleaſantly ſituate in the Valley of Slaughden, extending it ſelf near a Mile from North to South ; but is not very broad from Eaſt to Weſt. Its breadth has formerly been more than it is now, the unkind Ocean has in this Age ſwallowed up one whole Street. At preſent there are two Streets very near a Mile in length. The Town is meanly built, but very clean. The Ocean waſhes the Eaſt ſide of the Town, and the River Ald runs

not

not far from the South end thereof, affording a good
Key at Slaughden. The chief Trade of this Town is
Fishing for Herrings in the adjacent Seas, in their
Seasons; yet it trades for Coals to Newcastle, and
Corn is transported from hence to other Parts. It is
tolerably situate for Strength, and has several Pieces
of Cannon for its Defence. The Church stands on a
Hill a little West of the Town, and is a very good
Structure. It is a Town Corporate, governed by two
Bailiffs, ten capital Burgesses, and 24 inferiour Officers.
It enjoys divers Privileges, sending two Members to
Parliament &c. Here is a small Market weekly on
Saturdays; and two Fairs yearly, the one on the 3d
of September, and the other on the first Tuesday in
Lent.

T H U s much for Aldeburgh. We will next take
a Survey of the Road from Aldeburgh to Saxmundham.
RETURNING back from Aldeburgh Market Cross,
in the last mentioned Road, through Rushmer Street,
avoid the left hand Way at the entrance of the Walks
leading to Polesborough Gate. At 3 m. 1 ½ f. cross
the Road leading from Blithburgh to Melton, leaving
Polesborough Gate on the left near a Furlong, passing
over Friston Walks, at 4 m. is a Pound on the right;
the right goes to Knodishall; here turn on the left,
and avoiding the left hand Way leading to Snape Church,
turn again on the right through Friston Village, leaving the Church a little on the right. At 4 m. 3 f.
the right goes in at a Gate to Friston Moor; therefore turn on the left and pass by Friston Hall, (leaving
it 2 f. on the left,) and over the lower end of Friston
Moor. At 5 m. 6 f. the left goes to Snape; here turn
on the right. At 6 m. is Sternfield Church close on
the left; the Road right forward goes to Benhall,
therefore turn on the right. At 6 m. 4 f. is Mr. Long's
House, a little on the right. At 6 m. 6 ½ f. is Saxmundham Church close on the right; the right turns
to Leiston, wherefore turn on the left over the Brook.
At 6 m. 7 ½ f. is the Yarmouth Road at Saxmundham
Blacksmith's Shop.

RETURN we now to Wickham-Market, in order
to take a Survey of three Roads issuing out of the
Yarmouth

Yarmouth Road, leading from thence to Eye, to Needham, and to Harleston.

AND first of the Road from Wickham-Market to Eye. Passing along from the Crown Inn in Wickham-Market, avoid the right forward being the Saxmundham Road, and the left which goes to Dallingho; here cross the Hill. At 3 ¼ f. the left goes over Potford Green, toward Needham, of which anon. At 5 ¼ f. cross the River Deben at Glevering-Bridge. Passing along, leaving Glevering-Hall a little on the right, and the Mill a little on the left, at 1 m. 2 f. the right turns backward to Campsey-Ash. At 1 m. 3 f. is Easton Brick-Kiln close on the right. At 2 m. 3 ½ f. is Easton Church close on the right, and the White-House (the Earl of Rochford's Seat) close on the left; here the right goes to Parham, the left to Letheringham. At 2 m. 5 f. is a Pound on the right, were the right goes to Framlingham. At 3 m. 2 f. Letheringham-Abby is in View.

LETHERINGHAM, is of remark for a little Priory there founded by Sir John Boynet, but of what Order the Monks of it were, and to whom it was dedicated does not appear. Mr. Willis calls this Priory LEFRINGHAM, and says that William Clopton was Prior Anno 1510 Sir Anthony Wingfield obtained this Priory at the Dissolution of it, and Sir Henry Spelman tells us, that he left no Issue Male, which he accounts a Judgment upon him, for possessing himself of Lands dedicated to God's Service. This Priory was converted into a good Mansion, having been for some Ages, and now is, the Seat of the antient Family of the Nauntons, a Family as ancient as the Conquest, who formerly had their Seat at Alderton, in the Hundred of Wilford in this County. They have been Gentlemen greatly esteemed formerly, Sir Robert Naunton was in the Reign of King James the Ist Secretary of State, one of the Privy Council, and Master of the Court of Wards and Liveries. He died Anno 1630.

THUS much for Letheringham &c. At 3 m. 5 ¼ f. the left goes to Hoo, the right is a Spurway to Framlingham. At 3 m. 7 ½ f. is Kittleburgh Village, where
the

the right goes to Framlingham. At 4 m. 5 f. is Mr.
Sparrow's Manfion, clofe on the right; a little further
the left right forward goes to Debenham, therefore
turn on the right. At 4 m. 7 ¼ f. the left goes to
Debenham, the right to Framlingham, and leave
Brandefton-Hall about 1 f. on the left, of which more
in another Place. Keeping the Way right forward
over Brandefton-Green, pafs by a Manfion now called
the Firtree, formerly the Seat of the worthy Family
of the Stebbings. At 7 m. arrive at Earl-Soham Village, leaving the Church about 3 f. on the right.

EARL-SOHAM, probably the Place where Fe-
lix the firft Bifhop of Dunwich fometime refided. For
my Author fays, that Felix having governed in the
See of Dunwich 17 Years, died Anno 647, and was
bury'd in his Church there. His Body was afterward
removed to Soham, where he had his Seat fometime,
and was bury'd in the Monaftery there, which was
not long after demolifhed by the Danes. Capgrave
tells us, That fome Ages after, Abbot Ethelftan having with great Pains and Charge found out his Bones,
removed them to his Abby of Ramfey in the Reign
of King Canute. From all which 'tis probable 'twas this
Soham, or the other adjoyning called Monks-Soham,
it could not be the Soham near Ely; that being in
Cambridgefhire, and therefore not in the Diocefs of
Dunwich. The Lodge at Soham is a good old Building, but whether it was railed out of the Ruins of that
Monaftery is uncertain, however the Lord Vifcounts
Hereford had their Seat there before they removed to
Chrift Church in Ipfwich, and it now remains to that
Family. In this Parifh is a new Fair for Lambs on
the 12th Day of July yearly. Thus much for Soham.
    PASSING over a Brook avoid the left turning to
Afhfield. At 8 m 1 f. is Clough's-Corner, where the
left goes to Ipfwich. At 10 m. 1 f. is a Direction
Poft, the left goes to Debenham. At 10 m. 3 f. is
Kenton Church a little on the left; the left goes to
Debenham. At 11 m. 1 f. the right leads to Wor-
lingworth. At 11 m. 2 ½ f. the left forward to De-
benham, here turn on the right. At 11 m 7 ½ f. the
                                                    right

right goes to Worlingworth-Green. At 12 m. 1 f. the left forward goes to Kifhangles, therefore turn on the right, and avoid divers turning to the right and left. At 13 m. 3 f. is Occold Church clofe on the right. At 14 m. 5 f. the left acute backward goes to Thorndon. At 15 m. the left goes to Thorndon. At 15 m. 7 3-4 f. is a Direction Poft, where the right goes to Framlingham, therefore turn on the left paffing over the Bridge. At the entring into Eye-Street, the right goes paft Eye Church to Hoxne. At 16 m. 4½ f. is Eye Market-Crofs.

EYE, a Town fituate in a Bottom between two Rivers, is a Town Corporate governed by two Bailiffs, 10 Principal Burgeffes, and 24 Common-Councilmen. Enjoys divers Privileges now, but they were more extenfive formerly, reaching even to the Gates of York. It fend two Members to Parliament. The Town is meanly built, and the Streets dirty. Here is a mean Market weekly on Saturdays, and one Fair yearly on Whitfon-Monday.

As to the Antiquities of this Town; we find that Robert Mallet, a Norman Baron (whofe Father came in with the Conqueror) having fignallized himfelf in keeping King William on the Throne, has his Father had in fettling him on it, obtained of that King the Lordfhip of Eye, with all the Appendages of it, being 221 Manours, or the greateft Part of them. He being thus poffeffed of this Lordfhip, built the Caftle here, upon a Hill near the Weft end of the Church; fome of the ruinous Walls are ftill to be feen. This Robert was difherited of this Lordfhip of Eye by King Henry I, and it was by him given to Stephen Earl of Bologne who afterwards became King of England. He left it to his Natural Son William, who ftiled himfelf Earl of Bologne &c. but he dying without Heirs, Anno 1160, it reverted to the Crown. Afterwards Richard I. gave it to Henry V. Earl of Brabant and Loraine. How long it was in that Family we find not, but it appears that it was in the Kings Hauds 9th of Edward II, and fo continued, till Edward III. Reg. 4. granted it to John of Eltham Earl of Cornwall;

wall ; but he alfo dying without Iffue, the fame King granted this Town, Caftle and Manour of Eye to Robert de Ufford whom he had lately made Earl of Suffolk. He left it to his Son William, but he dying without Iffue it returned again to the Crown, and was given to the De la Pools Earls of Suffolk. It now remains (tho' not in the vaft extent it was in Mallets Time) to the Lord Cornwallis, who is ftilled Baron of Eye. This Town was a Borough before the Reign of King John, and is called in Writing the Town and Borough of Aye.

HERE appears on the Eaft Side of the Town, the Ruins of a Monaftery of Benedictine, or Black Monks, founded by the aforefaid Robert Mallet, who gave to it the Church of St. Peter in Eye, with divers other Churches, Lands &c. The Foundation of this Houfe was no fooner laid, than it found confiderable Benefactors ; for Ranulph de Glanvil one of the Barons (fo Lords of Manours or Gentlemen of Eftates were then called) of Robert Mallet the chief Lord of the Honour of Eye, gave thefe a Houfe in Jakefly. Hubert de Monchenfy gave them alfo about the fame time his own Houfe in the fame Place ; William Earl of Bolein confirmed to thefe Monks the Lordfhip of Acol (I fuppofe Occold) and Stoke. In the Reign of King Stephen all thefe Benefactions were confirmed to this Houfe, with a grievous Curfe to the Violaters of them. This Monaftery was a Cell to the Abby of Bernay in Normandy, whofe Abbots were the Patrons of this at Eye, and in Token of their Dominion, during the Vacancy of a Prior, ufed to Place a Porter at the Gate, to be maintained out of the Houfe, who at the Inftallment of the next Prior, was to receive 5 s to buy him an Ox. It was valued at its Diffolution at 161 l. 2 s. 3 ¼ d per Ann. fays Dugdale, and at 184 l. 9 s. 7 ½ d. Speed, Weaver. This alfo is now the Eftate of the Right Hon, the Lord Cornwallis.

THUS much for Eye. Return we now to Wickham-Market, and the Road leading from thence, to Needham by Way of Coddenham. Paffing from the Crown Inn in Wickham in the Road laft treated of, at 3 ¼ f. leaving the right going towards Eye, keeping
the

the right forward Way over Potford-Green, at 1 m. 3 f. is Letheringham-Park, the right goes to Lethering-ham Street, paſſing by the Park on the right. At 2 m. ¼ f. leave the Park, where the right goes to Lether-ingham. At 2 m, 6 ½ f. the right forward goes to Chars-field Church; therefore turn on the left over a Brook. At 3 m. 3 f. the right goes to Charsfield-Church. At 4 m. 4 f. is a Direction Poſt, the left goes to Wood-bridge. At 5 m. 3 f. a Blackſmith's Shop cloſe on the right, where the right goes to Hoo, the left to Clopton. At 6 m. is Catts-Hill, where the right turns backward to Moneden. At 6 m. 2 f. the left goes forward to Woodbridge, wherefore turn on the right. At 6 m. 7 f. the right forward goes to Otley Church, therefore turn on the left. At 7 m. 7 f. is a Dire-ction Poſt, the right goes to Helmingham, the left to Ipſwich. At 8 m. 3 f. the right goes to Aſhbock-ing, the left to Ipſwich. At 8 m. 7 ¾ f. is Heming-ſton Hare and Hounds Inn; the Road right forward goes to Henley; here turn on the right. At 10 m. 4 f. is Stonewall, a Blackſmith's Shop cloſe on the left, where the right goes to Helmingham, the left to Ipſwich. At 10 m. 7 f. the left goes to Heming-ſton. At 11 m. 3 f. the right goes to Gosbeck, there-fore take the left At 11 m 5 ½ f. is Coddenham-Crown, the right goes to Debenham, and a little fur-ther the left goes to Ipſwich. At 13 m. 1 ½ f. we croſs the Pye Road, of which hereafter. Paſſing along through the Fields at 14 m. 2 f. is Boſmere Mill. At 14 m. 7 f. is Needham Chapel.

RETURN we now to Wickham-Market, in or-der to take a Survey of the Road leading from thence to Harleſton.

PASSING from Wickham-Crown Inn in the Yar-mouth Road before diſcribed, over Wickham-Bridge, paſt the Blackſmith's Shop, at 5 ½ f. leave the Yar-mouth Road which is on the right, and take the left hand Way. At 1 m. ¼ f. are the four Croſs-ways, the right leads to Aldeburgh, the left to Eaſton. At 1 m. 7 ¼ f. is Hacheſton Church cloſe on the right, the left leads through the Fair Field to Eaſton.

G HACHESTON,

HACHESTON. Here is a confiderable Fair held yearly on the 2d and 3d Days of November.

At 2 m. 1 f. the right goes backward being the Road from Framlingham to Orford. At 2 m. 3 f. is Hackefton Village, where the right leads to Parham-Hall, the left to Eafton.

PARHAM, was the Lordfhip and Demefn of Robert de Ufford Earl of Suffolk, 9 Edward II. He died poffeffed of it 43 Edward III. and left it to his Son William, who built the Church here, but dying fuddenly in the Parliament Houfe, it defcended to his eldeft Sifter Cicily, who married Sir Robert Willoughby Knt. and carried it into that Family. Their Pofterity afterwards became Lords Willoughby of Eresby, and for fometime were in Poffeffion of this Manour, till Chriftopher Lord Willoughby of Eresby gave it to his youngeft Son Chriftopher, who took up his Refidence here, and for Diftinction was called Willoughby of Parham. This Chriftopher Lord Willoughby gave in his laft Will, dated May 8, 18 Henry VIII, Four Pounds a Year to the Church of Parham in Satisfaction of all Tythes and Offerings by him negligently forgotten. Sir William Willoughby his Son and Heir, was in the 1 Edward VI created Lord Willoughby of Parham, 20th of February in that Year, he died 16 Elizabeth, 1574. whofe Succeffors now enjoy that Honour. Parham-Hall and Manour, fince the Willoughby's, has been in feveral Families, and is now the Eftate of John Corrance, Efq;

THERE is a remarkable Piece of Curiofity in Parham Park, viz. a Thorn that every Year on the Eve before the Nativity of our Bleffed Saviour, Bloffoms, and very often blows out, befides its blowing at the ufual Time, which it always does very early.

IN this Parifh in the Autumn Quarter, 1734, out of a Gravel Pit, in a Field called by the Name of Fryers Clofe, was taken the Bones of a Man, an Urn and the Head of a Spear, fuppofed to be the fome Danifh Commander. Thus much for Parham. Purfuing our Journey to Framlingham,

At

A T 3 m. 2 f. we come to Parham-Bridge, the right goes to Cransford, the left to Eafton. At 4 m. 5 ¼ f. the left goes in at a Gate to Eafton ; therefore turn on the right over the River Ore at the broad Water. At 5 m. 3 ¼ f. leave the left going through Framlingham to Dennington. At 5 m. 7 ¼ f. is Framlingham Broad-Gates Inn.

FRAMLINGHAM, is a Town of a large extent, and in the midft of it is the Borough ; it is pleafantly feated, and well built, upon a Clay Hill near the Head of the River Ore, which rifing in the Hills on the North of the Borough, paffeth through the Town, and falleth into the Sea at Hollefley beyond Orford. The Market is weekly on Saturdays, and a Fair on Monday and Tuefday in Whitfon-Week (procured by Thomas de Brotherton, Earl of Norfolk) and another on the Feaft of St. Michael, Sept. 29. The Market Place is a very fpacious, being almoft an equilateral Triangle. Between the Market Place and the Church, ftood the Hall of the Guild, or Faternity called the Guild of the Bleffed Virgin in Framlingham.

T H E Church and Caftle are great Ornaments of this Town. The Church is indeed a ftately Building, built (as is fuppofed) by fome of the Mowbreys, Earls of Norfolk, as appears by their Arms at the bottom, and on the middle of the Steeple, but being not compleated, was finifhed by King Edward VI. In the Ifles lies bury'd feveral of the Earls and Dukes of Norfolk.

T H E R E are two Alms-Houfes, worth our remark in this Town ; the one erected by the Will, and at the Charge of Sir Robert Hitcham, for 12 of the pooreft and moft decrepit Perfons in Framlingham, and for their Maintenance they are allowed 2 s. per Week each, and 40 s. a Year for their Gown and Firing ; they are obliged to attend the Prayers of the Church daily, at Eight of the Clock in the Morning, and Four in the Afternoon ; which if they neglect to do, their weekly Allowance fhall be abated, except they can plead fuch Excufe as fhall be allowed by the Mini-

G 2

fter

ßer of the Town, and certain others mentioned In the
Will; and that Prayers be read conftantly, he fettled
for Ever upon the Reader or Curate 20 l. a Year, and
5 l. a Year upon the Clerk or Sexton.

The other Alms-Houfe, was built by the Truftees
of Tho. Mills, who had been a Wheelwright, but in
the late Times of diforder turn'd Teacher, or Holder-
forth among the Anabaptifts at Saxted near this Town,
in which Perfwafion he died Anno 1703, or there a-
bouts. A little after his Death his Truftees built this
Alms-Houfe, for eight Poor Perfons. His Servant
Francis Mayhew, (if I miftake nor) was at the Charge
of building two of thefe Apartments. Thefe Poor are
allowed Half-a-Crown a Week each, and yearly an
outward Garment, and 30 s. each for Firing. This
they are to enjoy during Life, unlefs they are turned
out by the Truftees for any Mifdemeanor.

Sir Robert Hitcham by his Will ordered a Free
School to be founded in this Town, with a Salary of
40 l. a Year to the Mafter, to Teach 40 of the pooreft Children of this Town, to Read, Write, and Caft
Accompts, and when they are perfect in them, to give
each 10 l. to bind them Apprentices.

As to the Antiquity of this Town, we are told
with fome probability that it was a Town of the Bri-
tons, and was conquered by the Romans, when they
defeated Boadicea the Britifh Amazon. The Caftle,
which is the moft remarkable Piece of Antiquity in
this Town, was built, as is fuppofed, by fome of the
Kings of the Eaft Angles, but which of them our Hiftories do not mention. But it may be not improba-
bly fuppofed to have been built by Redwald the greateft of them, who kept his Court at Rendlefham, as is
mentioned before; yet this is only Conjecture. This
Caftle is a large, beautiful, and ftrong Building, containing in Land an Acre, one Rood, and 11 Perches
within the Walls now ftanding, but formerly a greater quantity. The Walls are 44 Foot high, and 8
thick, which are now ftanding pretty entire; there
are 13 Towers 14 Foot higher than the Walls, two
of which are Watch Towers. It was Inacceffible on
the Eaft fide, becaufe of the Meer adjoyning, and on
the

the other fide it was fortified with a double Ditch, &c. and by the Situation of the Place it may reafonably be fuppofed to have been a very ftrong Fortrefs, King Edmund being befieged in this Caftle by the Danes, and finding himfelf not able to maintain it againft fo powerful an Enemy, deferted it, and they taking Poffeffion thereof, kept it in their Hands 50 Years, mightily harraffing the Country round about, 'till they were brought under the Obedience of the Saxons. William the Conqueror gave it to his Coufin Roger Bigod Earl of Norfolk: From the Bigods (who died without Iffue) it reverted to the Crown, 25 Edward I, and fo remained till Edward II, who in the 6th Year of his Reign gave it to his Brother-in-Law Thomas de Brotherton Earl of Norfolk. He left it to his two Daughters, Margaret and Alice, which Alice marrying Edward de Montacute, upon the Divifion of the Eftate, he obtained for his part this Caftle and Demefn. He left it, the 35 Edward V, to his Daughter Joan, who marrying William de Ufford Earl of Suffolk, carried it into that Family. From him it defcended to the Mowbreys Earls of Norfolk, who fometimes refided here. From the Mowbreys, it defcended to the Howards, Earls, (afterwards Dukes) of Norfolk. After them it was granted to the de Veres Earls of Oxford; then it returned to the Howards again, who fold this Caftle, Manour and Demefns to Sir Robert Hitcham aforefaid; and he gave it to Pembroke Hall in Cambridge. In this Town are feveral reputable Inns of Entertainment.

THus much for Framlingham. Now we will purfue our Journey to Harlefton from the Broad Gates, alias the Griffon Inn. Paffing over the River Ore,

At 2 ½ f. the left acute forward goes to Saxted. At 1 m. 1 f. the left forward goes towards Stradbrook, wherefore turn on the right. At 1 m. 4 f. is Durrance Bridge. At 2 m. ½ f. the right forward goes to Baddingham; here turn on the left. At 2 m. 4 f. is Dennington Rectory Houfe a little on the left, where the left forward goes to Brundifh; here turn on the right. At 2 m. 6 ½ f. the left turns acute backward to Saxted, and Dennington Church is clofe on the right. At

3 m.

5 m. 4 ¼ f. is Froizly Bridge, where the right goes to Baddingham, the left to Brundish. Here going up a Hill in a very indifferent Road, at 5 m. 7 f. the right goes to Laxfield Church. Here turn on the left through a way called Stirrup Street. At 6 m. 7 ½ f. is Laxfield White-Horse Inn, where the right goes to Laxfield Church ; here turn on the left. At 7 m. 1 f. the left forward goes to Stradbrook; here turn on the right, leaving the Seat of the late Archbishop Sancroft on the left 3 f. At 8 m. 6 f. the right goes to Cratfield ; here turn on the left. At 10 m. 3 ¾ f. the left goes to Stradbrook, the left forward to Eye ; therefore turn on the right. At 10 m. 4 ¼ f. is Fressing-field Church Close on the right.

FRESSINGFIELD, is a Town of Note for being the Birth and Burial Place of that truly Pious and most Reverend Father in God, Dr. William Sancroft, some-time Archbishop of Canterbury ; who lies buried in this Church-yard, on the South Side of the Church, under a Pillar of the same ; over whose Grave there is a handsome Monument. Passing through Fressing-field Street, the right goes to Cratfield ; therefore turn on the left, leaving a Blacksmith's Shop close on the left ; and over a Brick Bridge, where turn on the right through a pretty strait way. At 12 m. 6 f. the left goes to Weybread Church, leaving it on the left about 3 f. At 12 m. 6 ¾ f. the Road right forward goes to Wey-bread Mills. Here turn on the right, leaving a Black-smith's Shop close on the right. At 13 m. 2 f. the left acute backward goes to Hoxne. At 13 m. 3 f the right goes to Wethersdale ; pass along over Shottisford Heath, leaving a Wind-Mill a little on the right. At 13 m. 7 f. the right goes to Halesworth. At 14 m. is Shottisford Bridge; the right goes to Mendham, therefore turn on the left. At 14 m. 4 ½ f. the left acute backward goes to Scole Inn, of which hereafter, and at 14 m. 7 f. is Harleston Chapel.

HARLESTON, is a Town in Norfolk, situate on the North-side of the River Waveny 7 f. from Shottisford Bridge. The Town is compos'd of Harleston, Mendham, Red-

Redenhall, and Starfton; Harlefton being a very fmall Part of it, though it give Name to the whole. It is a tolerable well built Town, having a confiderable Market Weekly on Wednefdays, and two Fairs Yearly, the one on Midfummer Day, and the other on the 29th of Auguft, called St. Jones's; remov'd from Palgrave.

Now return we now to Ipfwich, to take a Survey of divers other Roads Iffuing therefrom.

And firft of the Road from Ipfwich to Landguard Fort. Paffing from the Market-Crofs, by the great White Horfe, down Brook-ftreet, through Tankard-ftreet, and fo through St. Clement's-ftreet, at 7 f. is the end of St. Clement's-ftreet at the Plough Inn. Pafs along from thence, avoiding the firft turning to the right leading to Downham Bridge, and the fecond leading to Nacton. At 2 m. 5 f. is the Warren Houfe clofe on the left. At 4 m. $\frac{1}{2}$ f. is Foxhall Bounds Poft. At 4 m. 5 f. is another Poft; here the right goes to Nacton, the left through Bucklefham to Woodbridge. At this Crofs-way are feven Hills, caft up in Memory of a Battle with the Danes, Anno 1010. At 5 m. 1 f. is the Half way Houfe clofe on the right. At 7 m. 5 $\frac{1}{2}$ f. the left acute backward goes to Woodbridge, of which anon. At 8 m. 6 $\frac{1}{4}$ f. is Trimley Mariners Inn clofe on the right, and the two Churches clofe on the left. At 10 m. 2 $\frac{1}{4}$ f. is Walton Crofs. At 10 m. 5 f. the Road right forward goes to Felixftow, therefore turn on the right, and at 13 m. 1 f. is Languard Fort.

LANGUARD FORT, was built in the Reign of King James I, for the fecurity of Orwell Haven, on the Bank or Point of Langarthfton by the Sea-fide, called in a Record 14th of Edward III. Le-Polles, and in a Patent of Henry VIII. Pollifhened in Alto Mari, which is the Boundary of the Admiralty Jurifdiction of the Town of Ipfwich. This was a large regular Fort with four Baftions mounted with 60 very large Guns, particularly thofe on the Royal Baftion, where the King's Standard was difplay'd, which would throw an eight and twenty Pound Ball over Harwich.

Harwich. It had a conftant Garrifon with a Chapel and many Houfes for the Governor and other Officers, Gunners &c. It was lately demolifhed, and a fmall Platform made inftead of it, by the Waters Side. This Fort is faid to lie in the County of Effex, and that Arm of the Sea, which runs up to Ipfwich, to have ran formerly between Langarthfton and the High-Land of Suffolk ; that Land does indeed appear to have been formerly a Cliff wafhed by the Sea, and I am well informed that it is within the Jurifdiction of the Bifhop of London.

THUS much for Landguard Fort opofite to which on the other fide of the Water is,

HARWICH in Effex, a Town ftrongly fituate by Nature being encompaffed almoft round by the Sea. It was formerly well fortified, but the Fortifications were demolifhed in the Reign of King Charles the II. but it has been fince ordered to be fortified again, and Ground has been bought accordingly to the King's Ufe, by Act of Parliament ; but there is nothing done in it yet. It was incorporated the 13th of Edward the II. The Harwich Men pretended a Grant from Edward the III. to take Cuftom-Duties for Goods coming into that Haven, 'till a Complaint was made by the Town of Ipfwich, that it was an Infringement upon their Liberties ; on which this King granted a Commiffion of Inquiry to John de Welnetham, John de Reckely and Robert de Clare, to appoint a Jury to enquire into this Affair and make their Report. And an Inquifition was taken at Ipfwich upon Monday in Whitfon Week, in the 14 of Edward the III. and the Report of the Inquifitors was, that the Town of Ipfwich had long before received the faid Duties for which they paid a Rent to the King, and that the Men of Harwich, a Hamlet of the Manour of Dover Court, holden of the King, on colour of certain Letters Patents of the 2d of June in the 12th Year of the Reign of our now Lord the King, by which certain Duties were granted to them for a certain time for the benefit of the faid Hamlet and Walling thereof, which Letters Patents were revoked by others

bearing

bearing date the 12th Day of July in the fame Year, and they were commanded to forbear levying the faid Duties, but that notwithftanding, they had levyed the fame at feveral Times mentioned in the faid Report; upon which it was decreed that this Right was folely in the Bailiffs and Burgeffes of Ipfwich. This Commiffion, executed by two of the abovenamed Commiffioners, with the Report figned by the Jurors, is now to be feen in the Records of the Town of Ipfwich. Harwich is a neat, clean, well built Town, and enjoys a good Maritime Trade. It is a Town Corporate, governed by a Mayor &c. and fends two Members to Parliament, has a Market every Tuefday, and Friday, and two Fairs Yearly, the firft on May Day, and the other on the 18th of October. Thus much for Harwich. Return we now to

WALTON, in which there ftill remains the ruins of a Priory, of Black Monks of Rochefter; dedicated to St. Felix the firft Bifhop of the Eaft Angles. The Bigods Earls of Norfolk are fuppofed to have been the firft Founders, or at leaft great Benefactors to this Priory. The Monks were called the Monks of Rochefter, becaufe Robert Bigod, their firft Founder, gave it as a Cell to the Monks of Rochefter, Anno Dom. 1105; the value we find not, it is now the Eftate of Mrs Atkinfon.

WALTON has been an Antient Market Town, and though the Market is now difufed, the Market-Crofs is ftill remaining.

IN the Neighbouring Parifh of Felixftow, on the Colnes fide of Woodbridge Haven, ftill appears the Ruins of a Quadrangular Caftle advantageoufly fituated. In the War between King Henry the II. and his Son Henry, Robert Earl of Leicefter (who was engaged for the Son) attempted this Caftle at his firft Landing here with a great Number of Flemings, and Normans, who though affifted by the Earl of Norfolk, whofe Demefn it then was, could not win it; but, marching off to Bury St. Edmunds, at the Battle of Fornham was encoutered by the King's Forces, his Army totally routed, himfelf and Lady taken Prifoners. It was a-

H   bout

bout this time, that the fame King demolifhed this Caftle, that it might not be an Harbour for Rebels.

THUS much for Walton. Return we now to Wood-bridge to take a Survey of the Road leading from thence to Landguard Fort.

FROM Woodbridge Crown Inn, paffing along in the Ipfwich Road, through Martlefham Village, up Mart-lefham Hill at 2 m. ¼ f. is a direction Poft, where the right goes to Ipfwich, therefore take the left Hand way, avoiding the turnings to the right and left. At 3 m. 2 f. is a direction Poft where the right goes to Ipfwich, the left to Hemly. At 3 m. 6 ¼ f. is Bright-well Park, where the right goes to Ipfwich, the left to Newbourn. At 4 m. 2 f. crofs Brightwell River, the Hall is a little on the left. Paffing thro' Bright-well ftreet. At 5 m. 1 f. enter the Commons; avoid the right clofe by the Hedge thro' Bucclefham to Nac-ton. At 6 m. 1 f. is another direction Poft, where the right goes to Ipfwich, the left to Kirton. At 6 m. 6 ½ f. is another direction Poft, here the firft right Hand Way goes to Ipfwich, the fecond to Levington, the left to Kirton. At 7 m, 4 ¼ f. come into the Road that leads from Ipfwich to Trimly. At 8 m. 3 f. is Trimly Mariners Inn. At 10 m 1 f. is Wal-ton Crofs. And at 12 m. 7 ¾ f. is Landguard Fort.

From Ipfwich to Landguard Fort is ——— 13 m. 1 f.
From Woodbridge to Landguard Fort is — 12 m. 7 ¼ f.
Woodbridge is neareft to Landguard-⎱ ——— 1 ¼ f.
Fort by the diftance of ————⎰

THUS much for thefe Roads. Return we now to Ipfwich, to take a Survey of the Road leading from thence to Scole-Inn called the Pye Road.

FROM the Market Crofs in Ipfwich paffing through St. Matthew's Street, at 2 ¼ f. is a Wheelwright's Shop, the left is the London Road; here take the way right forward. At 3 ¼ f. the left goes through Bramford to Bildefton of which anon, here leave Ipf-wich Street. At 2 m. 2 ¼ f. is Whitton Maypole, from thence paffing through Whitton Street leave Aken-ham

ham Church on the right near 6 f. At 3 m, 6 ¼ f. is
Claydon Village, where the left goes acute backward
to Bramford. At 3 m. 7 ¼ f. the left over Claydon Bridge
goes to Stow-Market, of which anon. At 4 m. is
Claydon Falcon Inn, a Houſe of good Entertainment.
From thence we go through the Turnpike, and at
4 m. 2 ¼ f. the right goes by Barham Church to Henly.
At 4 m. 7 ½ f. the right goes through Coddenham to
Debenham of which hereafter. At 5 m. 6 f. is a Blackſmith's Shop cloſe on the left; here the right goes to
Shrubland Hall. At 6 m. 1 f. the left goes to Needham. At 6 m. 7 ¼ f. the left goes to Needham, the
right to Coddenham, paſſing over a Brook. At 7 m.
2 ¼ f. croſs the Road leading from Wickham Market
to Needham by way of Catts Hill, which is before
treated of. At 7 m. 5 ½ f. is a Blackſmith's Shop cloſe
on the left. At 8 m. 2 f. is Creeting Black-Horſe-Inn.
From thence paſſing along leaving Earl-Stonham Church
on the left near 4 f. At 10 m. 1 ¼ f. is Stonham Turnpike, where the right goes to Stonham-Aſpall, the
left to Stow-Market. At 10 m. 5 f. the left goes to
Stonham-Parva. At 10 m. 7 f. is Stonham Pye Inn,
a Houſe of good Entertainment, cloſe on the left. At
11 m. 4 f. is the four Elms, now the Seat of Thomas
Blomfield, Eſq. At 11 m. 7 f. the right goes to Debenham, the left to Stow-Market. At 12 m. 5 f. the left
goes to Mendleſham. At 12 m. 6 ½ f. the left in at a
Gate to Capt. Gibſon's, and towards Mendleſham. At
13 m. the right goes to Brockford Green. At 14 m.
the right goes to Brockford Green; paſſing along, about
6 f. on the left offers itſelf to view,

MENDLESHAM, a Town ſituate in a dirty Place,
to which the Lord of it, Hugh Fitz Otho, or the Son
of Otho the Mint Maſter, procured the Privilege of
a Market, and Fair of King Edward I. The Market is Weekly on Tueſdays, and a very mean one it
is. The Fair is Yearly on the 21ſt of September.

In this Age ſome Perſons in digging here, found
an Antient Silver Crown weighing about 60 Ounces,
which is thought to have belonged to Redwald, or
ſome other King of the Eaſt Angles.

H 2　　　　　　　PURSUING

PURSUING our Journey in the same Road, at
14 m. 6 f. the right goes to Wetheringsett Church. At
14 m. 7 f. is Brockford Village, here the right goes to
Wetheringsett Church, the left to Mendlesham, passing
along leaving Thwaite Hall and Park on the left, at
15 m. 5 ¼ f. is Thwaite Buck's Head Inn.

THWAITE, this Village has been honoured with
the Residence of the Knightly Family of Reeve, who
had their Seat at the Hall here; Sir George Reeve
Knight was the 22d of January 1661 created a Baronet; this Family is now extinct. There are two Fairs
Yearly held here, the one on the 29th Day of June,
and the other on the 15th Day of November. Here
are two Houses of good Entertainment. At 16 m. 3 f.
the right goes to Thorndon, the left to Wickham Skyth.
At 16 m. 5 ½ f. the right goes to Thorndon, passing
from hence over a Brook, leaving Stoke Ash Church
a little on the right, at 17 m. 2 ¾ f. is Stoke White
Horse Inn, a House of good Entertainment; here the
right goes to Framlingham, the left to Thornham
Magna. At 18 m. 1 f. the right to Braisworth. At
18 m. 2 ¾ f. is Yaxley Bull Inn, where the right goes
to Eye, the left to Thornham Parva. At 19 m. 2 f.
is Yaxley Church close on the right. At 19 m. 4 f.
is Yaxley Pound, where the right goes to Eye, the
left to Melles; pass along leaving a Brick Kiln a
little on the left. At 20 m. 7 f. the right goes to Eye,
the left to Palgrave. Now passing over Great Lanthorn
Green, at 21 m. 1 3-4 f, is Broome Swan Inn, where
the right goes over the said Green to Eye. At 12 m.
2 3-4 f. is Stufton Stone, where the left goes in at a
Gate to Diss, of which anon. Passing from hence,
leaving Stufton Church about 2 f. on the left. At 22 m.
1 ¼ f. the right goes to Hoxne, the left to Diss. At
22 m. 3 f. here the Road comes in that leads from
Bury St. Edmunds, to Yarmouth; of which hereafter.
At 22 m. 5 f, enter Norfolk at Scole Bridge. And
at 22 m 7 f. is Scole-Inn.

OSMONDESTON, alias Scole, is remarkable for
that Spacious House and once beautifull Sign, called
Scole

Scole Inn, which is the only thing remarkable in this Parish; here is a Fair Yearly on Easter Tuesday, and a new erected Fair for Lambs, on the 27th of August, which is likely to continue and increase. Scole-Inn is a good House of Entertainment.

RETURN we now to Stuston Stone aforesaid, in order to pursue on our Journey to Diss.

TURNING in at the aforesaid Gate by the White-Stone, it being from Ipswich hither 21 m. 2 3-4 f. passing through the Fields and over Stuston Common, over the River Waveny and Diss Common, between the Windmills. At 2 m. 5 f. farther is Diss Church; making in all the Distance from Ipswich to Diss 23 m. 7 3-4 f.

DISS, is a Town in Norfolk, pleasantly situate on a rising Hill on the North Side of the River Waveny. It is a considerable large, and tolerably well built Town; the Church is a very good Structure; the Streets are now for the most part well paved, and very clean, the Meere on the South side of the Town is an Ornament to it. It has a considerable Market weekly on Fridays, well served with Flesh, Fish, and all other Provisions. It has but one Fair in the Year, and that is held on the Feast of St. Simon and St Jude. The chief Trade of this Town is in Linnen, Cloth, Yarn, &c. Here are divers reputable Inns of good Entertainment.

THUS much for Diss. We will now return to Ipswich to take a Survey of the Road leading from thence to Debenham.

PASSING along in the last mentioned Road through Claydon Village and the Turnpike as is aforesaid, at 4 m. 7 ½ f. leave the Pye Road which goes right forward, and turn on the right leaving Shrubland Hall and Park on the left. At 6 m. 4 f. the right turns to Hemingston; therefore turn on the left over a Brook and past Coddenham Church, where the left goes to Needham, cross the Pye Road before treated of. At 6 m 7 ½ f. is Coddenham Crown Inn, a good House of Entertainment, where the right goes by Stone Wall to Wickham Market as is before mentioned. At 7 m. 5 ½ f.

5 ½ f. the left goes to Crowfield Hall, here turn on the right. At 9 m. 2 ½ f. the right goes to Gosbeck.· At 9 m. 5 f. the left acute backward goes to Crowfield Chapel. At 10 m. ½ f. is Crowfield Rofe Inn. At 10 m. 3 f. the right goes to Helmingham. At 10 m. 6 f. is Pettangh Church a little on the right, where the right goes to Framfden. At 11 m. 5 ½ f. the right goes to Winfton. Pafs along leaving Winfton Church on the right about a Mile. At 13 m. the right goes to Winfton Church. At 13 m. 1 f. the right goes by Afhfield Swan to Wickham Market. And at 13 m. 5 ¼ f. is Debenham Market Crofs.

DEBENHAM, is a Town fituate on the River Deben, near the Head thereof and fo took its Name of Debenham. The Roads from this Town to all Parts are dirty and troublefome ; yet the Town itfelf is tolerably clean, being conveniently feated on a rifing Hill. Its Church is a good Building, and the Market Place indifferently well built, but the reft of the Town is meanly Built. Here is a Free School founded by the appointment of Sir Robert Hitcham's Will, with a Salary of 20 l. a Year to the Mafter. It has a mean Market Weekly on Fridays, and a Fair Yearly on June 24th.

ABOUT a Mile South Eaft of this Town is Crows Hall, formerly the Seat of the Knightly Family of the Gaudy's. We find Sir Charles Gaudy Knight, of Crows Hall was created a Baronet April 20. 1661. From the Gaudy's it defcended (by Purchafe) to that worthy Gentleman John Pitt, Efq; but he dying without Iffue Male it reverted to his eldeft Brother, a Gentleman of a vaft Eftate. To Crows Hall belongs the Manour of this Town. Thus much for Debenham.

RETURN we now to Ipfwich, to take a Survey of the Road iffuing therefrom to Bildefton.

PASSING from the Market Crofs in Ipfwich through St. Matthew's Street, and fo forward in the Pye Road. At 3 3-4 f. at the Towns end avoiding the great Road on the right which goes to Claydon, take the left hand Way. At 1 m. 3 f. the left goes to Sproughton. At 2 m. 3 ½ f. the right goes Whitton, therefore

turt

turn on the left. At 2 m. 5 f cross the River Orwell at Bramford Bridge. At 2 m. 6 ½ f. the left goes
through Sproughton to Copdock and into the London
Road, therefore turn on the right through Bramford
Village. At 3 m. 3 ½ f the right goes to Claydon and
the Pye or Norwich Road. At 4 m. 4 ½ f. the right
on Road goes through Blakendham magna to Needham and Bury. Here turn on the left, passing along
leave Blakenham parva Church near 1 f. on the right.
At 5 m. 7 ¾ f. is Somersham Church a little on the
left, where the left goes to Flowton. At 6 m. 3 f.
is Somersham Village, where the left goes to Flowton, the right to Nettlestead. At 7 m. ½ f. the left
to Elmset. At 7 m. 2 ¼ f. the Road right on goes to
Barking-Tye, therefore turn on the left by a Blacksmith's Shop. At 7 m. 3 ¼ f. the left goes to Offton-
Castle, Here turn on the right.

OFFTON, is remarkable for a Castle built on
a Chalky Hill, by Offa King of the Mercians, after
he had Slain Etheldred King of the East Angles.
This Castle is now so entirely demolished that not
the least Rubbish of it remains, It is now in the
Hands of several Trustees for Uses unknown to me.
This Town took its Name from King Offa, being
called Offa's Town, now corruptly Offton.
A T 7 m. 6 f. the right goes to Barking-Tye. At
7 m. 7 f. is Offton Church close on the left. At 9 m.
4 f. the right goes to Briset. At 10 m. 2 f.
the right goes to Briset. At 10 m. 4 f. the left goes
to Naughton. At 10 m. 6 f. the left goes to Naughton Church, leaving it on the left about 2 f. Now
passing over Nedging-Tye, leaving Wattisham Church
about 6 f. on the right, at 12 m. 6 ¼ f. is Bildeston Rectory House at the end of Bildeston Street ;
and at 12 m. 7 ½ f. is Bildeston Market-Cross.

BILDESTON, is a Town situate in a Bottom,
meanly built, and the Streets dirty. It appears to
have been more Populous formerly than it is now.
The Church is a very good Building, standing on a
Hill on the West side of the Town, near which is
the

the Manfion of William Alfton, Efq; defcended from the Alfton's formerly in Marlsford in the Hundred of Loes in this County. Here is a mean Market Weekly on Wednefdays, and two Fairs Yearly, the one on Afh-Wednefday, and the other one Afcenfion Day. Here are feveral Houfes of good Entertainment.

RETURN we now to Ipfwich, to Survey the Road leading from thence to Hadleigh,

FROM the Market-Crofs in Ipfwich pafting again through St. Mathew's Street, at 2¼ f. leave the Wheelwright's Shop on the right, and go in the London Road over Handford Bridge. At 6½ f. leave the London Road which goes on right forward, and turn on the right by Hanford-Hall. At 1 m. 4½ f. is a View of the Chantry, of which hereafter. At 2 m. 1½ f. is Captain Harland's Manfion on the left. At 2 m. 4 f. the right goes to Sproughton, the left to Copdock, At 3 m. 4¼ f. the right goes to Burftall Street. At 3 m. 7 f. crofs a Brook. At 4 m. ¾ f. the left goes to Wafhbrook. At 4 m. 7½ f. is Hintlefham George-Inn, where the left goes to Chattifham ; leave the Church clofe on the right. At 5 m. 1½ f. is a View to Hintlefham Hall, of which in another Place. At 6 m. ¼ f. the left goes to Chattifham. At 7 m. 6¼ f. the Road right on goes to Layham, therefore turn on the right. At 8 m. 4¼ f. the left to Layham. At 8 m. 5¼ f. the right goes to Hadleigh Place; here turn on the left. At 9 m. 3¼ f. enter Hadleigh Street ; here the left goes to Stratford; (of which hereafter) turn on the right, and at 9 m. 4¾ f. is Hadleigh George Inn.

HADLEIGH, or as the Saxons called it HEADLEGA, is a large Town extending it felf in length from South to North fomething more than a Mile. It is feated on the North fide of the River Breton. Its Church is a Sumptuous Building, graced with a Spire Steeple, and being near the middle of the Town is a good Ornament to it. 'Tis of fome Note now for the Manufacture of Woollen Cloths, but not fo much as formerly ; but our Antiquaries have a

great

great Refpect for it, it being the Burial Place of
Guthrum or Gormo the Dane. This Guthrum the
Pagan Danifh King, being over-come in Battle by King
Alfred, was by his Perfwafion Baptized, who after-
wards gave him freely the Country of the Eaft An-
gles to govern, which he did 12 Years ; and dying
in the Year 889, was bury'd in the Church here.
It alfo remembers the Martyrdom of Dr. Rowland
Taylor, who was Burnt at Aldham Common in this
Town, Anno Dom. 1555. On the Place where he was
Burnt I obferved a Stone with this Infcription, viz.

Anno 1555.
Dr. Taylor for defending what was good,
In this Place fhed his Blood.

IT has been a Town Corporate, governed by a
Mayor &c. But a Quo Warranto being brought a-
gainft their Charter, in the Reign of James II, they
have never renewed it fince. Here are two Markets
Weekly, on Mondays and Saturdays; the Market is
very confiderable on Mondays, (efpecially in the An-
tumn Quarter) whither the Merchants and Farmers
refort to Contract for large Quantities of Corn ; and
it is well ferved with all manner of Provifions. Here
are two Fairs Yearly, the one on Monday in Wit-
fon Week, and the other on the 29th of September.
The Town is indifferently built, and being in a
Bottom is generally dirty. Here are feveral Houfes
of good Entertainment.

THUS much for Hadleigh. We will now return
to Ipfwich, to take a Survey of the Road leading from
thence to Stratford in the London Road.

FROM the Market Crofs paffing through St Matthew's Street (in the laft mentioned Road) over Han-
ford Bridge, at 6 ½ f. avoiding the right turning to
Hadleigh, keep the Way right forward. At 1 m.
5 ¼ f. is a View to the Chantry on the right. At 2 m.
2 f. the right acute forward goes to Chattifham. At
3 m. 2 f. is Copdock Black-Boy Inn clofe on the
right, where the right goes through Bramford and

I   Claydon

Claydon into the Pye Road for Norwich. Here turn on the left over the Brook. At 3 m. 3 ½ f. the right goes to Wenham. At 3 m. 6 ½ f. the left goes in at a Gate to Belftead, At 3 m. 7 ¼ f. is Copdock White Elm Inn clofe on the right, a Houfe of good Entertainment, where the right goes to Chattifham. At 4 m. 7, 3-4 f. the right to Wenham. At 6 m. ¼ f. the left goes to Bently. At 6 m. 3-4 f. is Capel White-Horfe Inn, clofe on the right. Here the right goes to Wenham. At 7 m. 5 ¼ f. is Capel Brook. At 7 m.. 7 f. the right goes to Wenham, the left to Eaftbergeholt. Paffing by a Blackfmith's Shop clofe on the right, at 8 m. the left goes to Eaftbergeholt. At 8 m. 3, 3-4 f. here the right goes to Hadleigh, the left to Eaftbergeholt. At 8 m. 7 ¼ f. the right goes to Higham. At 9 m. the left goes to Eaftbergeholt. At 9 m 3-4 f. the left goes to Eaftbergeholt, of which hereafter. At 9 m. 7 ½ f. the left forward through a Watery Lane to Dedham. Here turn on the right, leaving Stratford Church clofe on the left. At 10 m. 1 ½ f. enter Stratford Street where the right goes to Higham. Paffing through the Street avoiding the right leading to Sudbury and Hadleigh, of which anon. At 10 m. 5 ¾ f. is Stratford Swan Inn, a Houfe of good Entertainment, and at 11 m. 1 ¼ f. is Stratford Bridge.

STRATFORD, is a through-fare Village, where the Inhabitants imploy themfelves in the Woollen Manufactury. There is a great Trafic through the Village. Stratford Fair is Yearly on the 11th of June.

RETURN we now to Ipfwich, to Survey the Road leading from thence to Cataway Bridge.

FROM the the Market-Crofs paffing through St. Nicholas's Street, at 3 ¾ f. is Stoke Bridge At 1 m. 6 f, is Bourn Bridge, the left by the Waters fide goes to Shotly, of which anon. Keep the Way right forward. At 2 m. 5 ¼ f. the left goes to Capt. Brand's, therefore turn on the right. Then avoiding divers turnings to the right and left, at 4 m. 5 ½ f. is

Sandy

Sandy Hill Inn, where the left goes to Tattingston Church. At 4 m. 7 f. is Bently Brook. At 5 m. 7 f. the right goes to Bently, the left to Tattingston. At 7 m. 3 f. is Brantham Bull Inn, where the left acute backward goes to Shotly, of which hereafter. At 7 m. 7 f. the right forward goes ro Eastbergeholt, therefore turn on the left. At 8 m. 1 f. is Brantham Church close on the left. At 8 m. 3 f. the right acute backward goes to Bently, the right forward to Eastbergeholt, therefore turn on the left. At 9 m. 3 f. the right goes to Eastbergeholt, of which hereafter. A 9 m. 3 ¼ f. is Cataway first Bridge, and at 9 m. 5 ¼ f. is the second Bridge, and about a Mile beyond is

MANINGTREE, a Town in Essex, situated on the Stoure, a large Navigable River. It is but meanly built, and on account of its lying very low, it is generally dirty. It is a Hamlet to Misley, which lies a little beyond it; however, it has a tolerable good Market on Thursdays, and two Fairs Yearly, one on the first Thursday in Whitson-Week, and the other on the first Thursday after Michaelmas-Day. Here are several good Houses of Entertainment.

WE will now return to Ipswich, and take a Survey of the Road leading from thence to Shotly-Gate.

PASSING from the Market-Cross in the last mentioned Road, at 1 m. 6 f. as aforesaid, is Bourn Bridge; avoiding the Road right forward leading to Cataway Bridge and Maningtree, take the left hand Way by the Water side. At 3 m. 4 ¼ f. is Freston Boot Inn. At 3 m. 7 ¼ f. the right goes to Freston Church, the Road right forward goes to Holbrooke, therefore turn on the left. At 6 m. 2 f. is Chelmondiston Lion Inn. Leave the Church about a Furlong on the left. At 7 m. ½ f. the left goes to Shotly Church. At 8 m. 6 f. is Arwerton Park close on the right. Here the right goes to Cataway Bridge, of which above, therefore turn on the left. At 8 m. 6 ¾ f. is

I 2

Shotly

Shotly Bull Inn. At 9 m. $\frac{3}{4}$ f. the left in at a Gate goes to Shotly Church, and at 10 m. 2 $\frac{1}{2}$ f. is Shotly Gate Inn, from whence is a Paſſage by Water to Harwich.

RETURN we now to Ipſwich, to take a Survey of the Road leading from thence to Bury St. Edmunds, being the laſt Road we ſhall treat of with relation to Ipſwich.

FROM the Market Croſs in Ipſwich, paſs through St. Mathew's Street into the Pye Road through Whitton, and in Claydon Village, at 3 m. 7 $\frac{1}{4}$ f. leave the Pye Road which goes right forward, and take the left hand Way over Claydon Bridge. At 4 m. 6 f. the left goes through Bramford, being the Road to London, therefore turn on the right. At 4 m. 7 $\frac{1}{4}$ f. is Blakenham Turnpike, leaving the Church cloſe on the right. At 5 m. 5 $\frac{1}{2}$ f. the left goes through the Fields to Bayleham. At 6 m. is a Blackſmith's Shop cloſe on the left, where the left turns acute backward to Bayleham. At 7 m. 6 f. the right goes to Coddenham, the left to Barking. At 7 m. 7 $\frac{1}{4}$ f. enter Needham Street, where the left goes to Barking. At 8 m. $\frac{1}{4}$ f. the right goes through Coddenham by Stone Wall to Wickham Market, which is before treated of, and at 8 m. 2 $\frac{1}{4}$ f. is Needham Chapel cloſe on the right.

NEEDHAM, is a through-fare Town, extending it ſelf on the Road above half a Mile. It has formerly traded conſiderably in the Woollen Manufactury, but that Trade is now in a manner loſt; however, it now appears to be a tolerably well built Town, in which are ſeveral conſiderable Dealers. It has a mean Market Weekly on Wedneſdays, but a conſiderable Fair Yearly the 28th, 29th, and 30th Days of October. Needham is a Hamlet of Barking, and in it are ſeveral Houſes of good Entertainment.

FROM Needham Chapel, paſſing through the Street and over a Brook, at 1 m. 1, 3-4 f. is a View to Badley Hall on the left. At 1 m. 3, 3-4 f. the right goes to Creeting St. Peter's. At 3 m. $\frac{1}{2}$ f. is Combs Village, where

where the left goes to Bildeston, (of which hereafter) the Road right forward to Finborough magna, therefore turn on the right over Combs Ford. Pass between Stow Windmills, and at 3 m, 4 ½ f, is Stow-Market Cross,

STOW-MARKET, so called to distinguish it from other Places of that Name in the County of Suffolk, as Stow-Langtoft, West-Stow &c. It is a tolerable large well built Town, very near the Center of the County (Needham being something nearer it.) It is situate near the Conjunction of the two chief Springs of the River Orwell. That Head that rises at Wetherden washes the East side of the Town, and the other that rises in Rattlesden runs into that at the South end of the Town at Combs Ford, between this Town and Combs. The greatest Ornament to this Town is its spacious Church and Spire Steeple, dedicated to St. Peter. But there was formerly another Church in the same Church Yard, dedicated to the Blessed Virgin. The Parishes of Stow-Market and Stow-Upland are now consolidated, but they have still distinct Officers for each Parish. There is a Hamlet on the North West side of the Town called by the Name of Chilton, which is now a Member of Stow-Market. Its Market is Weekly on Thursdays, and a very considerable one it is for Corn, and well served with all manner of Provisions. This Town has two Fairs Yearly, the one on the 29th of June, and the other (a Lamb Fair) on the first Day of August. Here are several Houses of good Entertainment. Thus much for Stow-Market.

FROM the Market-Cross in Stow, pass out at the North end of the Town, and at 1 m. 6 f. the right hand Way goes through Haughley to Botesdale, of which hereafter. At 2 m. 5 f. the right goes to Haughley, the left to Halston. At 3 m. 1 f. the left goes to Shelland. At 3 m. 3 ¼ f. the Road right forward goes through Wetherden to Ixworth, (of which hereafter) therefore turn on the left by Haughly Park, and pass over Wulpit Heath. At 5 m. is the end of the Heath, where the right goes to Elmswell, the
left

left to Shelland. At 5 m. 5 f. the left goes to Shelland. At 5 m. 6 f. is Wulpit Church close on the
right.

WULPIT, is a through-fare Village, extending it
self on the Road about a Quarter of a Mile. It has a
handsome Church and Spire Steeple. This Town is
by some supposed to be the ancient Sitomagus, by reason
of the present appearance of large and deep Ditches,
which are conjectured to be Roman Works. It is
as present of no remark but for making the best White
Bricks, and a Fair for Horses &c. Yearly, beginning
September the 6th, which holds a Week &c.

PROCEEDING from Wulpit Church, at $\frac{1}{2}$ f. the
left goes to Rattlesden; therefore turn on the right
through Wulpit Street. At 4 f. the right goes to
Elmswell, crossing over a Brook and leaving Toftock Church about 2 f. on the right. At 1 m. 1 f.
the right goes to Toftock Church. At 1 m. 4 f. the
left to Drinkston. At 2 m. 5 $\frac{3}{4}$ f. is Beyton Bull Inn,
where the right goes to Thurston, the left to Hessett.
At 3 m. 4 f. is a View on the right of Rougham-
House, the Seat of John Corrance, Esq; At 3 m. 7 f.
the right goes to Thurston, the left through the
Fields to Rougham Church, leaving the Mansion of
John Cook Esq; a little on the left. At 4 m. 3 f. is
a Blacksmith's Shop close on the right, where the
right goes to Ixworth, the left pass Bradfield Manger
Inn to Lavenham. Passing along at the entring of
the Heath the right hand Way leads into Bury St.
Edmunds through the East Gate; keep the right forward Way over the Heath, avoiding divers turnings
to the right and left. At 7 m. 1 $\frac{1}{2}$ f. is the River Lark;
here the left turns to Rushbrook. At 7 m 3 f. is
Bury St. Edmunds South Gate; here the left goes to
Lavenham, of which hereafter. Passing through the
South Gate Street, Church and Guild-Hall Streets, at
8 m. 2 $\frac{3}{4}$ f. is Bury St. Edmunds Market-Cross.

FROM

From Ipfwich to Needham Chapel ——— 8 m. 2¼ f.
From Needham to Stow-Market Crofs ——— 3 m. 4½ f.
From Stow-Market to Wulpit Church ——— 5 m. 6 f.
From Wulpit to Bury Market-Crofs ——— 8 m. 2¾ f.

From Ipfwich to Bury-Crofs ——————— 25 m. 7½ f.

THUS much for the Roads iffuing from Ipfwich. We will now Place our next Centre at Bury St. Edmunds.

BURY St. EDMUNDS, is fituate on the Weft fide of the River Lark, which is at prefent Navigable from Lynn to Fornham, a Mile North of the Town. It has a moft fruitful enclofed Country on the South and South Weft, and on the North and North Weft the moft delicious Champaign Fields, extending themfelves to Lynn, and that Part of the Norfolk Coaft. The Country on the Eaft is partly open and partly enclofed. It is fo regularly built, that almoft all the Streets cut one another at right Angles; and it ftands upon fuch an eafy Afcent, that an ancient Writer has recorded this Encomium of it: " That the Sun fhines not upon a Town more a- " greeable in its Situation.

THIS was the VILLA FAUSTINI of the Romans, and afterwards had the Name of BEDERICESWORTH, or BEODRICESWORTH, differently Spelt by different Authors, as Saxon Names frequently are, and taken, if we might credit the Records of the Old Monks, from one Beodricus, who being Lord and Proprietary of this Town made St. Edmund his Heir.

THE Abbey, which was once fo Illuftrious, was firft built by Sigebert King of the Eaft Angles, foon after Chriftianity was planted here by Felix the Burgundian, and being finifhed, King Sigebert, about the Year 638, retired into it and fecluded himfelf from all Temporal Affairs.

A s

As to St. Edmund, from whom this Town has ever since retained its Name, we may well suppose him to have descended from the Royal Blood of the Saxons; but the particular Account, that Alkumundus was his Father, especially that Siwara was his Mother, must be deemed Fabulous. He began to Reign, as King of the East Angles, Anno Dom. 855, in the 14th Year of his Age. Some have imagined that this was the Place of his Coronation: But our Zeal for the Honour of this Town (says my Author) ought not to lead us into so vulgar an Error; for this Ceremony was performed at Buers, not at Bury. Others have represented him as one abandoned to Luxury, and whose Courage was lost by the Effeminacy of those Times; but Asserius who was co-eval with him refutes this Calumny.

He reigned 15 Years, being killed Anno Dom. 870, in the 29th Year of his Age; and his Corpse having lain interred in the Town where he was killed (generally supposed to be Hoxne) 33 Years, was removed to Bury. On this Account, and thro' the Superstition of the Age, the Revenues of the Abby increased so fast, that the Monks, greedy to swallow all the Prey, accused the Seculars among other Things of Negligence and Irreverence to the Corpse of St. Edmund; and so petulant was the Accusation, so strong their Interest, as to procure Power and Authority to eject all the Seculars, and to fill their Places with those of their own, the Benedictine, Order; this they accomplished about the Year 1020, and in the 4th Year of King Canute, who then laid the Foundation of a more Magnificent Church to the Honour of this Martyr, the former in which he had been deposited being but a Wooden Building, or, at best, covered with Wood. The Expence for this Fabrick was raised by an annual Tax of no less than Four Pence on every Plough Land in Suffolk and Norfolk. It was finished in the space of about 12 Years, and consecrated by Æthelnoth or Agelnoth Archbishop of Canterbury, and dedicated to Christ, St. Mary and St. Edmund.

Uvius, Prior of Hulm, was consecrated the first Abbot, Anno Dom. 1020, and in the next Year this
Abby

Abby was exemped from all Epifcopal Jurifdiction by the Council of Winchefter. He firft encompaffed the Abby and a Part, if not the whole, of the Town with a Wall and Ditch, the Ruins of which are ftill to be feen in many Places.

Thus was the Grandeur of this Abby begun: Its Abbots were made Parliamentary Barons, and its Wealth yearly encreafed until its final Diffolution by Henry VIII, when its Valuation exceeded all, except Glaffenbury, it being then valued at 1659 l. 13 s. 11 ½ d. per Annum, according to Dugdale; but Mr. Speed and others fay at 2356 l. 16 s. When this Abby was in its Profperity, there was a Chapell at every one of the Gates, which are five in Number, the Eaft Gate, Weft Gate, North Gate, South Gate and Risby Gate. Some Perfons pretend to know the Names of thefe Chapells; but the Reverend Gentleman who favoured me with this Account of Bury, informs me, there is Foundation for this, therefore I forbear faying any thing further of them.

Instead of the many Chapels and Oratories which were formerly in this Town, there are now only two magnificent and ftately Churches ftanding in the fame Chnrch-Yard; the one dedicated to St. Mary, which is 139 Feet 2 Inches long, and the Chancel 73 Feet 10 Inches, in all 213 Feet. The widh of this Church is 67 Feet 6 Inches; the width of the Chancel, including the fide Ifles, 68 Feet. There is a fine afcent of fix Steps to the Altar, on the North fide of which is the Tomb of Mary Queen of France, Daughter to Henry VII, and afterwards married to Charles Brandon Duke of Suffolk. On her Leaden Coffin is this Infcription, MARY QUEEN, 1533, OF FRANCE. EDMUND. H. —— On the South fide of the Chancel is a large Monument of Roger Drury Efq; and Agnes his Wife, with this Infcription round about it, SUCH AS YE BE, SOMETYM WERE WE: SUCH AS WE ARR, SUCH SHALL YE BE. He died 1472, fhe in 1443. Over againft this on the North fide is another large Monument with this Infcription, WILLELMI CAREW MILITIS QUI OBIIT XXVI DIE MENSIS MAII 1501 — MARGARETE CONSORTIS SUE QUE OBIIT 20

K   DIE

DIE MENSIS JULII A.D. 1525. In the South East Corner of the South Isle is an old Monument of John Barret. The top of the Isle is handsomely illuminated, and his Motto, GRACE ME GOVERN, frequently repeated, and ORATE PRO ANIMA JOHANNIS BARRET.

THE other Church, dedicated to St. James, was built in the Reign of King Edward VI; the length of it is 137 Feet, and of the Chancel 56 Feet 8 Inches, in all 193 Feet 8 Inches; the width of the Church is 69 Feet, and of the Chancel 27 Feet 5 Inches. There is in this Church a convenient Library, but no Monument of Note.

THE rest of the Publick Buildings are the Abby Gate, which still speaks the former Grandeur of the Abby; the Guild-Hall; the Grammar School, endowed by Edward VI; the Market-Cross; the Wool-Hall and the Shire-House.

THE Civil Government of the Town is now lodged in the Hands of an Alderman, a Recorder, 12 Capital Burgesses, and 24 Common Burgesses. These have the sole Right of choosing their own Burgesses in Parliament.

THERE are two weekly Markets, on Wednesdays and Saturdays; the chief Market is on Wednesday, and a very considerable one it is, well served with all manner of Provisions. And three annual Fairs; the first on Easter Tuesday, the second for three Days before the Feast of St Matthew and three Days after, but this is generally protracted to an uncertain length, for the Diversion of the Nobility and Gentry that usually resort to it; and the third on St. Edmunds Day, November the 20th.

THE Benefactors to this Town are very numerous, and the Commemoration of them is annually celebrated on the Thursday in Plow-Monday Week.

THE agreeableness of its Situation has always induced many of the Nobility and Gentry to reside in this Town and in its Neighbourhood; and as it formerly gave Birth and Education to several Persons who were eminent in Church and State, so it has also lately; and I hope I may take its present flourishing Condition

tion as an earneſt of its future Proſperity and Suc-
ceſs.

THUS much for Bury St. Edmunds. We will now
take a Journey from thence to Yarmouth.

FROM the Market-Croſs in Bury, paſſing through
the Eaſt Gate Street, at 6 f. leave the Road going right
forward to Stow-Market, take the left hand Way.
At 1 m 3 ¼ f. is Bury Bounds Poſt-cloſe on the left;
paſſing along avoid divers turnings to the right and
left. At 2 m. 5 f. is Barton Church cloſe on the left,
beyond which avoid the firſt right hand Way leading through Pakenham to Finningham White Horſe
(of which hereafter) and divers other turnings to the
right and left. At 6 m. 2 ½ f. is Ixworth Bridge, and
at 6 m. 3 ¾ f. is Ixworth Pickerel Inn.

IXWORTH, is a through-fare Town, extend-
ing it ſelf about half a Mile on the Road. It is a
Market Town having a mean Market weekly on Fridays, if it may be called a Market. Here are two
Fairs yearly; the firſt on May-Day, and the other on
the 18th Day of October. It is a dirty mean built
Town; yet it is memorable for a Religious Houſe
founded by Gilbert de Blund, or Blount, in a pleaſant
Valley by the River ſide. Its Order was of Canons
Regular of St. Auſtin, and dedicated to the Bleſſed
Virgin Mary. What Benefactors this Houſe had we
find not, but it is probable it had not a few, being
valued at its Suppreſſion at 280 l. 9 s. 5 d. per Ann.
We have no Account to whom this Houſe was granted at its Diſſolution. It is converted into a neat Manſion, being now the Seat of Thomas Norton, Eſq; and
for ſometime has been the Seat of that Family.

LEAVING Ixworth Pickeral Inn, at 6 m. 5 ¼ f.
the right goes to Stow-Market, the left to Thetford,
of which hereafter. At 6 m. 7 ¼ f. take the middle
Way, the right leading to Walſham, the left to
Bardwell. At 9 m. 2 ¼ f. is Stanton Windmill cloſe
on the left, where the left goes to Gaſtrope Gate; the
left acute backward goes through Bardwell to Hon-
ington. At 9 m. 4 f. is Stanton Village, where the
right goes to Walſham.

K 2

STANTON,

STANTON, confifts of two Parifhes, Stanton St. John and Stanton All Saints. Here is a Fair year-ly on the laft Day of May and the firft Day of June.
PASSING along paft Stanton White Hart Inn, where the right goes to Walfham, leaving Hepworth Church on the left about 6 f. At 10 m. 7 ½ f. enter Hepworth Caufey. At 11 m. 4 f. leave it, and enter Whattisfield Caufey. At 12 m. leave the Seat of Mr. Baker on the right about 3 f. At 12 m 2¼ f. the right goes to Walfham, the left to Theluetham; leave Whattisfield Church a little on the right. At 12 m. 4¾ f. is a Blackfmith's Shop clofe on the right, where the left goes to Hindercley. At 14 m 1¼ f. the right to Walfham. At 14 m. 3¼ f. Rickin-gale Inferior Church clofe on the left, and at the end of Botefdale Street, the right goes to Stow-Market, of which hereafter. At 15 m. 2 f. is Bo-tefdale Crown Inn.

BOTESDALE, BOATESDELE or BOTULPHSDALE, is a long mean built, dirty through-fare Town, ex-tending it felf very near a Mile on the Road. The Town is Part Botefdale and Part Rickingale Inferior, Botefdale is the fmalleft Part, though it gives Name to the whole. It lies in two Hundreds, Botefdale is in Hartfmere Hundred, and Rickingale in Blackbourn. The Mother Church to Botefdale is Redgrave. There is a mean Market weekly on Saturdays, and a Fair yearly on Holy Thurfday. Here are feveral Inns of good Entertainment.
FROM the Crown Inn in Botefdale, pafs by Red-grave-Hall, a fine old Seat, leaving it on the left a-bout 2 f. of which more hereafter. At 1 m. 3½ f the right goes to Burgate. Pafs along over Wortham-Common. At 2 m. 6½ f. the right goes to Melles, the left to Difs. At 2 m. 7¾ f. the left acute forward goes to Palgrave. At 4 m. 3½ f. the right to Thrandifton, the left to Palgrave. At 4 m. 4 f. the right turns acute backward to Eye. At 4 m. 7 f. the right to Eye, the left to Palgrave. Pafs through Stufton Street. At 5 m. 5, 3-4 f. the right goes to Eye, the left to Difs. At 5 m. 7 f. the right leads through Broome to Hoxne, the

the left to Diſs. At 6 m. 3 ¾ f. enter the Pye Road leading from Ipſwich to Scole Inn, which is before treated of, and at 7 m. is Scole Inn.

PURSUING the Road from Scole Inn to Harleſton, avoid the Road right forward to Norwich, and turn on the right. At 1 m. ¼ f. is Billingford Horſe Shoes Inn, where the right goes to Broom, the left to Dickle-borough. At 2 m. 3 f. Thorp Abbots Church cloſe on the left. At 2 m. 5 f. the right to Hoxne, the left to Thorp Street. At 4 m. leave the right lead-ing over Syleham-Bridge to Stradbrook, and paſs along through Brockdiſh Village. At 5 m. 6 ½ f. is Need-ham Church cloſe on the left. At 6 m. 1, 3-4 f. the left goes to Starſton. At 6 m. 6 ¼ f. enter Har-leſton Street, where the right acute backward goes over Shottisford-Bridge to Framlingham, which is be-fore treated of, and at 7 m. ¾ f. is Harleſton Chapel.

AT 2 f. from hence leave Harleſton Street, avoid-ing divers turnings to the right and left. At 1 m. 3 ¼ f. is Redenhall Church cloſe on the right. At 2 m. 2 f. is Wortwell, a little Village ſo called, in Norfolk, where the right goes to Mendham, the left to Al-borough. At 2 m. 7 ¼ f. the right leads through Ho-mersfield and Flixton to Bungay. Paſs along in a to-lerable ſtrait Way, avoiding the turnings to the right and left. At 4 m. 1 ½ f. is Denton-Bridge, where the left goes to Denton Church. Here turn on the right, and paſs by Earſham Park on the left. At 5 m 2 f. the left is the neareſt Way from hence to Gilling-ham Village, and is the Coach Road from Bury to Yarmouth; but we ſhall take the right hand Way, deſigning to paſs through Bungay. At 6 m. 2 f. is Ear-ſham Queen's Head Inn, where the left goes from Bungay to Norwich, therefore turn on the right, and leave Earſham Church about 2 f. on the right. At 7 m. 1 f. re-enter Suffolk at Bungay Bridge, and at 7 m. 2 ¼ f is Bungay Market-Croſs.

BUNGAY, is a Town pleaſantly ſituate on the River Waveny which is Navigable for Barges from Yarmouth hither. The Town is well built; but the Streets are, moſt of them, unpaved. It conſiſts of two diſtinct Pariſhes and has two Pariſh Churches, one of
which

which is a fumptuous Structure, and its beautiful Steeple is a great Ornament to the Town.

THERE appear between these two Churches the Ruins of a Benedictine Nunnery, founded by Roger de Glanvil and Gundreda the Countefs, his Wife. But others will have it to be founded by the Anceftors of Thomas de Brotherton Earl of Norfolk. It was well endowed by a great Number of Benefactors, all whofe Gifts were confirmed to the Nuns and their Succeffors, to hold in pure and perpetual Alms, by King Henry II, in the 19th Year of his Reign. This Houfe was valued at its Suppreffion at 62 l. 0 s. 1½ d. per Annum, fays Dugdale, but Mr. Speed and others fay at 62 l. 2 s. 1 d.

THERE alfo remains the Ruins of a very ftrong Caftle, fuppofed to have been built by the Bigods, Earls of Norfolk. In the Barons Wars it was fortified, and made fo ftrong by Hugh Bigod, that he was wont to boaft of it as impregnable, faying in the Wars of King Stephen and the Emprefs,

> Were I in my Caftle of Bungay,
> Upon the River Waveny,
> I would ne care for the King of Cockney.

BUT notwithftanding his great Confidence in this his Caftle, when King Henry II came to the Throne (he having always fided with King Stephen) he was forced to compound with that King for a great Sum of Money, and give fufficient Hoftages to fave it from being demolifhed. But afterwards the faid Earl fiding with Richard Son of the faid King Henry II, againft his Father, he demolifhed his Caftle of Felixftow, and took from him his Caftles of Framlingham and Bungay. In the Reign of Henry III, this Caftle was demolifhed, and Roger Bigod Earl of Norfolk obtained a Licence of King Edward I, in the 10th Year of his Reign to embattle his Houfe in the Place where the Caftle had ftood. Afterwards it reverted to the Crown. But in 4 Richard II, we find that William de Ufford Earl of Suffolk died poffeffed of the Caftle, Burrough and Manour of Bungay. He married Joan
the

the Daughter of Edward Montacute by Alice his Wife, Daughter and Coheir of Thomas Brotherton Earl of Norfolk, and fifth Son of King Edward I, on whom 'tis probable that King fettled them. But now, if I miftake not, it remains to the Duke of Norfolk.

HERE is a Market Weekly on Thurfdays, well reforted unto by the Farmers in the Neighbourhood, and well ferved with all manner of Provifions. There are two Fairs Yearly, the one on the third Day of May, and the other on the 14th Day of September.

THERE is a large Common belonging to this Town (almoft encompaffed with the River Waveny) which is of great advantage to its Inhabitants.

ON the North fide of this Common, on the Norfolk fide of the River, about a Mile from the Town, is a Cold Bath, lately erected by Mr. King an Apothecary in Bungay, in a pleafant Situation, which is daily experienced to be of excellent Effect in curing many Difeafes incident to Human Bodies. Thus much for Bungay.

WE will now purfue our Journey to Beccles. At 2¼ f. from Bungay Market-Crofs leave Bungay Street, where the right goes to Homersfield, the left to Ditchingham. At 5¼ f. is Duke's Bridge. At 7½ f. the right acute backward goes to Homersfield. At 1 m. 1¼ f. the left goes to Wangford Mill. At 1 m. 6½ f. is Mettingham Church clofe on the right; about 6 Furlongs S. S. E. of which we obferved the Ruins of

METTINGHAM Caftle. It appears to have been a Square Building and of confiderable Strength. It was firft built by John, Sirnamed de Norwich, who obtained a Licence from Edward III to make a Caftle of his Houfes in this Town. He dying 36 Edward III, left it to his Grandfon John, who left it to his Coufin and next Heir Catherine de Brews; but fhe taking upon her the Habit of a Nun foon after, Robert de Ufford Earl of Suffolk, and Son of Margaret de Norwich, inherited this Caftle as next Heir. From the de Uffords it defended to the de Mettinghams, who being

ing

ing the Lords of this Town took their Name from it.
It is now the Eſtate of Tobias Hunt, Eſq;

IN this Caſtle was founded a College or Chantry,
by Sir John de Norwich Knight Vice Admiral of
England, dedicated to God and the Bleſſed Virgin
Mary. It was ſurrendred to King Henry VIII. in the
33 Year of his Reign, and then the Yearly Income
was found to be 202 l. 7 s. 5 ½ d Speed, Weav.

CONTINUING our Journey to Beccles. At 3 m.
½ f. is Ship Meadow Church cloſe on the right. At
3 m. 3 f. the left acute forward (with Barſham Church
on the right) goes to Beccles. At 3 m. 7 f. the right
goes to Reddiſham. Paſs by Barſham Church on the
left. At 4 m. 1 ¼ f the right goes to Ringsfield. At
4 m. 4 ½ f is a Brick Bridge. At 5 m. 2 f. is Roſe
Hall, the Seat of Sir Robert Rich Baronet, cloſe on
the left, where the right goes to Ringsfield. And at
5 m. 6 f. is Beccles Church. For the reſt ſee the Road
from Ipſwich to Yarmouth.

From Bury St. Edmunds to Boteſdale is — 15 m. 2 f.
From Boteſdale to Scole Inn is ——— 7 m
From Scole Inn to Harleſton is ——— 7 m. ¾ f.
From Harleſton to Bungay is ——— 7 m. 2 ¼ f.
From Bungay to Beccles is ——— 5 m. 6 f.
From Beccles to Yarmouth, as mentioned } 14 m. 3 f
in the Ipſwich Road is ———

From Bury Croſs to Yarmouth is —— 56 m. 6 f.

RETURN we now to Bury St. Edmund's, to take a
Survey of the Road leading from thence to Gaſtrope
Gate, being the Road from Bury to Norwich.

FROM the Market-Croſs in Bury. At 4 f. is the
North Gate. At 1 m. 1 f. the Road right forward
goes to Fornham, therefore take the right Hand way
over the River, and a little further turn on the left.
At 1 m. 5 ½ f. leave the Thetford Road going right
forward, and take the right Hand way, leaving Fornham St. Martin's Church a little on the left. At
3 m. 1 f. the right to Barton, the left to Timworth.
At 3 m. 4 ½ f. the right to Ixworth, the left to Timworth,

worth, leaving the Church on the left 2 f. At 3 m. 6 f. the right to Ixworth. At 5 m. 2 f. a Blackſmith's Shop cloſe on the left, where the right goes to Ixworth, the left to Livermore mag. leaving the Church on the left near 2 f. At 6 m. 2 f. is Troſton Bull Inn, cloſe on the right; here the left goes to to Rhymer Houſe, therefore turn on the right; and a little farther the right goes to Ixworth, the Road right forward to Ixworth Thorp, Here turn on the left in at a Gate, leave Troſton Church a little on the right. At 7 m. 2 $\frac{1}{4}$ f. the right to Bardwell, the left to Thetford. At 8 m the Road right acute back-ward to Ixworth. Here the Road comes in from Ix-worth to Thetford, of which hereafter; leave Hon-ington Church a little on the right. At 8 m. $\frac{1}{4}$ f. is Honington Street, where the left goes to Livermore parva; the Road right forward goes to Thetford. Here turn on the right over the River. At 8 m. 7 $\frac{1}{4}$ f. is Sapiſton George Inn. A 9 m. $\frac{3}{4}$ f. the right goes to Sapiſton, the left to Fakenham. At 9 m. 5 $\frac{1}{2}$ f. is a Brick Kiln cloſe on the right. Paſs by Barningham Park on the left. At 11 m. 4 f. the right to Barning-ham, the left to Thetford. At 11 m. 7 $\frac{1}{4}$ f. the right to Barningham, the left to Thetford. At 13 m. 3 $\frac{1}{4}$ f. the right to Hopton, the left to Ruſhford; leave Knettiſhall Church 1 f. on the right. At 13 m. 4 $\frac{1}{2}$ f. the right acute backward goes paſt Knettiſhall Church to Coney-Weſton, paſſing by a Pound on the right, where the right goes to Hopton, the left to Thetford, of which hereafter. At 13 m. 5 $\frac{1}{4}$ f. enter Norfolk, and at 13 m. 7 $\frac{3}{4}$ f. is Gaſtrope Gate Inn.

The next ſhall be the Road from Bury St. Ed-munds to Thetford.

From the Market-Croſs paſſing along in the laſt mentioned Road through the North Gate and over the River. At 1 m. 5 $\frac{1}{2}$ f. the right goes to Gaſtrope Gate being the Road laſt treated of; leave Fornham St. Mar-tin's Church cloſe on the left. At 1 m. 7 f. the Road right forward goes to Brandon, of which hereafter. Take the right Hand way, then leave the right to Timworth. At 3 m. 2 $\frac{1}{2}$ f. croſs a Brook by a Pound on the left; leave Timworth Church on the right near

L

3 f At 4 m. is Ingham Church close on the right. Passing from hence over an open Country, past a Place called the Seven Hills, at 7 m. 2 f. is Rhymer House a little on the right; here the right acute backward goes to Trofton. At 9 m. 5 f. is Barnham Crown Inn, where the right goes to Euston, the left to Elvedon; from hence passing over Sandy Lands, at 11 m 5 ½ f. enter Thetford Street, leaving St. Mary's Church close on the left, where the right acute backward goes through Euston to Ixworth, of which hereafter, and at 11 m. 7 f. is Thetford Bridge.

THETFORD, a Town Part in Norfolk and Part in Suffolk, is of great Antiquity; for in Edward the Confessor's Time there were found in it 947 Burgesses, and in the Conqueror's Time 720 Mansions, and the chief Magistrate called a Consul; by which it may be concluded to have been a Town of the Romans. Besides other tokens of Antiquity there is a great High Mount artificially raised up, which was formerly strengthened with Walls &c. This Town is situate on the Little Ouse, which is Navigable from Lynn hither.

THE Town at present is but meanly built; but by the Ruins of the Churches and Monasteries now remaining, it may be concluded to have been formerly very Magnificent. There are at present but three Parish Churches standing entire, two on the Norfolk side, and one on the Suffolk. It is probable when the Bishops had their See here the greatest Part of the Town was on the Suffolk Side, where now remain six Ruins of Churches and Monasteries, besides St. Mary's Church now standing intire, viz. the Cathedral Church or Episcopal See, dedicated to the Holy Trinity; the House of Benedictine Nunns, dedicated to St. George, now called the Place; the House of Black Canons, dedicated to St. Sepulchre; on the right Hand side of the Road from Thetford to Brandon, between that and the Hospital or School, was the House of Fryars Preachers, called God's House; The Hospital, in which was founded a Free Grammar School by Sir Richard Fulmerston, Knt. in the Reign of King James I. and St. Etheldred's Church. There were two other Churches
further

further towards Barnham, so entirely demolished tha there is not a Stone remaining, but the Foundations are plowed over.

I T is a Town Corporate, governed by a Mayor, 10 Aldermen, and 20 Common Council Men ; sends two Members to Parliament ; has a plentiful Market weekly on Saturdays, and three Fairs Yearly, the first on the third of May, the second on the 22d Day of June, and the third on the 14th of September. The Lent Affizes for the County of Norfolk are held here. Thus much for Thetford.

W E will now return to Bury St. Edmund's to Survey the Road leading from thence to Brandon : From the Market Crofs in Bury, paffing out at the North Gate in the laft mentioned Way to Fornham St. Martin's Village, at 1m. 5 $\frac{1}{2}$ f. avoiding the right going to Thetford, laft treated of, take the Road right forward. At 2 m. 3 $\frac{1}{4}$ f. the left acute forward goes to Fornham All Saints. At 2 m. 7 f. leave Fornham Genoveve Church 2 f. on the left. At 4 m. 2 $\frac{1}{4}$ f. is Culford Church, 2 f. on the left. At 4 m 4 $\frac{1}{4}$ f. the right forward Road goes to Thetford, therefore turn on the left. At 4 m. 7 f. the left to Weftow, the right to Ingham. At 5 m. 4 f. is Wordwell Church clofe on the left. At 8 m. 5 f. the right goes to Thetford, the left to Icklingham. At 9 m. 3 f. the right acute forward to Elvedon. At 10 m. 2 f. crofs the Road from Newmarket to Thetford, of which hereafter. Paffing along over Sandy Lands, at 15 m. $\frac{1}{4}$ f. is Brandon Maiden's Head Inn, where the left goes to Mildenhall, of which hereafter, and at 15 m. 3 f. is Brandon Bridge.

BRANDON, is fituate on the Little Oufe, which is Navigable from Ely and Lynn to this Town. It is a through-fare Town, tolerably well built, the Road lying through it from Bury St. Edmunds to Lynn. The Church is a very good Structure, fituate about 3 f. on the Weft fide of the Town. Near 2 f. Weft of the Church is the Seat of Jofeph Birch, Efq; This Town has a fmall Market weekly on Fridays, and three Fairs yearly, the firft on Valentine's Day Feb.

14, the second on St. Barnabas's Day June 11, and the third on St. Martin's Day Nov. 11.

IT was first honoured in giving the Title of a Baron to Charles Gerrard, who for his faithful Services to his Royal Master King Charles I, was by him created Lord Gerrard of Brandon. He was afterwards by King Charles II created Earl of Macclesfield; but that Family being Extinct, Queen Anne, Anno Dom. 1711, created Duke Hamilton a Peer of England by the Stile and Title of Baron of Dutton and Duke of Brandon, whose Succeffor now enjoy that Title.

THIS Town furnished London with a Lord Mayor Anno Dom. 1445, who was John Eyre, Son of John Eyre of this Town, Draper. He built Leaden-Hall for the Use of the City, and left besides that 5000 Marks (a Prodigious Sum in those Day) to Charitable Uses. He died Sept. 18. 1459. Here are several Inns of good Entertainment.

LEAVING Brandon, we will now return to Bury St. Edmounds, to take a Survey of the Road leading from thence to Mildenhall.

FROM the Market-Cross in Bury pass out at the Risby-Gate through the Risby Street. At 3¼ f. the right to Fornham All-Saints, the left goes to Horningsheath. At 6 f. the left to Saxham. At 1 m. 6 3-4 f. the left to Westly. At 2 m. leave the Road right forward leading to Newmarket, and take the right hand Way. At 3 m. 3¾ f. is Risby Church close on the right. Pass through Risby Street, and along in an open Country, and at 7 m. 1 f. is Cavenham Church close on the right, where the right goes to Lackford, the left to Higham Green. Leave the Mansion of Richard Webb, Esq; close on the left. At 8 m. 7 f. the left turns backward to Barrow. Here turn on the right. At 8 m. 7¾ f. is Tuddenham Church close on the right. At 9 m. 3-4 f. the right to Ichlingham, the left to Kentford. At 9 m. 4 f. the left acute forward goes to Worlington. At 10 m. 7 f. is Barton-Mills Inn, a House of good Entertainment; where the left forward goes to Newmarket, of which hereafter, therefore turn on the right, over the River

ver. At 11 m. the Road right forward goes from Newmarket, to Brandon, and Thetford, of which hereafter. Here turn on the left. At 11 m. 6 f. enter Mildenhall Street, where the Road from Brandon to Mildenhall comes in, and at 12 m. 2 f. is Mildenhall Market-Cross.

MILDENHALL, situate on the River Lark, is a very large Town in Bounds, and a half Hundred of it self. The Burrough (commonly called High Town Mildenhall) is a pleasant well built Town. Its noble Church and tall Steeple are good Ornaments to it. There is a plentiful Market weekly on Fridays, well served with Fish, Wild-Fowl and all other Provisions. Its Fair begins yearly on the 29th of September, and a very considerable one it is, lasting four Days. Here are several Houses of good Entertainment. Towards the Fens are several large Streets as big as ordinary Towns, called by the Inhabitants Rows, as West-Row, Beck-Row and Hollywell-Row.

THE Lordship of this Town, in the 9 Edward II, did belong to the Abbot of Bury St. Edmunds. Who it was granted to at the Dissolution of that Abbey we find not; but afterwards it descended to the noble Family of North; from them it descended to Sir Thomas Hanmer, Bart. who now mostly resides there in a noble Mansion a little North of the Church.

THIS Town furnished London with two Lord Mayors, viz. Henry Barton, Son of Henry Barton of this Town, who was Lord Mayor Anno Dom. 1428, and William Gregory, Son of Roger Gregory of this Town, was Lord Mayor Anno Don. 1451. May 17. Anno Dom. 1507, a great Part of this Town was consumed by Fire.

RETUNING from Mildenhall to Bury, we will now take a Survey of the Road leading from thence to Newmarket. Passing from the Cross in Bury through the Risby Gate in the last mentioned Road, at 2 m. leave the Road on the right to Mildenhall, keeping the right on Way. At 2 m. 3 f. the left goes to Saxham. At 3 m. the right goes to Risby, the left to Saxham. Leave Risby Church on the right about 3 f.

At

At 5 m. 1, 3-4 f. is Barrow-Bridge. At 6 m. 6 f. the right goes to Tuddenham, the left to Higham Green. Paſſing along and avoiding divers turnings to the right and left, go directly for Kentford Church; leave Barrow and Gazely Churches on the left about a Mile. At 8 m. 2, 3-4 f. the right goes through Tuddenham to Icklingham, the left to Gazely. At 9 m. 3 ½ f. is Kentford Church cloſe on the right. At 9 m. 4 f. enter Cambridgeſhire at Kentford Bridge. At 9 m. 5 f. the right goes to Kennet, the left through Moulton to Lidgate. At 10 m. 4 ½ f. the right goes to Freckingham, the left to Cheevely. At 11 m. 1 f. the right goes to Chippenham, the left to Woodditton. At 13 m. 5 f. is the end of Newmarket Town, where the right acute backward goes to Thetford, the left acute backward goes to Sudbury, of both which we ſhall treat hereafter, and at 13 m 6 ½ f. is Newmarket Greyhound Inn.

NEWMARKET, is no antient Town, as the very Name imports. It is a handſome well built through-fare Town, having as great Traffic through it as moſt Towns in England. It conſiſts chiefly of one Street about half a Mile in length, and is ſo ſituate that the North ſide of the Street is in Suffolk, the South in Cambridgeſhire. There are two Churches St. Mary's and All-Saints; the firſt of which is Parochial and Inſtitutive; the other belongs to Woodditton, as the Mother Church. His Majeſty has a Palace here for his Reception during the Time of the Horſe Races.

Our antient Hiſtorians ſpeak little of this new beautiful Town: Yet we find that in the Reign of King Henry III. Robert de Inſula (or Liſle) gave one half of it to Richard de Argenton (from whom the Allingtons are deſcended) in Frank Marriage with his Daughter Caſſandra; from which Marriage proceeded Richard de Argenton, who procured, 21 Edward I, a Charter for a Fair to be held here yearly on St. Barnabas's Day, June 11. But how long this Fair has been diſuſed we know not; there are now held here two Fairs yearly, the firſt on Tueſday in Whitſon Week, the

the other on the Feaft of St. Simon and St. Jude, October 28. There is a very good Market Weekly on Tuefdays, well ferved with all manner of Provifions. Here is a Free School endowed by King Charles the II.

THIS Town hath not grown up to its Height by any Manufactures ufed in it, or any particular Merchandize, but by its fituation upon a confiderable Road, and affording Conveniencies for Paffengers ; but chiefly from the frequent refort of the Court or Nobility thither Twice a Year for Horfe Racing and other Diverfions, upon thofe fpacious Plains which furround this Town, called Newmarket Heath, which draws Multitudes of Spectators thither to fee them.

AT 2 f. from the Greyhound Inn in Newmarket leave the Street and the left hand Way which is the London Road. At 5 ½ f. is the Stand clofe on the right. At 2 m. pafs through that Noble Rampart called by the Vulgar the

DEVILS DYKE, becaufe they look upon it a work of Devils rather than Men. It is alfo called Reche Dyke from Reche a little Market Town at the beginning of it. From Reche is croffes Newmarket Heath near to Stechworth. It was formerly the Boundary between the Kingdoms of the Eaft-Angles and Mercians, and now is the Boundary between the Bifhopricks of Norwich and Ely. It is uncertain who was the Founder of fo great a Work : Some afcribe it to King Canute ; but that cannot be true, becaufe Abbo, who mentions it, died before Canute began his Reign. It is moft probable it was caft up in the Reign of King Edmund, for Matthew Florilegus declares, that the Battle againft Ethelwolf was fought between St. Edmund's two Ditches ; the other Ditch is about 5 Miles further towards Cambridge, now called 7 Mile Dyke, but formerly Fleam Dyke. At 4 m. 3 f. is a Stable clofe on the right. At 6 m. 2 ½ f. is Bottifham Village At 8 m. 4 f. Qui Church clofe on the right, and at 13 m. is Cambridge Market Crofs,

From

From Bury St. Edmund's to New Market—13 m. 6 ½ f.
From New Market to Cambridge ————— 13 m.

From Bury St. Edmund's to Cambridge ——— 26 m. 6 ½ f.
From Ipswich to Bury St. Edmunds is ——— 25 m. 7 ½ f.

From Ipswich to Cambridge ——————— 52 m. 6 f.

RETURN we now back to Bury St. Edmund's to Survey the Road leading from thence to Clare Market Cross. At 2 ¼ f. from the Market Cross in Bury St. Edmunds is the West Gate, a little beyond which the right goes to Chevington. At 5 ¼ f. is Standford Bridge. At 6 f. the left acute forward goes to Hawstead; a little further the right is the Road to Horningsheath. At 1 m. 2 f. is Bury Bounds Post. At 1 m. 4 f. the right acute forward to Horningsheath. At 3 m. 3 f. is a direction post, where the Road right forward goes to Brockley. At 4 m. 1 ¼ f. the left leads past Whepstead Church to Nowton; turn on the right; leave Whepsted Church about 2 f. on the left. At 4 m. 4 ¼ f. the right goes to Chevington. At 6 m. 5 f. the right goes to Reed Church, leaving it on the right about a Furlong. At 7 m. 3 f. is Brockley Direction Post, where the left goes to Brockley. At 8 m. 3 ¼ f. is Hawkedon Church a little on the left. At 8 m. 4 f. the left acute backward goes through Somerton to Hartest, the Road right forward to Glemsford, therefore turn to the right. At 9 m. 2 ¼ f. is a Direction Post, where the right goes to Burntash Bridge, through Wickham Brook, to Newmarket of which hereafter. Leave Stansfield Church a little on the right. At 9 m. 4 ¼ f. the right through Denston to Straddishall, the left to Hartest. Cross over the Brook. At 9 m. 5 f. the left goes to Boxsted. At 9 m. 6 ¼ f. the right goes to Kedington. At 12 m. 1 f. the right goes to Hundon. Leave Poslingford Church a little on the right. At 12 m. 2 ¼ f. the left to Glemsford. At 13 m. 2 ¼ f. the right through Chilton Street goes to Kedington; turn on the left past Chilton Chapel (now a dwelling House) and at 14 m. ¼ f. is Clare Market Cross.

CLARE

CLARE, an indifferent large Town fituate on the Stour is is now of no great note, but formerly was for its Owners and the Earls defcended from them. It was the Poffeffion of Richard Fitz Gilbert, Sirnamed Crifpin, who, being a Kinfman of William Duke of Normandy and one of the Principal Perfons by whofe Affiftance he gained the Crown of England in the Battle of Haftings, was greatly advanced by him both in Honour and Poffeffions. In this County he had ninety five Manours given him, and among them this of Clare. He was the firft Earl of Clare, but having his Refidence at Tonebruge (now called Tunbridge) he went ufually by the Name of Richard de Tunbridge. He dying the 14th of King Stephen, his Son Richard Sirnamed Strongbow fucceeded him. To him fucceeded Ifabel his Daughter and Heirefs, who married William Marfhall Earl of Pembroke. His Unele Richard, Son of the aforefaid Gilbert de Tonebruge fucceeded him. To him fucceeded Gilbert his Son, Earl of Clare, who died without Iffue, A.D. 1151, was buried at Clare and was fuceeded in this Honour by Roger his Brother. To Roger fucceeded Richard his Son, who departed this Life in the 8th of King John, and was buried at Clare. To him fucceeded Gilbert, and Richard his Son; Gilbert, who was poyfoned Anno Dom 1262, left Maud his Wife behind him, who had this Manour of Clare for part of her Dowry. Richard left for his Heir Gilbert, Sirnamed the Red, who married Joan D'Acres Daughter of King Edward I, by whom he had his Son and Succeffor Gilbert, who dying without Iffue Male, the Houour became extinct. Afterwards Lionel the third Son of King Edward III. in the 36 Year of the Reign of the faid King was created Duke of Clarence. He firft Married Elizabeth the Daughter of William de Burch Earl of Ulfter and by her had a Daughter Philippa, who was his Sole Heirefs. She marrying Edward Mortimer Earl of March carried the Lordfhip into his Family, who enjoy'd it a few Succeffions. This Dukedom being extinct by the Death of the faid Lionel was not reftored till the 13 Henry IV, when Thomas the fecond Son of that King

M

was

was advanced to the Title of Duke of Clarence; but he dying without Iſſue Male the Title of Clare lay again dormant awhile. In this interval the Caſtle and Town of Clare where the Demeſne of Edmund Mortimer Earl of March, who dying without Iſſue, George Plantagenet Duke of York and Brother of King Edward IV, was created Duke of Clarence. But being afterwards attainted and impriſoned in the Tower he was drowned (as 'tis ſaid) in a Butt of Malmſey Wine. Thus the Title of Clarence lay dormant a third time, till the 22d of King James I, when Sir John Hollis of Hougton in Nottinghamſhire was created Earl of Clare. To him ſucceeded John his Son, who marrying Elizabeth one of the Coheireſſe's of Horace Lord Vere of Tilbury had two Sons, John who died in his Infancy, and Gilbert who ſucceeded him in his Honour and Eſtate, and by Grace his Wife the Daughter of the Earl of Kingſton, he had ſeveral Sons, of whom the Eldeſt, John, who ſucceeded in this Earldom 1688, married Margaret third Daughter to Henry Cavendiſh Duke of Newcaſtle. He was after the Death of his Father in Law, in 6th of King William III, created Marquis of Clare and Duke of Newcaſtle. He died July 17, 1707, being ſuppoſed the richeſt Peer in England of his Time; having no Iſſue Male he left the bulk of his Land Eſtate to Thomas Hollis Pelham, Son of his youngeſt Siſter Grace; he was by King George I, created Earl and Marquis of Clare, and afterwards Duke of Newcaſtle.

SOUTH Eaſt of this Town, between it and the River, are ſtill the Ruins of a very ſtrong Caſtle, as may be reaſonably ſuppoſed by its Situation. Who was the Founder of this Caſtle we find not; but it is certain it was built by ſome of the Noble Perſons aforementioned, who were Earls of Clare.

There was alſo a Monaſtery of Canons Regular of St. Auguſtine, (Dugdale puts it under the Order of St. Benedict) founded in the Year 1248, by Richard de Clare Earl of Glouceſter. This Houſe being an Alien Priory and a Cell to the Abbey of Beckeherlewin in Normandy, was naturalized by King Richard II. Reg. 19. and by him given as a Cell to St. Peter's at Weſtminſter. This Houſe had divers other

Benefactors

Benefactors whose Gifts were all confirmed to the Monks by Pope Alexander. Afterwards it was changed from a Priory of Monks to a College of a Dean and Secular Canons.

This House was valued at its dissolution at 324 l. 4s. 1½d. per Ann. Dugd.

As to the present Condition of this Town, It is but meanly Built or Inhabited ; the Streets not paved, but dirty ; Its Church is a very good Structure, which with the Ruins of the Castle and Monastery are the only things worthy Notice here; it has a mean Market weekly on Fridays, if it deserves that Name, and two Fairs Yearly, the one on Easter Tuesday, and the other on July the 26. The General and Spiritual Courts are held here for this Part of the County. Here are several Houses of good Entertainment.

WE will now return to Bury St. Edmund's and take a Survey of the Road leading from thence to Sudbury. From the Market Cross in Bury at 7 ¾ f. is the South Gate, where the left turns to Stow-Market, of which before ; keep the Road right forward. At 1 m. ¼ f. the right goes to Nowton. At 1 m. 4 ¾ f. is Bury Bounds Post. At 2 m. 2 ¼ f. the right goes to Hawstead ; leave Rushbrook Park close on the left. At 2 m. 7 f. cross a Brook at Sicclesmore Village. At 3 m. the left goes to Welnetham Parva ; leave a Pound on the left. At 3 m. 7½ f. the Road right forward goes through the Bradfields to Felsham, therefore turn on the right. At 5 m. 1¼ f. the left goes to Bradfield St. George. At 5 m. 2 f. is Bradfield Manger Inn, a House of good Entertainment; leave Bradfield Combust or Burnt Bradfield Church close on the right. At 6 m. the right goes to Stanningfield. At 6 m. ¼ f. is a Direction Post, where the left turns through Cockfield to Lavenham, of which anon ; keep the Road right forward. At 6 m. 6½ f. is Lawshall Post. At 7 m. 3 ¼ f. the right goes to Lawshall. At 7 m 4 ¾ f. the left goes to Cockfield ; here turn on the right. At 7 m. 7 ½ f. the right goes to Shimpling street, the left to Cockfield. At 8 m. 2 ¾ f. is Shimpling Post. At 9 m. 4 3·4 f. the right goes to Shimpling. At 10 m. 7 3-4 f. is Alpheton Bridge in Bridge street, where the

left

left goes to Lavenham; therefore turn on the right, and a little further, at the Top of the Hill, the right going to Shimpling; turn on the left. At 11 m. 1 3-4 f. is Melford Bounds Poft. Pafs along in a tolerable Strait way over Melford Green, leaving the Church on the right and the Hall on the left. At 13 m. 1 ¼ f. is Melford Bull Inn, where the left goes to Lavenham, the right acute backward over Melford Green to Clare.

MELFORD, above a Mile in length from North to South, is a pleafant Village, and perhaps the largeft in England that is not a Market Town. Melford Hall is a noble Old Seat, Sir William Cordell had a great Kindnefs to this Town, and as he fettled his Family at the aforefaid Hall, fo he built an Hofpital here for the Poor, which is a noble Foundation. He was Mafter of the Rolls in the Reigns of Queen Mary and Queen Elizabeth. His defcendant Robert Cordell Efq; refiding then at Melford-Hall was made a Baronet June 22 1660. From the Cordells it defcended into the Family of Firebrace, and is now the Seat of Sir Cordell Firebrace Bart. one of the Reprefentatives in Parliament for this County of Suffolk. At the South End of the Town is an old Seat, where the Family of Martin have long refided; for we find that Roger Martin, Mercer, Son of Laurence Martin of this Town, was Lord Mayor of London Anno Dom. 1567. his Defcendant Roger Martin of this Town Efq; was Created a Baronet March 28 Anno Dom. 1667. It is now the Seat of Sir Roger Martin Bart.

KENTWEEL HALL, another Noble Old Seat in this Town, was formerly the Seat of the Lady Rivers. Afterwards it defcended to the Family of Robinfon; my Author informs me that Thomas Robinfon of Kentwell Hall Efq; was Created a Baronet January 26 1681. But the faid Sir Thomas, or his defcendant Sir Thomas Robinfon now living, Purchafing an Eftate at Worlingworth near Beccles and removing thither, fold this Manfion and his other Eftate in thefe Parts to John Moore, Efq; who now refides here.

THE

THE Church is a very beautifull and Noble Structure, ftanding at the North End of the Town. This Town furnifhed London with another Lord Mayor, which was John Milbourn, Draper, Son of John Milbourn of this Place. He was Lord Mayor Anno Dom. 1567. Melford Fair is Yearly on Tuefday in Whitfon Week. Here are feveral Inns of good Entertainment. Paffing along through Melford ftreet, at 14 m. 4¾ f. the right goes to Borely in Effex, the left to Acton, and at 16 m. 2½ f. is Sudbury Market Crofs.

SUDBURY is fituate on the River Stour Navigable for Barges from Maningtree hither, which adds greatly to its Trade. It was anciently called South-Burgh, in Oppofition to Norwich, which is faid to have been the North-Burgh or Village. It is a very ancient Town, and at prefent confifts of three diftinct Parifhes, having therein three beautiful and large Parifh Churches, St. Gregory's, St. Peter's, and All-Saints. The Town is tolerably well built, but the Streets (being moftly unpaved) are dirty. It has a fair Bridge over the Stour, where the Road leads through Ballingdon into Effex.

THIS Town was one of the firft Places where King Edward III plac'd the Dutchmen, whom he had allur'd by his Emiffaries to come into England, out of the Netherlands to teach the Englifh to Manufacture their own Wool, which they were wholly Ignorant of before; and here the Woollen Trade hath continued ever fince in a flourifhing Condition; the Inhabitants at prefent imploy themfelves in making Says &c.

IT is a Town Corporate, governed by a Mayor, 6 Aldermen, 24 Capital Burgeffes and other Sub-Officers, enjoys divers Privileges, fends two Members to Parliament, and is honoured in giving the Title of a Baron to his Grace CHARLES Duke of GRAFTON.

Simon Tibold, or Theobald, Surnamed Sudbury, Archbifhop of Canterbury, tranflated thither from the See of London, June 6. 1375, was a Native of this Town. He was murdered by the Inftigation of one John Ball, a feditious Malecontent and Fanatical

Preacher

Preacher in Wat Tyler's Rebellion. The King fent to know the occafion of their Rifing; they required him to come to them and he fhould know it. The Archbifhop and Sir Robert Hales, Lord Treafurer, advifed his Majefty not to Truft his Perfon with them. Upon this they came to the Tower of London, where the Court was, demanded the Archbifhop and Sir Robert Hales, whom they dragged to Tower-Hill and beheaded. The Archbifhop kneeled down, and received the firft Blow without falling, he put his Hands to the Wound faying, "A ha! it is the Hand of God." The fecond Blow cut off his Fingers ends and felled him to the Ground, and at the eighth Blow they got off his Head, nailed his Hood upon it, and fixing it upon a Pole fet it upon London Bridge. One John Starling, who boafted he had beheaded him, loft his Head for the fame a few Days after. He was a moft Reverend, Wife, Learned, Eloquent, Liberal and Merciful Man; he built the upper end of St. Gregory's Church in this Town, where his Head is fhown to this Day; it was not long fince entire, covered with the Flefh and Skin dried by fome Art, the Mouth wide open, occafioned by the dying Convulfions. He founded in the fame Place where his Father's Houfe ftood a goodly College, which he furnifhed with Secular Priefts and other Minifters, and fo bountifully endowed it, that at the Suppreffion it was valued at 122 l. 18 s. per Annum, Speed, Weaver, Goodwyn; it is now in Ruins.

HERE was alfo a Priory dedicated to the Honour of our Saviour and St. Bartholomew the Apoftle, of the Order of St. Auguftine, founded (as Mr. Speed fays from Leland) by the fame Archbifhop Sudbury and one John de Chertfey; but Mr. Weaver from his Manufcript tells us, That it was founded by one Baldwin de Shipling, or Simperling, and Chabil his Wife only, who lie buried in the Priory-Church with many others of Note. This Priory (fays Mr. Weaver) was furrendred to King Henry VIII. Reg. 36. Dec. 9. and was found in Annual Rents worth 222 l. 18 s. 3 d. To whom this Priory was granted at its Diffolution we know not. It is now a very good old Building

and

and is the Manſion of Denny Cole, Gent. the preſent Town Clerk of Sudbury.

RETURNING to Bury St. Edmunds, our next Buſineſs ſhall be to take a Survey of the Road lead-ing from thence to Lavenham.

FROM the Market-Croſs in Bury St. Edmunds, paſſing out at the South Gate, and in the laſt men-tioned Road, through Sicclemore Village, and paſt Brandfield Manger Inn, at 6 m. ½ f. come to the afore-ſaid Direction Poſt ; here avoiding the Road right for-ward leading through Melford to Sudbury, which was laſt treated of, take the left hand Way and paſs through a Village called Cockfield-Croſs, and by a Manſion a-bout a Furlong on the left, being the Seat of the Harvey's. At 6 m. 7 ¾ f. is Cockfield Crown and Punch-Bowl Inn, on the left of which 2 f. is Cock-field Church. At 7 m. 3 ½ f is Cockfield Windmill, where the left goes to Felſham. At 8 m. 1 ½ f. the right goes to Alpheton, the left to Felſham. At 8 m. 2 ¾ f. is a Blackſmith's Shop cloſe on the left. At 8 m. 6 ¼ f. the right goes to Alpheton. At 10 m. 6 f. is the end of Lavenham Street, where the left goes to Preſton. At 11 m. ½ f. is Lavenham Swan Inn.

LAVENHAM, LANHAM or LEVENHAM, an in-different large well built Town, ſtanding upon a Branch of the River Breton or Bret. It is ſituate on a Hill of an eaſy aſcent, on the top of which is a ſpacious Market Place, whoſe Market, being weekly on Tueſ-days, was formerly very conſiderable, but now ſcare deſerves the Name of a Market. The Fair is yearly on the 29th of September, which is of great Repute, eſpecially for Butter and Cheeſe.

THE Staple Trade of this Town for Blue Cloths was anciently very famous and much enriched it. It was then, for the better regulating their Manufacture and employing and providing for their Poor, divided into three Guilds or Companies, who had each of them diſtinct Conſtitutions and Orders, viz. 1. The Guild of St. Peter, granted by John Earl of Oxford 2 Edward VI, whoſe Hall was in the High Street. 2. The Guild of the Holy Trinity, granted by the ſame

Earl,

Earl, 6 Edward VI, whofe Hall was in Prentice Street. 3. The Guild of Corpus Chrifti, granted by another Earl of Oxford, 21 Henry VIII, whofe Hall is in the Market Place. Thefe Companies have been long out of ufe, but the Town is ftill governed by fix Capital Burgeffes or Headboroughs, who choofe inferior Officers, hear and regulate the Complaints of the Poor, and preferve good Orders in the Town. But the Woollen Manufacture is not quite loft ; for though Blue Cloths are not made here as heretofore, yet here is a Staple Trade carried on for making Serges, Shalloons, Says, Stuffs, and Spinning fine Yarn for London, which has of late flourifhed very much, by fetting up a a Hall for felling Wool; which being conveniently fituate for the Traders of the adjoyning Parts of the Country, many Hundred Loads of Wool are Sold out to Tradefmen in a Year.

THE Church and Steeple juftly accounted the fineft in the County, are fituate upon a Hill on the Weft fide of the Town, the Steeple lifting up a Majeftick Head of 137 Feet in height, over-looking a fine fruitful Country. They are noble Pieces of Architecture, and were beholden to the de Veres Earls of Oxford, and the Springs for their Grandeur, who were great Benefactors to them, as may be fuppofed from their Arms being on divers Parts of the Church, Chancel and Steeple. In the Steeple are fix large tunable Bells, of which the Tenor hath fuch an admirable Note, as perhaps England has none to compare to it. It weighs but 23 C. but founds like a Bell of 40 Hundred weight.

THE Charities to this Town are many and exemplary, and may be reduced under three Heads. 1. For the Maintenance of the Poor, the Inhabitants of the Town purchafed 80 l. per Annum for repairing the Alms Houfes, and maintaining fuch as are put into them. Dr. Coppinger, once Rector here, gave 10 l. a Year for ever for the Maintenance of 4 Poor Perfons in this Town. John Carder, gave, 12 Charles I, 40 s. per Aunnm for ever, to be given to the Poor in Bread in Time of Lent ; and Mr. John Cream gave 40 l. towards the Maintenance of 12 Widows of this Town. 2. Richard Peacock of Lavenham gave, 23 Charles II,

5 l.

5 l. per Annum for educating five Poor Boys in the Grammar School ; and Edmund Colman of Furnivals Inn, Esq; gave, the 8 William III, 200 l. to the which the Inhabitants and some other Pious Persons gave such Additions as purchased a convenient Dwelling and School-house, and an Annuity of 30 l. a Year for the Master. 3. Robert Rice, Gent. gave 5 l. a Year for ever for binding out two Poor Boys of Preston, where he lived; and for want of such there, of Lavenham. Edward Colman, Esq; aforesaid gave 200 l. to be laid out in Land for binding out one Poor Boy yearly of 14 Years of Age, born and brought up in Milden, Brent-Ely or Lavenham. This Town furnished London with a Lord Mayor Anno Dom. 1463, who was Thomas Cooke, Draper, Son of Robert Cooke of this Town.

THE Generals and Spiritual Courts are held here for this Part of the Arch-deaconary of Sudbury. Here are several House of good Entertainment.

THUS much for Lavenham ; we will now take a Survey of the Road leading from thence to Sudbury.

FROM the Swan Inn in Lavenham, avoid the left hand Way leading to Bildeston, of which hereafter. Pass right forward, leaving the Church close on the right. At 2 f. the Road right forward goes to Alpheton ; therefore turn on the left. At 4¼ f. is a direction Post where the right goes to Melford. At 1 m. ½ f. enter Washmore Green, where the left goes cross the Green through Waldingfield Parva, over Cornerd Heath, to Bures. At 2 m. 7½ f. is another direction Post, where the left turns acute backward through Waldingfield Parva to Bildeston. At 3 m. 2⅘ f. enter Babergh Heath, where on the right is the Mansion of Roger Kedington, Gent. Here the right goes over the Heath through Acton to Melford. the left through Waldingfield Magna, past the Mansion of Joseph Alston, Esq; in Edwardston, to Kersey and Hadleigh, being the nearest way from Melford to Ipswich. Pass directly forward over the Heath. At 4 m. 1 f. the Road right forward goes to Colchester ; here take the right hand way. At 4 m. 7½ f. is a view of

N   Chilton

Chilton Hall, about a furlong on the left, and at 6 m. 2 ½ f. is Sudbury Butter Cross.

From Bury St. Edmunds to Lavenham aforesaid is	11 m. 0 ½ f.
From Lavenham to Sudbury is	6 m. 2 ½ f.
From Bury to Sudbury by way of Lavenham is	17 m. 3 f.
From Bury to Sudbury, by way of Melford is	16 m, 2 ½ f.
'Tis the neareſt Way from Bury to Sudbury by Way of Melford by the Diſtance of	1 m. 0 ½ f.

HAVING finiſhed the Survey of the Roads iſſuing from Bury St. Edmunds we will now make Sudbury the next Centre, and take a Survey of three Roads iſſuing from thence, viz. to Haverhill, Hadleigh, and through Bures and Neyland to Stratford Swan Inn. And firſt of the Road leading through Clare to Haverhill. Paſſing back in the forementioned Road leading from Bury to Sudbury, through Melford Village, over the River, leave Melford Hall and the Bury Road on the right. At 3 m. 3 3-4 f. is Melford Black Lion Inn; here turn on the left. At 4 m. the right goes through Stansfield and Wickham Brook towards Newmarket, of which hereafter. At 4 m. 6 3-4 f. is Glemsford Bridge. At 5 m. 1 f. the right goes to Glemsford; paſſing along leave Pentlow Church in Eſſex, about 2 f. on the left. At 6 m. 7 f. the left goes to Foxerd or Foxearth. At 6 m. 7 3-4 f. croſs a Brook at the end of Cavendiſh ſtreet, where the right goes to Glemsford. At 7 m. 1 ¼ f. is Cavendiſh Church cloſe, on the right, where the right goes to Poſlingford.

CAVENDISH, a Village ſituate upon the Stour, is memorable for giving Name to the noble Family of Cavendiſh. Sir John Cavendiſh Born in this Place was Lord Chief Juſtice of the King's Bench 46 Edw. III, and continued in that Station till the 5 Rich. II. He was honeſt and learned, great faults in thoſe
unhappy

unhappy Times. For which Qualifications he was beheaded by the Rebellious Crew headed by John Raw,
a Prieſt, and Robert Weſtbroom, at Bury St. Edmunds.
From this Learned and upright Judge deſcended William Cavendiſh, who was the 3 Jac. I. advanced to
the Dignity of Baron Cavendiſh of Hardwick and
Earl of Devonſhire, whoſe Succeſſor is now Duke
of Devonſhire.

PURSUING our Journey to Clare, we leave a
Windmill cloſe on the left ; a little beyond, croſs a
Brook, at the entrance of Clare, where the right goes
to Chilton ; leave the Ruins of Clare Caſtle on the left.
At 9 m. 5 ¾ f. is Clare Half Moon Inn. Paſs
through Clare ſtreet, at the end of which avoid the
left going through Braintree in Eſſex towards London.
At 11 m. 2½ f. the right goes to Hundon, therefore
turn on the left. At 12 m. 1 f. is Stoke Church cloſe
on the left, where the left goes over the Stour into
Eſſex.

STOKE Juxta Clare, is of Remark for a Priory
tranſlated from the Caſtle of Clare thither by Richard
de Tonbruge, Earl of Clare. It was of the Benedictine
Order. Edmund Mortimer Earl of March, changed
it from a Priory to a Collegiate Church of a Dean and
Secular Canons, Pope John XXIII and Martin V
ratifying this Change. It was valued at its Diſſoltion at
320 l. 4 s. 1 d. per Annum. Dudgale. Who this College
was granted to at its Diſſolution we know not. If it was
not then granted, it afterwards came to the Family of
Elwes, for Jervaiſe Elwes, Eſq; of Stoke Juxta Clare
was created a Baronet, July 22d, 1660, whoſe Succeſſor
Sir Harvey Elwes now enjoys the Honour and Eſtate.
He reſides in a good old Seat where the Priory ſtood.
Stoke Fair is on Monday in Whitſon-Week.
PASSING from Stoke, leave the Priory on the left.
At 13 m. 13-4 f. the right goes through Kedington to
Newmarket ; here turn on the left over the Stour; enter
Eſſex. At 13 m. 3¼ f. is Bathan Inn, cloſe on the left,
where the Road right forwards goes to Colcheſter ;
therefore turn on the right ; leave Whixoe Church about
3 f. on the ſame hand. At 14 m. 1 f. the right to

Whixoe

Whixoe Mill; here turn on the left. At 14 m. 3 f. the Road right forward goes to Bumſtead, wherefore turn on the right. At 14 m. 5 f. is Whatsfar Bridge. At 14 m. 7 f. the right goes to Whixoe. At 15 m. 4¼ f. is Sturmer Village, where the right goes to Kedington, the left to Bumpſtead. At 16 m. 3 3-4 f. re-enter Suffolk at Haverhill Bounds. At 16 m. 5 ¾ f is the end of Haverhill-Street; where the right goes to Kedington, and at 17 m. 3½ f. is Haverhill Church.

HAVERHILL, or as in old Records HAVER-HULL or HAVEREL, is a long through-fare mean built Town, about a Mile in Length. The South End of of the Street is part in this County, and part in Effex. The North End is wholly in Suffolk. It has a mean Market weekly on Wedneſdays, and two Fairs yearly, the one on May the 1ſt, and the other on Auguſt the 15th. Here is nothing in this Town worthy of remark, at preſent; but it ſeems to have been larger than it is now, by the Ruins of a Church or Chapel, ſtill remaining

RETURN we now to Sudbury to Survey the Road leading from thence through Boxford to Hadleigh. From the Butter Market-Croſs in Sudbury, leaving the Bures Road turning to the right; paſs out at the Eaſt end of the Town. At 5 f. the left goes to Chilton. At 6¼ f. is a Brick Kiln cloſe on the right. At 1 m. 5 f. enter Cornerd Heath, where the left goes over the Heath to Waldingfield Parva At 1 m. 7½ f. the right goes to Bures, the left over the Heath through Waldingfield and Lavenham to Bury St. Edmunds, being the Common Road from Bures to Bury. At 2 m. 1¾ f. is the End of the Heath where the left acute backward goes over the Heath, to the Waldingfields. At 2 m. 6 f. is Newton Saraſens Head Inn. Paſs over Newton Green; leave the Church about 3 f. on the left. At 3 m. ½ f. leave the Green, where the right goes acute backward to Bures. At 3 m. 5½ f. the Road right forward goes through Stoke to Dedham, being the common Road from Sudbury thither; therefore turn on the left. At 4 m. ¾ f. the left goes to Newton Church. At 5 m. the right goes to Affington. At 5 m. 2¼ f. is a
Pound

Pound on the right; where is a view of Coddenham Hall on the right Pass from hence by a Wind-mill on the left and Boxford Church on the right. At 6 m. 3-4 f. is Boxford Bridge.

BOXFORD, a neat well built Village situate in a bottom between two Brooks, (who have their conjunction a little below it) is a Place of great Traffick, and considerable Trade; here are two Fairs Yearly, the one on Easter Monday and the other on the Feast of St. Thomas, September 21.

ABOUT a Mile South East of this Village, situate in the Parishes of Boxford, Stoke and Assington, we observed Peyton Hall, granted by William I, to Robert Mallet, a Norman Baron, a Progenitor of the ancient Family of Peyton, from which descended the de Uffords Earls of Suffolk, who assumed the Surname of Peyton, according to the Custom of those Times. From the Peytons it came to the Dashwoods, and is now the Lordship and Demesne of George Dashwood, Esq; who has a Seat in or near Sudbury, called by the name of Wood-Hall.

SOUTH West of Boxford Church we observed Coddenham Hall, a very good Seat, formerly the Lordship and Demesne of Sir Joseph Brand, now of Thomas Bennet, Esq.

AT the East End of Boxford Street is another very neat Mansion, now the Seat of Henry Benyon, Esq.

PASSING from Boxford, where the left goes through Lavenham to Bury, take the right hand Way past the Fleece Inn, a House of good Entertainment; avoid the left going to Groton; pass by the Mansion of Henry Benyon, Esq; At 6 m 2 f. the Road right forward goes to Stratford, therefore turn on the left. At 6 m 7 f. the left goes to Groton. Pass along over Wickerstreet Green. At 8 m. 2 f. is Colt's Tye, where the right goes to Polstead, the left to Milden. At 8 m. 4½ f. on the left comes in the Road before mentioned leading from Melford, through Acton, over Babergh Heath, past Waldingfield magna Church, and the Mansion of Joseph Alston, Esq; through Hadleigh, to Ipswich. At 8 m. 5¼ f. the right goes to Polstead.

At

At 8 m. 7 ½ f. is Samfons Hall clofe on the right. At 9 m. 4 f. is Kerfey Church, a little on the left ; here the left turns through Kerfey to Seamer, therefore turn on the right.

KERSEY, is memorable only for a Priory of Monks of St. Benedict, of which we obferve nothing more but that Nefta de Cokefield, Widow of Thomas de Burgh, gave to God and the Church of St Mary and St. Anthony in this Place, and to the Canons ferving God there, divers Lands of which fhe and her Hufband paffed a Fine 4 Henry III. Here is a Fair yearly on Eafter Tuefday.

PURSUING our Journey to Hadleigh, at 10 m 2 f. the left goes to Bildefton, of which hereafter; here turn on the right. At 11 m. 1 f. is the end of Hadleigh Street, where the right goes to Polftead; here turn on the left over Hadleigh Bridge. At 11 m. 2 3-4 f. the Road right forward goes to Aldham; turn on the right, and at 11 m. 4 3-4 f. is Hadleigh George Inn.

From Ipfwich to Hadleigh is ———— 9 m. 4 ¾ f.
From Hadleigh to Sudbury is ———— 11 m. 4 ¾ f.

From Ipfwich to Sudbury is ———— 21 m. 1 ½ f
From Sudbury to Clare is ———— 9 m. 5 ¾ f.
From Clare to Haverhill is ———— 7 m. 5 ¾ f.

From Ipfwich to Haverhill by Way of Sudbury is ———— 38 m. 5 f.

WE will now return to Sudbury, to Survey the Road leading from thence through Bures and Neyland to Stratford Swan Inn.

FROM the Butter Crofs pafs out at the Eaft end of the Town; avoid the laft mentioned Road leading to Boxford, going on the left. At 4 ½ f. the left goes to Chilton. At 7 ¼ f. is Cornerd magna Church clofe on the left. At 1 m 1 ½ f. is a Blackfmith's Shop clofe on the right, where the right goes to Cornerd Mill, the left to Cornerd Street. At 1 m. 5 ¼ f. the right goes to Amey Mill, the left to the laft mentioned Street ;

Street; paſs over Cornerd Mere. At 1 m. 7¼ f. is another Blackſmith's Shop on the right. At 2 m. 1 3-4 f. the left goes to Little Cornerd. At 3 m. 3-4 f. the left goes to Little Cornerd. Paſſing along, avoiding divers turnings to the left, keep the Road turning to the right. At 5 m. 1½ f. enter Bures Street, where the left goes acute backward to Boxford. At 5 m. 3 f. is Bures Church cloſe on the right; here the right goes over Bures Bridge to Colcheſter.

BURES, a Villiage on the Stour, over which it has a fair Bridge leading through Bures Hamlet (in Eſſex) to Colcheſter. Galfridus de Fontibus (who wrote about the Year 1156) tells us, That King Edmund who was cruelly murdered by the Danes at Hoxne in this County, was Crowned here. His Words are theſe, " Edmund being unanimouſly approved by the Eaſt " Angles (who had been without a King 60 Years) " they brought him to Suffolk, and in the Village " called Burum made him their King; and the Ve- " nerable Prelate Hunibert attending, he anointed and " conſecrated him. Now Burum is an ancient Royal " Ville, the known Boundary between Eaſt Saxe and " Suffolk, and ſituate upon the Stour, a River very rapid " both in Summer and Winter." Which Paſſage (ſaith the Author of the Additions to Cambden) is the more obſervable, becauſe it ſhews what we are to under- ſtand by Burva, in Aſſerius's Life of Alfred; that it is not Bury, as ſome have conjectured, nor yet Bourn in Lincolnſhire, as others have aſſerted; but this Bures, or Buers, as Matthew Weſtminſter calls it.

THE Church and Spire Steeple were great Orna- ments to this Village, but in the Year 1733 the Spire was ſet on Fire by Lightning and burnt down to the Steeple; the Bell Frames were likewiſe burnt, the Bells melted, and the Steeple much damaged. Bures Fair is yearly on Holy Thurſday.

AT Small-bridge in this Pariſh long reſided the ancient Family of Waldgrave, which is now extinct.

PASSING through Bures Street, at 5 m. 5¼ f. is Bures Pound cloſe on the right, where the right goes to Bures Mill. At 6 m. 4¼ f. croſs over a Brook. At

7 m.

7 m. 5 f. the left goes to Newton, therefore turn on the right. At 8 m. 1 ½ f. the Road right forward goes to Affington ; here turn on the right ; leave Wifton Church on the right 2 f. At 8 m. 6 ½ f. the right leads to it ; here turn on the left. At 8 m. 7 ½ f. the left goes to Affington. At 9 m. 6 ½ f. enter Neyland Street. At 10 m. ½ f is Neyland Crofs Street, where the right goes paft the Church over the Bridge to Colchefter, the left through Stoke and Boxford to Lavenham and Bury.

NEYLAND, a Town fituate on the Stour over which it has a fair Bridge leading into Effex ; it is tolerably well built and inhabited. The Church and Spire Steeple ftanding near the middle of the Town are good Ornament to it. The Woolen Manufacture has flourifhed here, but now not fo much as formerly ; yet the Inhabitants at prefent imploy themfelves in making Bays and Says. Here is a mean Market weekly on Fridays, and one Fair Yearly on September the 21.

CONTINUING our Journey towards Stratford, at 10 m. 1 3-4 f. is the End of Neyland ftreet. At 11 m. is Stoke Park, where the right goes to Thurfton alias Thirteen ftreet ; crofs a Brook ; leave Sir John Williams's fine Seat on the right, and Stoke Church on the left. At 11 m. 6 ¼ f. is Stoke Village, where the Road right forward goes to Hadleigh, the left goes through Affington and Newton to Sudbury, being the Common Road from Stratford thither ; therefore turn on the right.

STOKE JUXTA NEYLAND, called in our Hiftories Stoke-Neyland to diftinguifh it from other Villages of that Name in this County, as Stoke by Clare &c. Its Church and Steeple are noble Structures ; the Steeple lifting up a Majeftick Head is feen at a confiderable diftance, and affords a good Profpect. Stoke Fairs are Yearly on the 24 February and May 1.

SIR John Capel, Draper, Lord Mayor of London, Anno Dom 1503, was a Native of this Place, from whom is defcended the prefent Earl of Effex.

GIFFARD's Hall in this Parish is a noble old Seat, and for some time has been the Seat of the Knightly Family of the Mannocks, for Francis Mannock of Giffard's Hall in Stoke Neyland, Esq; was created a Baronet June 1, Anno Dom. 1627, whose Successors have enjoy'd the Honour and Estate ever since, and it is now vested in Sir Francis Mannock, Baronet.

TENDRING HALL in this Parish is another good Seat; it has for some time been the Seat of the Family of Williams, and is now the Seat of Sir John Williams, Knt. one of the present Aldermen of London. Passing along leave the Park on the right. At 12 m. f. is the end of the Park, where the right goes to Neyland. At 13 m. 1 f. the right goes to Boxsted, the left to Hadleigh. Pass through a Village called Thurston alias Thirteen Street and over a Brook. At 13 m. 7 $\frac{1}{4}$ f. the right goes to Langham. At 14 m. 5 $\frac{1}{4}$ f. is Higham Bridge. At 14 m. 7 3-4 f. is Higham Village, where the left goes to Hadleigh, of which hereafter; the Road right forward goes to Ipswich; therefore turn on the right past Higham Church on the same hand. At 15 m. 4 $\frac{1}{2}$ f. the left goes to Holton, the Road right forward to Ipswich; here turn on the right, and at 16 m. 1 f. is Stratford Swan Inn.

From Sudbury to Bures is ——————— 5 m. 3 f.
From Bures to Neyland is —————— 4 m. 5 $\frac{1}{2}$ f.
From Neyland to Stratford Swan Inn is —— 6 m. $\frac{1}{2}$ f.

From Sudbury to Stratford by way of Bures is 16 m. 1 f.

BEING arrived at Stratford we will now take a Survey of the Road leading from thence through Eastbergholt, Brantham, Stutton and Holbrook, to Shotley Gate Inn. Go into the Road before treated of leading from Ipswich through Stratford to London, past Stratford Church. At 1 m. 5 f. leave the Ipswich Road which goes right forward and turn on the right. At 2 m. 6 3-4 f. is Eastbergholt Bull Inn.

EASTBERGHOLT, is a large well built Village situate about half a Mile North of the Stour. The

O

Cloth

Cloth Manufacture formerly flourished here, and there is something of it still remaining; it is supposed to have been a Market Town, but the Market is now disused. Here is a Fair Yearly at Whitsontide. The Church is a very good Structure, but the Steeple is in ruins; yet there is a good Ring of Bells in a Cage in the Churchyard, which are rung by Hand. A little South of the Church is a neat Mansion built not many Years since by ____ Chaplin Esq; from whom it descended to Sir Henry Hankey, Knt. one of the present Aldermen of London. It is now a Country Seat for that Family.

PASSING from the Bull Inn aforesaid out at the East end of the Street over a Common, corruptly called Barfield Heath, at 5 m. 3-4 f. is Cattaway Bridge close on the right, where the right goes over it to Manningtree, therefore turn on the left passing along in the aforementioned Road from Ipswich to Cataway Bridge, past Branham Church. At 7 m. 3-4 f. is Brantham Bull Inn close on the right. Here leave the Ipswich Road going towards the left, keeping the Road right forward. At 8 m. 1 ¼ f. is Stutton Hall about 3 f. on the right; Pass through Stutton Village, at the End of which the left goes to Ipswich; here turn on the right, and a little further the Road right forward goes to Stutton Church, therefore turn on the left. At 10 m. 2 ¼ f. cross the River at Holbrook Mill. At 10 m. 3 ¾ f. the Road right forward goes through Holbrook Street to Ipswich. Here turn on the right. At 10 m. 6 f. is Holbrook Hall, where the left goes to Ipswich; therefore turn on the right leaving the Hall close on the left. Avoid divers turnings to the left; leave Harkstead Church about 3 f. on the left. At 13 m. 7 ¾ f. the Road right forward goes to Chempton or Chelmondeston; here turn on the right. At 14 m. 1 3-4 f. is Arwerton Queen's Head Inn. At 14 m. 5 f. is Arwerton Church close on the right. Passing along through Arwerton Hall Yard leaving the Hall close on the right (of which hereafter) pass by the Park on the right at the Corner of which the Road from Ipswich to Shotley Gate comes in on the left. Pass along to the right in the said Road. At 15 m. 5 ¼ f. is Shotley Bull Inn, and at 17 m. 2 f. is Shotley Gate Inn.

From

From Stratford Swan Inn to Eaftbergholt Bull Inn is	3 m. $6\frac{3}{4}$ f.
From Eaftbergholt Bull Inn to Brantham Bull-Inn is	4 m. 2 f.
From Brantham Bull to Shotley Gate-Inn is	10 m. $1\frac{1}{4}$ f.

From Stratford Swarn to Shotley Gate is — 17 m 2 f.

RETURN we now to Lavenham to take a Survey of the Road leading from thence of Bildefton. From the Swan Inn avoid the Road right forward going to Sudbury, which is before treated of; turn on the left at the Corner of the Houfe, and pafs on through the Street. At $1\frac{3}{4}$ f. is the End of the Street, where the Road right forward goes to Kettlebarfton; here turn on the right. At 7 f. crofs Brent-Ely firft Bridge. At 1 m. $3\frac{1}{2}$ f. crofs over the fecond Bridge. At 2 m. $\frac{3}{4}$ f. the right goes to Waldingfield Parva; here turn on the left, paffing by Brent-Ely Church and Hall on the left. At 2 m. $\frac{3}{4}$ f. avoid the Road right forward going over the River to Prefton; turn on the right through Burnt-Ely Village. At 2 m. 3 f. the Road right forward goes to Milden; here turn on the left over the River. At 3 m. $3\frac{1}{4}$ f. the right goes to Milden, the left to Kettlebarfton. At 3 m. 7 f. is Monks-Ely Church a little on the left, where the left goes to Kettlebarfton. At 4 m. 2 f. the right turns over Monks-Ely Bridge through Hadleigh to Ipfwich, it being the common Road from Lavenham thither; but we keep the Road right forward. At 4 m. $6\frac{3}{4}$ f. the left forward goes to Kettlebarfton. At 4 m. $7\frac{1}{2}$ f. is Chelfworth Church a little on the right. At 5 m. the right goes to Seamer; a little further the left to Bildefton Church. At 5 m. 1 f. the right goes to Nedging; crofs a Brook. At 5 m. $7\frac{1}{2}$ f. enter the Road leading from Bildefton to Hadleigh, of which anon; here turn on the left. At 6 m. $\frac{1}{2}$ f. is the end of Bildefton Street, where the right leads to Ipfwich which is before treated of, and at 6 m. $1\frac{3}{4}$ f. is Bildefton Market Crofs.

O 2

WE

W E will now return to Newmarket to take a Survey
of the Road leading from thence to Sudbury. From the
Grey-hound Inn in Newmarket return in the Bury Road.
At 1 ½ f. leave the same and take the right hand
way over Champain Plains, avoiding divers turnings
to the right and left ; leave Cheevely Church about a
Mile on the right. At 3 m. 5 ¼ f. is the Ruins of a
Chapel a little on the right. At 4 m. 4 f. is also the
Ruins of Silvery Church a little on the left. At 6 m.
3 f. cross a Brook. At 6 m. 4 f. is Lidgate Church,
a little on the left.

LIDGATE. Here we obferved a Mount moated
in near the Church, on which remain the Ruins of a
very ftrong Caftle, as may be conjectured by its fituation. But this Parifh is more memorable for giving
Birth and Name to John Lidgate : He was a Benedictine Monk of the Abbey of Bury St. Edmund's,
and thirfting after Knowledge he travelled through
France and Italy to learn the Languages and Arts
there profeffed, and became an elegant Poet, an eloquent Orator, an expert Mathematician, an acute Phi-
lofopher, and no mean Divine. He departed this Life
Anno Dom. 1440, in the 60th Year of his Age. On
whofe Tomb this Epitaph is faid to have been written, viz.

' Dead in the Word, yet living in the Skie,
        Intombed in this Urn doth Lidgate lie,
    In former Times fam'd for his Poetry
            All over England.

PASSING along through Lidgate Village, at 10 m.
is Wickham Brook Church clofe on the right. At
10 m. 4 f. is the Plumbers Arms Inn, where the right
goes to Straddifhall, the left through Depden to Bury.
At 12 m. 6 f. is a direction Poft where the left goes
to Bury St. Edmunds. Paffing along in the aforementioned Road from Bury St. Edmunds to Clare, at
12 m. 7 f. is Stansfield Church clofe on the right ; crofs
a Brook. At 13 m. 1 f. the Bury Road turns on the
right towards Clare ; avoid divers turnings to the right
and left. At 17 m. 7 ¼ f. is Glemsford Church clofe
                                                    on

on the right. At 18 m. 4 f. the left goes to Bury St. Edmunds; leave Stanstead Church on the left near 4 f. At 20 m. 3 ¾ f. enter the Road leading from Sudbury to Clare, which is before treated of. At 1 m. is Melford Black Lion Inn; from thence pass through Melford Street in the aforementioned Road from Sudbury to Clare. And at 24 m. 3 3-4 f. is Sudbury Butter Market Cross.

RETURNING back to Newmarket we will now Survey the Road leading from thence to Thetford. At 1 ½ f. from the Grey-Hound Inn avoid the Road on the right going acute forward to Sudbury, last treated of, and the Road right forward leading to Bury; take the left hand way at the end of the Street. Pass over Champain Plains leaving Kennet Church near a Mile on the right. At 5 m. 1 f. re-enter Suffolk at a Brook. At 5 m 2 ¼ f. the left goes to Mildenhall; leaving it on the left about a Mile, pass by a Warren House on the left; leave Barton Mills Church a little on the left. At 8 m. 4 ¼ f. is Barton Mills Inn, where the Road right forward goes to Bury St Edmunds, therefore turn on the left over the River. At 8 m. 5 ¼ f. leave the left hand Roads, the one going to Mildenhall, the other towards Brandon, take the right hand Way by the Side of the Hill; leave a Shepperd's Lodge close on the left; pass over an open Country directly for Elveden Church, avoiding divers turnings to the right and left. At 15 m. 3 f. cross the Road that leads from Bury to Brandon, which is before treated of. At 15 m. 7 f. is Elveden Church close on the left; pass through the Street over Sandy Lands. At 19 m. 4 f. is the end of Thetford Street, where the left goes to Brandon, of which anon, and at 19 m. 5 f. is Thetford Bridge.

WE will next Survey the Road leading from Thetford Bridge to Brandon. Returning backward to the last mentioned Road, at 1 f. avoid the Road going right forward to Bury St. Edmunds; here turn on the right leaving on the same hand the Ruins of the Houses of Fryers Preachers and Black Canons; enter in at a Gate. At 1 m. ¼ f. the Road right forward goes to Lakenheath, the right to Downham; take the middle

Way

Way directly for the Warrener's Lodge. At 2 m. $\frac{1}{2}$ f. is the Lodge clofe on the right. At 2 m. 7 3 4 f. is another Lodge or Farm Houfe clofe on the right. And at 5 m. 7 f. is Brandon Maiden's Head Inn, where the left goes to Mildenhall, the right to Downham.

FROM the Maiden's Head in Brandon we will next Survey the Road leading from thence to Mildenhall. Leave Brandon Church on the right near 6 f. At 4 m. 5 $\frac{1}{4}$ f. the left goes to Bury St. Edmunds, the right to Lakenheath; leave Erefwell Church about a Mile on the right. At 8 m. 3 f. the left acute backward goes to Thetford. At 8 m. 4 f. the Road comes in on the left at the end of Mildenhall Street from Bury St. Edmunds, which is before treated of, and at 9 m. is Mildenhall Market Crofs.

RETURN we now to Thetford to Survey the Road leading from thence to Gaftrope Gate Inn. From Thetford Bridge take the firft right hand Way; pafs out at the Eaft end of the Town. At 5 $\frac{1}{2}$ f. crofs over Melford Bridge; avoiding the left going to Shadwell Lodge and the right leading to Eufton, take the middle Way; leave a Shepperd's Lodge near half a Mile on the right going on directly for Rufhford. At 3 m. 5 $\frac{1}{4}$ f. is Rufhford Church and College on the right, where the left goes to Shadwell. At 3 m. 6 $\frac{1}{2}$ f. reenter Suffolk at Rufhford Bridge; leave the Red-Houfe clofe on the left; pafs over Champain Lands having the Little Oufe River on the left. At 6 m. 6 $\frac{1}{4}$ f. is a Pound where the right goes from Gaftrope Gate to Bury; here turn on the left, over the laft mentioned River into Norfolk. At 7 m. 1 $\frac{1}{2}$ f. is Gaftrope Gate Inn.

WE will now take a Survey of the Road leading from Bungay to Halefworth. From the Market Crofs in Bungay pafs out at the South end of the Town; avoid the firft right hand Way leading through Flixton to Harlefton, and take the Way right forward. At 5 f. the right goes to Homersfield, the left to Beccles. At 2 m. 1 f. is St. John's Church clofe on the left; here the Road right forward goes to St. Andrew's, therefore turn on the right throught a ftrait
Way

Way called Stone Street. At 3 m. is St. Lawrence's Church on the left about 1 f. here the left goes to St Lawrence. At 4 m. 1 ½ f. is the Half-way Houſe cloſe on the right, where the right goes to St. Margarets. At 5 m. 2 ½ f the left goes to St. Andrew's. At 7 m. 2 ½ f. is the Fairſtead Gate on the right. At 7 m, 6 ½ f. is a Direction Poſt where the left acute back ward goes to Beccles. At 8 m. ½ f. the left to Holton. At 8 m 5 f. enter Haleſworth Street, where the left goes to Loweſtoft of which anon ; here turn on the right over the River, and at 8 m. 7 ½ f, is Haleſ worth Market Croſs.

HALESWORTH, by the Saxons called HEALS-WORDA, a large and pretty well built Town, is ſitu ate in a bottom, upon the River Blyth which runs through it. The Streets are part of them paved and generally clean. It has a conſiderable Market weekly on Tueſdays, procured by the Lord of the Manour Richard de Argenton. In the Time of Henry III, Reginald de Argenton obtained a Fair to be held here yearly on the Eve Day and Morrow after the Feaſt of St. Luke, October 18, which is ſtill very conſiderable for Lean Cattle. From the Argentons the Lordſhip of this Town deſcended to the Allingtons, and now belongs to Thomas Betts, Eſq; The Church is a very good Structure, and very beautiful within. In this Town are ſeveral Houſes of good Entertainment.

BEING arrived at Haleſworth, we will next take a Survey of the Roads iſſuing from thence to divers Places in theſe Parts ; and firſt of the Road leading from thence to Yoxford. At 3 f. from the Corner of the Church Yard, by the Alms-Houſe, is a Direction Poſt, where the left is a Spur-Way from Haleſworth, through Bramfield, and over Sibton Green to Yoxford. At 1 m. 3 ¼ f. the Road right forward goes to Cookley ; here turn on the left over the River. At 1 m. 4 ½ f. the Road right forward goes to Bramfield, therefore turn on the right. At 1 m. 6 ½ f. the left acute backward goes to Holton ; paſs by Walpoole Church on the right. At 2 m. 4 f.

is

is Walpoole Village, where the Road right forward
goes through Huntingfield to Cratfield; here turn on
the left, avoiding the firft left hand Way leading to
Bramfield. At 2 m. 5½ f. the right goes through
Heveningham and Ubbefton to Laxfield. At 4 m. is
Threadbare Hall clofe on the left. At 4 m. 3 f. the
right goes to Heveningham, the left to Sibton Green;
enter in at a Gate; pafs through the Fields. At 5 m.
3 f. the right goes through Heveningham Long-Lane
to Ubbefton; here turn on the left through Boy Street.
At 5 m. 5¼ f. the right goes through Peafenhall
and Baddingham to Framlingham. At 5 m 7. 3 4f.
is a Gate to Sibton Abbey.

SIBTON or SIBETON, is of Note for a Cefter-
tian Monaftery dedicated to the Virgin Mary by
William Cheney, fays Mr. Cambden, but Leland tells
us that the Lord D'acres was the Founder of it. This
Lord D'acres was Heir to the faid William Cheney
of Horfeford in Norfolk, and therefore it may be probable that Mr. Cheney might begin to build, and
his Heir the Lord D'acres finifh this Monaftery. Mr.
Speed fays it was valued at its Diffolution at 250 l.
5 s. 7½ d. per Annum.

To whom this Monaftery was granted at its Dif-
folution we know not; it is at prefent a good old
Houfe, and for many Years has been the Seat of the
Family of Scrivener, and is now the Lotdfhip and
Demefne of Charles Scrivener, Efq;

LEAVING the Abbey on the left, at 6 m. 1 3-4 f.
is Sibton Church clofe on the right. At 7 m. 1½ f.
is a Direction Poft, where on the left comes in the
laft mentioned Spur way leading from Halefworth to
Yoxford, and at 8 m ¼ f, is Yoxford Church.

RETURNING back to Halefworth we will next
Survey the Road leading from thence to Southwould.
From the Market Crofs returning back in the Bungay Road over the River, avoid the Roads to Wiffet
and Bungay, both going to the left; keep the right
hand Way through the Street. At 1 m. 2¼ f. is
Holton Blackfmith's Shop, where the left goes through
Brampton to Beccles, of which anon; leave the Wind-
mill

mill on the right; pass by Blythford Church a little on the right. At 2 m. 7¼ f. the right goes over Blythford Bridge to Wenhaston; a little further the left goes to Sotherton Moore; passing along in a tolerable strait Road, avoiding divers turnings to the right and left, at 4 m. 1¼ f. cross the Coach Road from Ipswich to Beccles. At 5 m. 7 f. is Wolsey-Bridge, and at 8 m. 6 f. is Southwould Market-Cross.

RETURNING to Halesworth we will now take a Survey of the Road leading from thence to Lowestoft. From the Market Cross in Halesworth, passing along in the said Road, leading from Halesworth to Southwould. At 4 m. 1¼ f. cross the Road leading from Blithburgh to Beccles, leave the Road going on the right over Wolsey Bridge to Southwould, pass along, leave Henham Park on the left. At 6 m. 6½ f. is Wangford Church loss on the right; here the right goes through Raydon to Southwould, which is before treated of, keep the Road right forward. At 6 m. 7 f. the right goes to Southwould, the left to Uggeshall. At 8 m. 2½ f. the left goes to Frostendon Common, here turn on the right. At 8 m. 4½ f. the right goes to South Cove, therefore turn on the left. At 8 m. 7 f. the right goes past Wrentham Spread Eagle Inn to Benacre. At 9 m. 6 f. is Wrentham Church close on the left; leave the Hall a little on the right; pass over Satterly Common. At 11 m. 6 f. the right goes to Benacre Waluntree Inn, the left past Hinstead Church to Beccles; leave Hinstead Church a little on the left. At 13 m. 1 f. is Rushmer Church close on the right. At 14 m. 7 f. is a Blacksmith's Shop close on the right, and Carlton Colvile Church a little on the left. At 15 m. ¼ f. is the five Cross Ways, where the right acute backward goes to Southwould, the right to Peakfield, the left to Beccles, of which anon. At 16 m. 6 f. is Mutford Bridge, where the Road right forward goes to Yarmouth, of which anon. Here turn on the right, and at 18 m. 7 f. is Lowestoft Queen's Head Inn.

THE next Road that shall be Surveyed is the Road leading from Halesworth to Beccles. From the Market-Cross returning back in the last mentioned Road, at 1 m. 2¼ f. as aforesaid is Holton Black-

P

smith's

smith's Shop ; avoid the laſt mentioned Road going to the right, and Holton Church about 1 f. on the left. At 4 m. 4½ f. is Weſthall Church cloſe on the left, and the Hall a little on the right. At 5 m. 1½ f. is Brampton Church. Enter the Road from Ipſwich to Beccles ; here turn on the left paſt the Church; for the reſt ſee the Road from Blithburgh to Beccles. And at 10 m. 6 f. is Beccles Church.

WE will how Survey the Road leading from Lowe-ſtoft to Beccles. Returning back in the laſt Road treated of over Mutford Bridge, avoid the turnings to the left at the five Croſs-ways. At 3 m. 6¾ f. is Carlton Ship Inn. At 5 m. is Barnby Blind-Man Inn. At 5 m. 5 f. is Barnby Church cloſe on the left. At 5 m. 5½ f. is Barnby White Hart Inn. At 6 m. 7 f. is North-Cove Church cloſe on the right. At 8 m. is Worlingham Church cloſe on the left, and the Hall a little on the right, and at 9 m. 4 3-4 f. is Beccles Church.

RETURN we now from Beccles to Haleſworth, and the laſt Road we ſhall Survey iſſuing therefrom ſhall be from that to Harleſton. From the Market Croſs in Haleſworth paſs through Cheddiſton or Cheſton Street ; leave the Manſion of Walter Plumber, Eſq; about 3 f. on the right. At 2 m. ¼ f. is Cheddiſton Church cloſe on the right. At 3 m. 3¼ f. is Linſtead Chapel cloſe on the right. At 7 m. 1¼ f. is Metfield Church cloſe on the left. At 8 m. 6¼ f. is Wetherſdale Croſs, where the right goes to Mendham, the left to Freſſingfield. At 10 m. 7 f. is Shottisford Bridge, and at 11 m. 6 f. is Harleſton Chapel.

FROM Blithburgh White Hart Inn we will now Survey the Road leading from thence to Yarmouth by Way of Mutford Bridge. Paſſing along from Blithburgh White-Hart Inn as mentioned in the Road from Southwould to Blithburgh, at 2 m. 5 3-4 f. is Wangford Church on the right. At 5 m. 5¼ f. is Wrentham Church on the left. At 7 m. 5¼ f. is Henſtead Church on the left. At 9 m. ¼ f. is Ruſhmer Church cloſe on the right. At 10 m. 6¼ f. is Carlton Blackſmith's Shop on the right. At 12 m. 5¼ f. is Mutford-Bridge ; avoid the Road on the right going to
Loweſtoft

Loweftoft. At 13 m. ¼ f. is a Blackfmith's Shop clofe
on the right, where the right goes to Loweftoft.
At 14 m. 1 f. the right goes to Loweftoft, the left to
Oulton ; leave Oulton High-Houfe on the left; pafs
through a tolerable ftrait Way, and over Lound-
Common. At 17 m. 2 ¼ f. is Hopton White-Hart Inn,
where the right goes as aforefaid to Loweftoft; for
the reft fee the Road from Yarmouth to Loweftoft.
At 21 m. 7 ¼ f. is Yarmouth Bridge.

From Blithburgh to Yarmouth by Way
  of Beccles is ——— ——— ——— —— 24 m. 1 f.
From Blithburgh to Yarmouth by Way
  of Mutford Bridge is —— ——— — 21 m. 7 ¼ f.
'Tis the neareft Way from Blithburgh
  to Yarmouth by Way of Mutford 2 m. 1 ½ f.
  Bridge by the diftance of —— ——

WE will now return to Stow Market and Survey the
Roads leading thence to Botefdale, Thetford, and Stratford Swan Inn. And firft of the Road leading from
Stow to Botefdale. From the Market Crofs in Stow pafs
along the Bury Road. At 1 m. 6 f. leave the Bury
Road going right forward, and take the right hand
way over the River. At 2 m. 4 ¼ f. enter Haughley
Street, where the right acute backward goes to Newton. At 2 m. 6 f. is Haughley Church, a little on
the left the Road right forward goes to Wetherden,
here turn on the right.

HAUGHLEY, or as it written in Records Haughle
and Haghele. Here remain ftill the Ruins of a very
ftrong Caftle as may be conjectured by its Situation.
This Caftle did antiently belong to the De Uffords
Earls of Suffolk, who died feized of it the 43 Edward
III. Afterwards this Caftle and Manuor defcended to
the De Greys Dukes of Suffolk; it came to the Crown
by the Attainder of the Lady Jane Grey, and was
granted by Queen Mary I, to Sir John Sulyard of
Wetherden Hall, who built Haughley Hall, (there being before only a Keeper's-lodge in the Park) removed

from

from Whetherden Hall thither and made it his Seat, in which Family it has continued ever since.

The Manour is large and extensive, the Lord of it formerly had a Jurisdiction of Oyer and Terminer, trying all Cases in his own Court. We find in the Court Books, at a Court holden 15 Edward IV. It is commanded to seize all the Lands and Tenements, Meadows, Feedings and Pastures of John Buxton of Stow, because that he unjustly enforced and vexed one William Turner by the Writ of our Sovereign Lord the King contrary to the antient Customs and Ordinances of this Manour, that no Tenant should Prosecute any other Tenant in any Court saving this. And 6 Henry V, 17 Henry VIII, 2, 4, and 11 Elizabeth to the same Purpose.

At another Court held in the same Year, it was ordered that the Abbot of Hales in Gloucestershire should erect a new pair of Gallows in Luberlow Field in Haughley under the Penalty of 40 s. The 8 Edward IV William Paxteyn held certain Lands by the Service of finding a Ladder to the Lords Gallows.

It was an antient Market Town out of the ruins of which Stow seems to have risen; for we find, 3 Edward IV, William Hoxon of Stow, was fined because he lay wait near the Town of Haughley and bought Eggs, Chickens &c. And at another Court held the 31 Henry VIII. the Butchers of Stow were amerced 3 s. 4 d. because they Sold out of the Market their Meat on the Market Day, contrary to the Custom of this Manour. And the Year following it was advanced to 6 s. 8 d. How long this Market has been disus'd we know not. There is still a Fair Yearly August 15.

In this Parish is the Seat of Charles Knipe Esq.

Thus much for Haughley: From hence let us pursue our Journey towards Botesdale. At 3 m. 3-4 f. the right goes to Newton; here turn on the left; pass over Haughley Green. At 4 m. ½ f. is a Blacksmith's Shop close on the right, where the right goes to Mendlesham; leave a Windmill close on the left. At 4 m. 4 f. leave Haughley Green. At 5 m. 6 3-4 f. the left goes to Wyverston. At 6 m. 3 ½ f. is Bacton Bull Inn, where the left goes to Wyverston, the Road right forward

ward to Wefthorp, therefore turn on the right ; leave the Seat of Barham Prettyman, Efq; clofe on the left, and Bacton Church clofe on the right. At 7 m. the Road right forward goes through Cotton to Mendlefham, here turn on the left over a Common called by the Name of Middlegate way. At 7 m. 5 ½ f. the right goes to Mendlefham. At 8 m. ½ f. the right goes to Wick-ham Skyth, the left to Wyverfton, where is the End of Middlegate Green. At 8 m. 1 ¾ f. is Finningham White Horfe Inn (a Houfe of good Entertainment) where the left goes to Bury, (of which hereafter) the right to Thornham Magna.

FINNINGHAM Hall, is the Seat of Edmund Frere, Efq; here is a confiderable Fair Yearly for Cattle beginning Auguft 24. Leaving Finninham White Horfe Inn pafs by the Church on the right. At 8 m. 3 ½ f. the right goes to Giflingham; leave Finningham Hall on the left. At 9 m. 6 f. en-ter Alud Green. At 10 m. 6 ¼ f. leave it. At 12 m. 2 f. is Rickingale fuperior Church on the right ; the Road right forward goes to Whattisfield, therefore turn on the right. At 12 m. 4 ¾ f. is the Road from Bury to Yarmouth before treated of ; here turn on the right through Botefdale Street, and at 13 m. 3 f. is Botefdale Crown Inn.

RETURN we now to Stow Market to take a Sur-vey of the Road leading from thence through Ixworth to Thetford. From the Market Crofs in Stow paffing along in the laft mentioned Road. At 1 m. 6 f. go paft the aforefaid Road on the right which goes through Haughley to Botefdale, and keep the Road right forward being the Bury Road before treated of, but at 3 m. 3 ¼ f. avoid the left going to Wulpit and Bury and keep the right forward Road. At 3 m. 7 f is Wetherden Village, where the right goes paft the Church towards Haughley Green, Wulpit. At 5 m. 1 3-4 f. the right goes to Elmfwell Green, the left to Wulpit. At 5 m. 4 f. the right acute backward goes to Elmfwell Green ; leave the Church clofe on the right. At 5 m. 4 ½ f. the Road right forward goes to Toftock, here take the right hand way. At 7 m. 6 ½ f. the right goes to Afhfield, the left to Bury and Norton Dog Inn, clofe

clofe on the right. At 8 m. 3 ¼ f. is a view of Dr. Macro's Manfion, where a Gate on the left leads to it.
At 8 m. 7 ¾ f. the right leads in at a Gate through the
Fields to Stow-langtoft. At 9 m. 2 f. come at the Road
leading on the right through Stow-langtoft to Finningham White Horfe Inn, the left through Pakenham to
Bury, of which hereafter. At 9 m. 4 ½ f. crofs a
Brook and pafs over the Fieldings, and at 11 m. 2 ¾ f.
is Ixworth Street, where the right goes to Botefdale,
the left to Bury.

    From Ixworth let us proceed to Thetford. At 3 ¼ f.
crofs the River and leave the Mill on the left; avoid
the left going to the Livermers, keep the Road right
forward. At 1 m. 4 f. is Ixworth Thorp Church clofe
on the left; pafs along over a Common. At 2 m. 6 f.
on the left comes in the Road from Bury to Gaftrope
Gate Inn before mentioned; leave Hunnington Church
clofe on the right. At 2 m. 6 ¾ f. here the Road
from Bury to Gaftrope Gate Inn turns to the right;
the left goes to Livermer, therefore keep the Road
right forward. At 4 m. 4 ¼ f. the right acute backward goes to Sapifton; leave Fakenham Church clofe
on the right; pafs over Champain Lands; leave Eufton
Church and Hall (the Seat of his Grace the Duke of
Grafton) on the right, of which hereafter. At 6 m. ¼ f.
the left goes to Barnham; turn on the right over
Eufton Bridge, having the Park clofe on the right.
At 6 m. 1 ¼ f. the Road right forward goes to Barningham; here turn on the left through Eufton Village.
At 6 m. 7 3-4 f. enter Norfolk at Carlford Bridge;
avoid the Road right forward going over Melford-
Bridge into Thetford; take the left hand Road over
the Warrens. At 8 m. 4 3-4 f. re-enter Suffolk at
Folly-Bridge; pafs by the Place formerly a Houfe of
Benedictine Nuns clofe on the right, and at 9 m. 3 ¼ f
is Thetford-Bridge.

From Stow-Market to Ixworth is —— 11 m. 2 ¾ f.
From Ixworth to Thetford is —— 9 m. 3 ¼ f.
_____
From Stow-Market to Thetford is —— 20 m. 6 f.

W E

WE will now return back to Stow-Market, and Survey the Road leading from thence to Bildeſton. From the Market Croſs take the Ipſwich Road, paſſing over Combs Ford. At 4 f. leave the left going to Ipſwich, and the right going to Finborough magna, and keep the Road right forward. At 7½ f. is a View of Combs Hall on the left about 2 f. paſs along avoiding divers turnings to the right and left. At 3 m. 6 3-4 f. enter Battisford Tye, where the Road right forward croſs the Tye goes to Ringſhall, therefore take the right hand Way over the Tye. At 4 m. 3¼ f. leave it at a Carpenter's Shop on the right. At 5 m. 1 3-4 f. is a Direction Poſt on Charles's Tye. At 6 m. 3 3-4 f. is Wattiſham Church cloſe on the left. At 6 m. 6½ f. is a Blackſmith's Shop cloſe on the left. At 7 m. 3 3-4 f. is a Direction Poſt, where the left acute backward goes to Needham, and at 8 m. 2 3-4 f. is Bildeſton Market-Croſs.

FROM Bildeſton we will now Survey the Road leading to Hadleigh. Paſſing from the Croſs in Bildeſton at 1¼ f. avoid the left going towards Ipſwich, and at 2¼ f. the right towards Lavenham, both which are before treated of, leaving Nedging Church about 2 f. on the left; paſs over Seamer-Bridge. At 1 m. 7 3-4 f. is a Blackſmith's Shop cloſe on the right. At 2 m. 3½ f. is a Direction Poſt, where the right goes to Kerſey. At 2 m. 6 f. is another Direction Poſt, where on the right comes in the Road from Lavenham through Monks-Ely and Kerſey to Ipſwich. At 3 m. ½ f. the left goes to Naughton. At 3 m. 3½ f. the right goes to Kerſey, the left to Colford Bridge. At 3 m. 7 3-4 f. on the right comes in the Sudbury Road to Hadleigh, and at 5 m. 1¼ f. is Hadleigh George Inn.

THE laſt Road we ſhall Survey ſhall be that leading from Hadleigh George Inn to Stratford Swan Inn. Avoid the right hand Way going through Layham to Stoke. At 1½ f. avoid the left leading to Ipſwich, and keep the Road right forward. At 4½ f. is the end of the Street; leave Layham Church about 2 f. on the right. At 1 m. 7 f. croſs a Brook
where

where the Road right forward goes to Eaſtbergholt, here turn on the right. At 2 m. 6½ f. the right, forward goes to Shelly; turn on the left, leave the Church and Hall 2 f. on the right. At 3 m. croſs another Brook, paſs by a Blackſmith's Shop on the left. At 3 m. 1 3-4 f. the left goes to Raydon; turn on the right. At 4 m. 6½ f. the left to Holton. At 4 m. 7¼ f. is Higham Village, where the right goes to Stoke, as is aforeſaid, the left to Ipſwich, and at 6 m. ½ f. is Stratford Swan Inn.

HAVING finiſhed the Survey of all the Roads of any conſiderable Traffic, and given a ſhort Hiſtorical Account of all the Market and other conſiderable Towns in the County, with what is or has been of any Remark in them, our next Buſineſs ſhall be to treat of the Hundreds, and thoſe Towns in them, not before taken Notice of, in an Alphabetical Order.

BABERGH

BABERGH Hundred,

IS bounded on the Eaſt by the Hundred of Samford, on the Weſt by the Stour and part of Risbridge Hundred, on the North by the Hundreds of Thingoe and Thedweſtry, and on the South with the Stour dividing it from Eſſex. It is in length 12 Miles, in breadth 11, making the Circumference 42 Miles. The Towns and Villages in this Hundred are, viz.

ACTON; the Manour of this Pariſh in 9 Edward I, was the Inheritance of Robert de Buers or Buris. King Edward IV afterwards gave it to Henry Lord Bourchier. He dying, 23 Edward IV, left it to Henry his Grandſon; to whom it deſcended afterwards we find not. Acton-Place is a noble Building, and is now the Seat of William Jennens, Eſq; by whom it was lately Built. On the ſide of Babergh Heath in this Pariſh is the Seat of Ambroſe Kedington, Eſq.

ALPHETON, formerly the Lordſhip of John de Welnetham.

ASSINGTON, the Lordſhip of Roger Corbet 9 Edward I, but in later Times it has been the Seat of the Family of Gurdon, Men of Figure and Eſtate in this County. John Gurdon of this Place, Eſq; was High Sheriff for this County 26 Queen Elizabeth; they are ſtill in Repute in this Place; the preſent Poſſeſſor is John Gurdon, Eſq.

BOXFORD, See Page 93.

BOXSTEAD, formerly the Lordſhip of the Abbot of Bury St. Edmunds, but afterward, (by what means is uncertain) the 9 Edward I, it was granted to Robert Harleſton, Eſq; who being Attainted in the Reign of Edward IV, it was granted to Richard Duke of Gloceſter, Brother to the ſaid King. It is now the Seat of   . Pooley, Eſq.

BURES or BUERS, See Page 95.

BRENT-ELY, a Village and Manour belonging

Q   the

the Anceſtors of Sir Henry Shelton, who procured a Market for it of King Henry III, long ſince diſcontinued. His Poſterity flouriſhed here a long time ; but afterwards it deſcended to the Family of Colman who now enjoy it ; the preſent worthy Gentleman reſiding at the Hall is Edward Colman, Eſq.

CAVENDISH, See Page 93.

CHILTON, the Hall appears to be a good old Seat, it was formerly the Seat of the Knightly Family of Crane, for Sir John Crane of this Place, Knt. was created a Baronet May 11, Anno Dom. 1627 ; but that Family being extinct, to whom it now belongs we know not.

COCKFIELD, COKEFIELD or COOK-FIELD, formerly the Lordſhip of the de Vere's Earls of Oxford ; for Edward de Vere Earl of Oxford died poſſeſſed of it 24 Edward I ; afterwards John Earl of Oxford, taking Part with the Lancaſtrians againſt Edward IV, forfeited his Eſtates to the ſaid Victorious Edward, who ſeized them and gave this Manour to his Brother Richard Duke of York. But Henry VII, reſtoring him to his Honour and Eſtate, his Succeſſors enjoyed this Manour till the Death of Awbery de Vere the laſt Earl of Oxford. To whom it deſcended afterwards we know not ; but the Family of Hervey has a good Seat here.

CORNERD Magna, formerly the Lordſhip of the Abbot of Malling ; to whom it now belongs we know not.

CORNERD Parva, formerly the Lordſhip of Thomas Grey, but whoſe now we know not.

EDWARDSTON, a Village of Note for the Lords formerly inhabiting in it, called MONTE CANISIO commonly called Mont or Monchienſy ; from the Monchienſys, it deſcended to the Waldgraves, and afterward to the Alſtons. Joſeph Alſton, Eſq; now reſides in a neat Manſion in this Pariſh. A little North of Mr. Alſton's Manſion is the Ruins of St. Edwards Place, formerly a Religious Houſe and a Cell to the Abbey at St. Alban's ; what the Revenues of this Houſe was at its Diſſolution we know not. It is now the Eſtate of the aforeſaid Joſeph Alſton, Eſq. GLEMSFORD,

GLEMSFORD, or GUTHELNESFORD, one of thofe Manours which Odo Earl of Champaign, a near Kinf-man of William the Conqueror, was found poffefs'd of when the General Survey of England called Doomsday Book was taken. Afterwards it belonged to the Bifhops of Ely; but whether fo now, we know not.

IT is a very large Town, in Bounds and very full of Inhabitants; but the Houfes are fcatteringly fitu-ate, which were they Contiguous it is fuppos'd there would not be four larger Towns in this County. The Fair is yearly June the 24th.

GROTON, formerly the Lordfhip of the Abbot of Bury St. Edmonds; who it defcended to at the Diffolu-tion of that Abbey we know not. It is now the Lord-fhip of Thomas Warren, Efq; who refides in the Place; a good old Manfion, a little North of the Church.

HARTEST, formerly the Lordfhip of the Bifhop of Ely; but whofe at prefent we know not.

LAVENHAM, See Page 87.

LAWSHALL, formerly the Lordfhip of the Abbot of Ramfey; but to whom it belongs at prefent we know not.

MELFORD, See Page 84.

MILDEN, formerly the Lordfhip and Demefne of Remigius de Milding or Milden, who took his Name from this Place. Afterwards it defcended to the Allingtons; from them by purchafe to the Fa-mily of Canham. It is now vefted in John Canham, Efq; who has his Seat at the Hall.

MONKS-ELY, fo called becaufe the Lordfhip formerly belonged to the Monks of St. Peter's in Can-terbury. To whom it belongs at prefent we know not.

NEWTON, formerly the Lordfhip of William Butvillein; but to whom it now belongs we know not.

NEYLAND, See Page 96.

POLSTEAD, formerly the Lordfhip of James Lamburn, Efq. It is at prefent of Remark for its Cher-ries. Here is the Seat of Jacob Brand, Efq

PRESTON, formerly the Lordfhip and Eftate of the Hofpital of St. John of Jerufalem 9 Edward I, but afterward of the de Veres Earls of Oxford; but to whom it defcended after we know not.

SHIMPLING.

SHIMPLING or SIMPLING, in the Conqueror's Time the Lordship of Odo de Campania, Earl of Albemarle and Holderness. How long it remained in that Family we find not. It afterwards descended to the Lords Fitz-water. It is now the Inheritance of the Plampyns, and William Plampyn, Esq; has now his Seat here in a Mansion called by the Name of Cheracre (or Shadacre) Hall.

SOMERTON, of which we have nothing to Remark, but that it was formerly the Lordship of Thomas de Burgh.

STOKE by Nayland. See Page 96.

SUDBURY. See Page 85.

WALDINGFIELD Magna, formerly the Lordship and Estate of James Butler Earl of Wiltshire, and afterwards of the Earls of Essex; but to whom it now belongs we know not.

THIS Village furnished London with a Lord Mayor Anno 1594, viz. Roger Spencer Cloth-worker, the Son of Richard Spencer of this Place.

WALDINGFIELD Parva, the Lordship of William Beauchamp and William Fitz Ralph 9 Edward I. In this Parish is the Seat of　Warner Esq.

WISTON, formerly the Lordship of Michael Lord Poinings, who leaving it to his Son and Heir Thomas Lord Poinings, he left it to his Son and Heir Michael. In the 9 Edward II, Agidia de Horkesly was Lady of this Manour; but who now we know not.

THIS Hundred contains 34 Parishes.

BLACKBOURN Hundred,

Is bounded on the East with the Hundreds of Hartsmere, and by Stow on the South, by the Hundred of Lachford and Thedwestry on the West, and on the North by the Little Ouse dividing it from Norfolk. Its greatest length is 16 Miles; its greatest breadth is 9 Miles, making the Circumference 52 Miles. The Towns and Villages in this Hundred are, viz.

ASHFIELD.

BADWELL-ASH, the Lordship of William Creketote 9 Edward I, but to whom it belongs now we know not.

BARDWELL was, the 9 Edw. III, the Lordship of

of John Packenham and Ifabella de Wykes; afterwards it came into the Family of Read; one of which married the Daughter and Heirefs of William Crofts of Saxham Magna in this County, who was by King Charles II at Brabant, May 18, 1658, created Lord Crofts of Saxham, from which Marriage they took the Sirname of Crofts. It is now the Lordfhip of Thomas Crofts Read, Efq.

BARNHAM, confifting of two Parifhes, viz. St. Martin and St. Gregory, having formerly had two ParifhChurches; but St Martin's Church is now in ruins. It was formerly the Lordfhip of James de Shrylle, and now belongs to his Grace the Duke of Grafton.

BARNINGHAM, formerly the Lordfhip of John de Montfort, and the Prior of Blefworth, in the 9 Edw. I. The Family of the Sheltons have long refided in this Village; the prefent Gentleman of that Family, Maurice Shelton, Efq; refides in a good old Seat near the Church, who is now Lord of this Manour we know not; but the Duke of Grafton, lately purchafed of the faid Mr. Shelton the Meffuage and Eftate in or near this Parifh called by the Name of Barningham Park.

CONY-WESTON, formerly the Lordfhip of the Abbot of Bury St. Edmunds.

CULFORD, or CULFORTH, was formerly the Lordfhip of the Abbot of Bury St. Edmunds, a Village adorned with a neat Seat built by Sir Nicholas Bacon. The Lords Cornwallis for many Years Honoured this Village by refiding in this Manfion.

ELMSWELL, formerly the Lordfhip of the Abbot of Bury St. Edmunds, now of Charles Wood, Efq.

EUSTON, was formerly the Lordfhip and Demefne of a Family of that Name; afterwards it defcended to the Family of Pattifhall, from them it defcended to Sir Henry Bennett, who, as a Reward for his faithful Services to his Royal Mafter King Charles I, was by his Son, King Charles II, made Secretary of State, created Lord Arlington, Vifcount Thetford, and Earl of Arlington. He being induced by the pleafant Situation of this Village raifed a
noble

noble Structure there, calling it Euston House or Hall, adorning it with pleasant Gardens, &c. He leaving only one Daughter Isabella, who being married to Charles Fitz-Roy, one of King Charles IId's Natural Sons by the Dutchess of Cleveland, he was by his Father created Earl of Euston and Duke of Grafton; and it now remains in his Son by the said Isabella, Charles Fitz-Roy, the present Duke of Grafton.

FAKENHAM, formerly the Lordship and Demesne of Gundred de Warren, descended from the Earls of Surrey; afterwards by Marriage to the Nevils; from them it came to the Crown; was granted by Henry VI to Reginald de Weste. His Son, a great Favourite to Henry VII, enjoyed it. To whom it descended afterwards we know not. It is now the Lordship and Demesne of his Grace the Duke of Grafton.

HEPWORTH, formerly the Lordship and Demesne of the Abbot of Bury St. Edmunds; but whose now we know not.

HINDERCLAY, formerly the Lordship of the Abbot of Bury St. Edmunds.

HOPTON, formerly the Lordship and Demesne of the Abbot of Bury St. Edmunds, but whose now we know not.

HUNNINGTON, also the Lordship and Demesne of the Abbot of Bury St. Edmunds

HUNSTON, anciently the Lordship and Demesne of William de Langham; but to whom it belongs at present we know not; but   Heigham, Esq; now resides in a good old Seat in this Parish.

INGHAM, formerly the Lordship and Demesne of John de Ingeham; to whom it descended afterwards we know not. It is now the Lordship of the Right Hon. the Lord Cornwallis.

IXWORTH. See Page 67.

IXWORTH-THORP, a Village of small Remark.

KNETTISHALL, of no great Note at present, but formerly gave Name to a Family who were Lords of the Manour.

LANGHAM,

LANGHAM, formerly the Lordſhip of William de Criketote. Who is Lord of this Manour at preſent we know not; but John Turner, Eſq; has a Seat here.

LIVERMERE Parva, antiently gave Name to Bartholomew de Livermere, who was Lord of the Manour; to whom it deſcended after I am not informed. It is now the Lordſhip and Demeſne of Baptiſt Lee, Eſq; who has lately erected a neat Manſion there, and made it his Seat.

NORTON, was the Lordſhip of John de Pakenham, 9 Edward III. How long it remained in that Family we know not. Here is now the Seat of Cox Macro, D. D.

RICKINGALE Inferior, antiently the Lordſhip and Demeſne of Ulfkettell Earl of the Eaſt Angles and Norfolk. He being killed in the Battle of Aſſendon in Eſſex, left this Manour to the Monks of Bury St. Edmunds; but whoſe it is now we know not.

SAPISTON. The Lordſhip of this Pariſh did formerly belong to the Crown; but whether ſo at preſent we know not.

STANTON { St. John, All-Saints. } See Page 68.

STOWLANGTOFT, ſo called to diſtinguiſh it from other Towns named Stow in this County; of which the Hall or Manour Houſe was the Seat of Jeffrey Peche 9 Edward III, but afterwards of the Family of D'ewes. The learned Sir Simon D'ewes, of this Place, Knt. was created a Baronet, July 15, 1641. That Family is now extinct. The Lordſhip and Demeſne of this Town now belongs to Thomas Norton, Eſq;

THELNETHAM, corruptly called FELTHAM, antiently the Lordſhip and Demeſne of John de Thelnetham; but to whom it remains at preſent we know not.

TROSTON, formerly the Lordſhip of the Abbot of Bury St Edmunds; but for ſome Time it has been in the Family of Maddox. The Hall is now the Seat of Robert Maddox, Eſq;

WALSHAM in the Willows, the Lordſhip of Edmund de Pakenham 9 Edward III; but afterwards of William de la Pole Earl of Suffolk, who died ſeized
of

of it the 28 Henry VI. leaving it to his Son John de la Pole, who married Elizabeth the Sister of King Edward IV. He adhering to the York Family was Slain in the Battle of Stoke, 2 Henry VII. His Brother Edmund who succeeded him was in the 5th of Henry VIII beheaded. The Lordship of this Place being thus brought into the King's Hands, was granted to George Earl of Shrewsbury, in which Family it remained some descents; but of late it has been in the Family of Hunt, and is now vested in a Maiden Lady of that Name.

WHATTISFIELD, corruptly call'd WATCHFIELD, the Lordship and Demesne of the Abbot of Bury St. Edmunds, as were the Stantons adjoyning, the 9 Edward I; to whom it descended afterwards I am not informed. There is a good old Seat in this Parish belonging to the Family of Baker; but in whom the Lordship of this Parish is now vested, we know not.

WESTON-MARKET, antiently the Lordship of Hugh Hovell; afterwards it descended to the Family of Bokenham, and now is vested in Thomas Tyrell alias Bokenham Tyrell, Son of Thomas Tyrell of Gipping in this County, Esq;

WEST-STOW, formerly the Lordship of the Abbot of Bury St. Edmunds. To whom it was granted at the Dissolution of that Abbey we know not, unless to the Family of Herbert. Sir Sydenham Fowke, Knt. is now Lord of the Manour, and has his Seat at the Hall, whose Lady was an Heiress by Name, Herbert.

WORDWELL, antiently the Lordship of Thomas de Wordwell. To whom it descended from them we know not. It is now vested in the Right Hon. the Earl of Bristol.

THIS Hundred contains 35 Parishes.

BLITHING Hundred,

Is bounded on the East by the Ocean, on the West and South by the Hundreds of Hoxne and Plomesgate, and on the North by the Hundreds of Mutford

and

and Wangford. Its greatest length is 16 Miles, its greatest breath 13. making the Circumference 48 Miles.

THE Towns and Villages in this Hundred are, viz.

ALDRINGHAM a Village of no Remark. The Manour there belonged to the Priory of Leiston, and is now vested in the Lady Anne Hervey, Relict of the late Daniel Hervey, Esq.

BENACRE, antiently the Lordship and Demesne of Simon de Pierpoint. Afterwards it came into the Family of North, and from thence descended to Thomas Carthew, Esq; now residing in the Hall, which he lately Built.

BRAMPTON we find of no remark but for being the Residence of a Branch of the Family of Leman. The present Gentleman of that Family is Robert Leman, Esq; who having his Residence at the Hall, in the Year 1733 had the Misfortune to have it consumed by Fire.

BLITHBURGH. See Page 20.

BLYTHFORD, formerly the Lordship and Demesne of Thomas Bavent &c. now of Charles Wood, Esq;

BRAMFIELD, the Manour of Nicholas de Sergave 9 Edward II, but soon after of Walter de Norwich. He died the 2d of Edward III, left this Lordship to Sir John de Norwich; from them it descended to the de Uffords Earls of Suffolk. Who are the Lord or Lords of this Manour at present we know not, but the Family of Reginald Rabbett, Esq; as also that of the Neals have resided here some time, and Neal Ward, Gent. is now vested in the Seat and Estate lately belonging to the Family of the Neals.

BULCHAMP, a Hamlet of Blithburgh.

BUXLOW, a Hamlet of Knodishall.

CRATFIELD, the Lordship of John de Cove 9 Edward II; but we find that Thomas de Brotherton Earl of Norfolk, and fifth Son to Edward I, died possessed of it the 12 Edward III, leaving his second Wife Mary surviving; who for her Dowry, among other Estates, had an Assignation of a yearly Rent of 6 l. 1 s. 1 d. out of this Manour; and upon her Death it descended to Joan the youngest Daughter of Thomas de Brother-

R   ton.

ton. Afterwards it defcended to the Family of Coke, and is now vefted in the Right Hon. the Lord Lovel.

COOKLY, of which there is nothing Remarkable.

COVEHITH, at prefent of fmall Remark; but it appears to have been of Note formerly, by the Ruins of the Church now remaining, befpeaking its antient Grandeur.

CHEDDISTON, antiently the Lordfhip of Hugh Hovell, now Walter Plumer, Efq; who lately rebuilt the Hall in a beautiful Manner and made it his Seat.

DARSHAM, formerly the Lordfhip of the Prior of Thetford. To whom it was granted at the Diffolution of that Priory we find not. It afterwards came into the Family of Bedingfield, and from them defcended to the Knightly Family of Roufe, to whom it ftill remains, being vefted at prefent in Sir Roufe, Bart. a Child, being the only Son of the late Sir Robert Roufe, deceas'd. In this Village is alfo the Seat of George Purvis, Efq.

DUNWICH. See Page 27.

EASTON-BAVENT, the Lordfhip of Thomas de Bavent 9 Edward I, now Thomas Carthew, Efq. This Village is almoft fwallowed up by the Ocean, there remaining at prefent only a few mean Cottages.

FORDLEY, now of no Remark.

FROSTENDON, formerly the Lordfhip of Richard de Biskete. Afterwards it defcended to the Family of Glover; for we find that John Glover, Efq; fome time Servant to Thomas Howard Earl of Norfolk, having built the High Houfe in Campfey-Afh, his Succeffor fold it and removed to this Place, where the Family now remains.

HALESWORTH. See Page 103.

HEVENINGHAM, formerly of Note for giving Name to the Family of Heveningham. From the Heveninghams it defcended by Purchafe to John Bence, Efq; and now is the Lordfhip and Demefne of George Dafhwood, Efq; who has his Seat there.

HENHAM, 9 Edward I, was the Lordfhip of Robert Lord Kerdefton, in whofe Family it remained fome defcents; afterwards it belonged to the de la Pole's Earls of Suffolk; but for fome time has been the Seat of of the Family of Roufe. John Roufe of Henham, Efq; was created a Baronet Auguft 17, 1660. In whofe Family it now remains.

HENSTEAD, of no remark at prefent.

HINTON, a Hamlet of Blithburgh.

HOLTON, of no great remark.

HUNTINGFIELD, formerly the Lordfhip and Demefne of a noble Family of that name; afterwards it defcended to the Family of de Norwich, but has been for fome time the Lordfhip and Demefne of the Lord Lovels Anceftors, and is now vefted in that Noble Lord.

KNODISHALL, where we obferved a good Old Seat much decay'd, which for fome Ages has belonged to the Family of Jenny, and now remains to that Family.

LEISTON, See Page 29.

LINSTEAD Magna, and

LINSTEAD Parva, of no remark at prefent.

MELLS, a Hamlet of Wenhafton; the Church is now in Ruins, and as the Corn Tithes of Wenhafton now belong to Mells Church or Chapel, it may from thence be fuppofed it was antiently the Mother Church.

MIDDLETON, at prefent of no remark; South of Middleton Church in the fame Church-yard remain the Ruins of Fordley Church.

PEASENHALL, of which we have nothing to remark.

RUMBURGH, worthy of remark for a Benedictine Monaftery founded by Stephen Earl of Bretagn, and by him dedicated to God and the Bleffed Virgin Mary. What the Revenues of this Houfe were at its Diffolution, and to whom it was then granted does not appear. It was afterwards the Eftate of the Earls of Oxford, and was lately purchafed by Mr. Corbold a wealthy Quaker.

RAYDON, at prefent of no remark.

SIBTON. See Page 104.

SIZEWELL, a Hamblet of Leifton.

SOTHERTON.

SOUTHWOULD. See Page 26.

SOUTH COVE.

SPEXHALL.

R 2 STOVEN.

STOVEN.

THEBBERTON.

THORINGTON, formerly the Lordſhip and Demeſne of Walter de Norwich; afterwards of the de Uffords, and now is the Lordſhip and Seat of Alexander Bence, Eſq.

THORP, a Hamlet of Aldringham.

UBBESTON, of remark for having been ſome time the Seat of the Family of Sir Robert Kemp Baronet, which antiently had their Seat at Giſſing in the County of Norfolk.

UGGESHALL.

WALPOOLE.

WANGFORD. See Page 26.

WENHASTON.

WRENTHAM, antiently the Lordſhip and Demeſne of Simon de Pierpoint, afterwards it deſcended to the Poinings, from them to the Piercys Earls of Northumberland. It has been for ſome time in the Brewſters Family, and now belongs to Humphry Brewſter, Eſq.

WESTLETON.

WESTHALL, antiently the Lordſhip and Demeſne of Hubert de Burgh Earl of Kent. But ever ſince the 25 Henry VIII. has been the Reſidence of the Family of the Bohuns to whom it now remains.

WISSET, at preſent of ſmall remark.

YOXFORD, See Page 19.

THIS Hundred contains 53 Pariſhes or Hamlets.

BOSMERE and CLAYDON Hundred

Is bounded on the South by the Hundred of Samford, on the Weſt by the Hundreds of Cosford and Stow, on the North by the Hundred of Stow and Hartſmere, and on the Eaſt by the Hundreds of Thredling and Carlford. Its greateſt length is 12 Miles, its greateſt breadth 10 Miles, making the Circumference 45 Miles.

THE Towns and Villages in this Hundred are viz.

AKENHAM, formerly the Lordſhip of Philip Barnard Eſq; who had his Seat at Rice Hall, a Gentleman of a vaſt Eſtate, ſaid to have been owner of moſt

of

of the Lands between Woodbridge and Stowmarket. It was afterwards the Seat of the Family of Hawys, and now belongs to Walter Plumer, Esq.

ASH-BOCKEN, at present of small Remark.

BADLEY. Here is a good Seat where the Family of the Poleys have for some time resided. But it has been lately Purchased by Madam Crowley.

BARHAM has nothing more worthy of Remark at present, but that here is the Seat of Simon Dove, Esq.

BATTISFORD; the Hall is the Seat of Philip Bacon, Esq. a Grandson of Sir Nicholas Bacon Knight of the Bath.

BARKING. Here is a Seat late John Crowley's, Esq; which now remains to his Family.

BAYLEHAM, of which we have nothing to Remark.

BLAKENHAM Magna.

BLAKENHAM Parva.

BRAMFORD, 22 Edward I, was the Lordship and Demesne of Robert de Tibetot, but for some Ages the Family of Acton has had their Seat at the Hall in this Parish, and it is now vested in William Acton, Esq.

BRISET, of Remark for a Priory founded by Radulphus Fitz-brian and Emma his Wife, and by them dedicated to God, St. Mary and St. Leonard. They endowed it with divers Lands and Tythes, among which were the Tythes of Smithfield in London. What the Revenues of this Priory were at its Dissolution, or to whom it was granted, we know not.

CLAYDON, a through-fare Village on the Road from Ipswich to Norwich and Bury.

CODDENHAM, another through-fare Village on the Road from Ipswich to Debenham.

SHRUBLAND-Hall in this Parish is a good old Seat, and has been for some time the Seat of the Bacons, now remaining to Nicholas Bacon, Esq; whose Grandfather, Sir Nicholas Bacon, was created Knight of the Bath at the Coronation of King Charles II.

CREETING All-Saints,

CREETING St. Mary's,

CREETING St. Olave's, and

CREETING

CREETING St. Peter's, have nothing remarkable.

CROWFIELD, a Hamlet of Coddenham, or rather Coddenham to that, (for that is said to be the Mother Church) has nothing worthy of remark, but the Hall, now the Seat of Henry Harwood, Esq

DARMSDEN is a Hamlet of Barking.

EARL STONHAM, antiently the Lordship of the de Brotherton's Earls of Norfolk; to whom it descended from them we find not. It is now vested in the Person of Thomas Driver, Esq.

FLOWTON.

GOSBECK. Here is the remains of a Seat of the Styles, who removed from hence to Hemingston.

HEMINGSTON, a Manour held by Baldwin le Petteur (that is the Farter, Mr. Cambden bids us observe the Name) by Serjeantry (as the Book expresses it) for which he was obliged every Christmas-Day to perform before our Sovereign Lord the King of England one Saltus, one Sufflatus, and one Bombulus; or as it is read in another Place, that he held it by a Saltus, a Sufflatus and a Pet, that is (as Mr. Cambden interprets the Words) he was to Dance, make a Noise with his Cheeks puffed out, and let a Fart. Such was the plain jolly Mirth of those Times. It was many Years in the Family of the Styles lately extinct, but it is now the Lordship of Nathaniel Acton, Esq; whose Seat formerly went by the Name of Style.

HELMINGHAM, a Place honoured many Ages past with the Residence of the antient Family of Tallemach, who before they settled here had their Seat at Bently, in the Hundred of Samford. Lionel Tallemach of this Place, Esq; was created a Baronet the 22d of May 1611. But since, this Family has been enobled by the Earldom of Dysert in Scotland. The Noble Lord who now enjoys it being the Right Hon. Lionel Earl of Dysert, who succeeded his Grandfather of the same Name, and he inherited it from his Mother, Elizabeth Dutchess of Lauderdale.

HENLEY, where the Veres have for many Years had a Seat, it being now vested in Thomas Vere, Esq; now Mayor of Norwich, and Member of Parliament for that City.

MICKFIELD,

MICKFIELD.

NEEDHAM, a Market Town, yet a Hamlet of Barking, fee more Page 60.

NETTLESTEAD. From the Family of the Wentworths of this Place defcended the Right Hon. Thomas the prefent Earl of Strafford. He marry'd Anne fole Daughter and Heirefs of Sir Henry Johnfon of Frifton Hall in this County, Knt. which Anne, in right of her Grandmother, Anne, Daughter and fole Heirefs of Thomas Wentworth Earl of Cleveland, was in 1702 declared Baronefs Wentworth of Nettleftead, now living.

OFFTON. See Page 55.

RINGSHALL, is now of Note for being the Refidence of Sir William Barker, Bart.

SOMERSHAM.

STONHAM - ASPALL. A branch of the moft antient Family of the Wingfields of Wingfield-Caftle, before the Conqueft, has a Seat here. The Hall is now the Seat of John Wingfield, A. M.

STONHAM Parva, is of Note for the Refidence of the Family of the Blomfields or Blondevilles, an antient Family near as old as the Conqueft ; the eldeft Branch of which Family has ever fince refided at a Manfion in this Parifh, called the Four Elmes; which is now the Refidence of Thomas Blomfield, Efq.

THE Family of Gibfon has alfo a Seat in this Parifh, which now remains to Barnaby Gibfon, Efq;

SWILLAND.

WESTERFIELD, Part in this Hundred and Part in the Liberties of Ipfwich. In or near this Parifh is the Seat of Milefon Edgar, Efq.

WILLISHAM, remarkable for the Birth and Burial of the Right Reverend and very Pious Bifhop Brownrigg, ejected in the Great Rebellion.

There are in this Hundred 33 Parifhes, and Part of the Parifh of Wefterfield.

CARLEFORD

CARLEFORD Hundred

Is bounded on the South by the Hundred of Colnes, on the Eaſt with the Hundreds of Wilford and Loes, on the North and Weſt by the Hundred of Boſmere and Claydon, and the half Hundred or Liberties of Ipſwich. Its greateſt length is 8 Miles, its greateſt breadth 6 Miles, making the Circumference 29 Miles.

There being no Market Towns in this Hundred, the Villages are, viz.

BEALINGS Magna, antiently the Lordſhip of Robert de Tuddenham; afterwards it deſcended into the Family of Clynch; from them to the Webbs; from the Webbs it came by Purchaſe to John Pitt, Eſq; who removed from Crows-Hall near Debenham hither, and made Bealings Hall his Seat; but he dying without Male Iſſue, after the Death of his Lady (who now reſides in the Hall) it reverts with his other Eſtates to his Elder Brother.

BEALINGS Parva.

BRIGHTWELL, antiently the Lordſhip of John de Lamputt; afterwards it deſcended to the Wingfields; from the Wingfields it deſcended by Purchaſe to the Barnardiſtons. Sir Samnel Barnardiſton of this Place, Knt. was created a Baronet May 11, 1663, which Honour is now extinct, but the Eſtate is ſtill in that Family, and is at preſent veſted in Arthur Barnardiſton, Eſq.

BURGH.

CLOPTON.

CULPHOE.

FOXHALL, formerly a diſtinct Pariſh of it ſelf, but now a Hamlet to Brightwell.

GRUNDISBURGH, of Note for being the Lordſhip of the Family of Blois, who had their Seat at the Hall in this Pariſh. Charles Blois of this Place, Eſq; was created a Baronet April 15, 1686, now reſiding at Cockfield-Hall in Yoxford.

HASKETON.

KESGRAVE.

MARTLESHAM.

NEWBOURNE.

OTLEY,

OTLEY. Here is a good old House formerly the Seat of the Gosnolds. There is a Monument in the Church, with this Inscription: " Here resteth interred
' the Body of JOHN GOSNOLD, Esq; third Son of
" Robert Gosnold of Otley, Esq; and URSULA his Wife,
" born of the right antient and worthy Families of
" Naunton and Wingfield of Letheringham. His ten-
" der Years he spent in good Studies at Oxford and
" London; his riper Years he spent in Court, where
" he served in Place of Gentleman Usher in Ordinary
" the Majesties of Queen Elizabeth and King James;
" and was afterwards a Gentleman of the Privy-Cham-
" ber in Ordinary to King Charles. He married
" Winifred the Daughter of Walter Windsor, Esq;
" and of Margaret his Wife Daughter of Sir Jeffery
" Poole, Knt. Son of Sir Richard Poole, Knt. and the
" Lady Margaret Countess of Salisbury his Wife,
" Daughter of the Right Noble Prince George Duke
" of Clarence, Brother to King Edward IV of Eng-
" land. He departed this Life 17 Feb. Anno Dom.
" 1628, aged 60 Years.

THIS Family having suffered very much by Se-questration in the Time of the Great Rebellion, Otley Hall was Sold by the Rev. Mr. Lionel Gosnold the late Rector of this Parish, whose Grandfather Robert Gosnold, Esq; was Son to the abovementioned John Gosnold, and his Grandmother was Sister to Sir Lio-nel Tallemach of Helmingham, which see in Bos-mere and Clayton Hundred.

PLAYFORD, anciently the Lordship and Demesne of John de Playford. But for some descents has been the Seat of the Feltons. Henry Felton of Playford, Esq; was created a Baronet July 20, 1620. But the the Heirs Male of that Family failing by the Death of Sir Compton Felton, it now remains to the Right Hon. the Earl of Bristol, whose Lady was Daughter and Heiress to Sir Thomas Felton the preceeding Baronet, and Brother to Sir Compton.

RUSHMERE.
TUDDENHAM.
WALDRINGFIELD.

S   WITNESHAM,

WITNESHAM, antiently the Lordfhip and Demefne of Edmund de Bacun, afterwards of Bartholomew Lord Berghefh. The Family of Meadows has
for fome time had their Seat here.

THIS Hundred contains 18 Parifhes.

COLNES Hundred

Is bounded on the South by the Ocean, and the
River Orwell dividing it from the Hundred of Samford on the Weft; by the half Hundred or Liberties of Ipfwich and by Carleford Hundred on the
North, and on the Eaft by the River Deben dividing it from the Hundred of Wilford. Its length is
$6\frac{1}{2}$ Miles, its breadth 6 Miles, making the Circumference 25 Miles.

THE Villages in this Hundred are

BUCKLESHAM, antiently called BULECAMP.

FELIXSTOW.

HEMLEY.

KIRTON.

LEVINGTON. Sir Robert Hitcham was a Native of this Place; of whom fee more in the Account
of Framlingham, Page 43.

NACTON, is of remark for being the Birth Place
of Sir Robert Broke, who was Lord Chief Juftice of
the Common Pleas in the Reign of Queen Mary I.
One of his Pofterity Robert Broke of Nacton, Efq;
was Knighted by King Charles II, foon after the Refto-
ration, who dying without Male Iffue, his Nephew Robert Broke, Efq; who had married his Daughter and
Heirefs, left three Sons, one of which Philip Broke,
Efq; a worthy Member of the laft Parliament, refides
now in the Seat of the Family.

N. B. There is a Baronets Patent here, before Sir
Richard Broke the Grandfather of Sir Robert, perhaps
this Honour may be maintained by fome elder Branch,
which may be the Chefhire Family, unlefs it lies neg-
lected here.

Edward Vernon, Efq; another worthy Member of
the laft Parliament, does likewife Honour this Parifh
with his Refidence, having built a neat Manfion Houfe
here.

TRIMLEY

TRIMLEY confifts of two Parifhes, St. Martin's and St. Mary's. It is no fmall Honour to this Place that it give Birth to Thomas Cavendifh, Efq; who let Sail from Plymouth July 21,1586, to make a Voyage round the Globe, which he compleated in little more than two Years. Landing fafely at Plymouth Sept. 9, 1588. But defigning to make further Difcoveries, he fet out a fecond time from Plymouth, Auguft 26, 1591,‡ and in the Straits of Magellan in November following, was feparated from his Company, and never heard of after.

THE Barkers had their Seat formerly at Grimfton Hall in the Parifh of St. Martin in Trimley. John Barker of this Place, Efq; was created a Baronet March 17, 1621. The Honour and Eftate now remains to Sir John Barker, Bart.

WALTON. See Page 49.

THIS Hundred contains 9 Parifhes befides Hamlets, of which more at the end of this Treatife.

COSFORD Hundred,

Is bounded on the South by the Hundreds of Samford and Babergh; on the Weft by the Hundred of Babergh; on the North by the Hundreds of Thedweftry, and Stow, and on the Eaft by the Hundreds of Bofmere and Claydon, and Part of the Hundred of Samford; extending its felf in length 10 Miles, in breath 5 Miles, making in Circumference 28 Miles.

THE Towns and Villages in this Hundred are,
ALDHAM.

BILDESTON. See Page 55.

BRETTENHAM, fuppofed to be the antient COMBRETONIUN of Antoninus. At prefent of no great remark, but for the Family of Wenyeve who have their Seat here, which is now vefted in John Wenyeve, Efq.

CHELSWORTH.

ELMSET, at prefent of no remark, but for a Fair held yearly on Tuefday in Whitton Week.

HADLEIGH. See Page 56.

HITCHAM.

KITTLE-

KITTELBARSTON, antiently the Lordſhip of the Waldgraves, who had their Seat at the Hall; afterwards it deſcended to the Lemans; from them to the Beachcrofts, in which Family it now remains.

KERSEY. See Page 94.

LAYHAM.

LINDSEY.

NAUGHTON.

NEDGING.

SEAMER.

THORP, antiently the Lordſhip and Demeſne of Hugh de Moneux, and perhaps from him might derive the Name of Thorp Moreux.

ʰWATTISHAM.

WHATTISFIELD, WOTFIELD or WHEATFIELD at preſent of no great remark, but for its excellent Seed, Wheat.

THIS Hundred contains 17 Pariſhes.

HARTSMERE Hundred

Is bounded on the Eaſt by the Hundreds of Hoxne and Loes; on the South by the Hundreds of Thredling, Boſmere and Claydon; on the Weſt by the Hundred of Blackbourne, and on the North by the River Waveny dividng it from Norfolk. Its length is 11 Miles, its breadth 8 Miles, making the Circumference 35 Miles.

THE Towns and Villages in this Hundred are, viz.

ASPALL, or ASPALE, a Village ſituate at the River Deben. The Hall here was formerly the Seat of the Noble Family of the Brookes Lords Cobham; which Family being extinct, who it deſcended to from them we know not. It is now veſted in Clement Chevalier, Eſq; who has his Seat there.

BACTON, antiently the Lordſhip and Demeſne of the Biſhop of Norwich, but whether ſo at preſent we know not. Here is now a neat Manſion being the Seat of Baron Pretyman, Eſq.

BOTESDALE. See Page 68.

BRAIESWORTH.

BROOME, in this Village is a noble old Manſion, which for many Ages has been the Seat of the

Noble

Noble Family of Cornwallis. My Author informs me
that Sir John Cornwallis of Broome Hall, Knight, was
Steward of the Houshold to Prince Edward, afterward
King Edward VI.

His Son Sir Thomas Cornwallis being High Sheriff of Norfolk and Suffolk in the last Year of King
Edward VI. raised considerable Forces against the Op-
posers of Queen Mary's Title, Robert Gosnold of Otley
Hall, Esq; raising a Troop of Horse at his own Charge,
and by their Assistance set her on the Throne of her
Ancestors. He was promoted by that Queen to be
one of her Privy Council, Treasurer of Callis, and Comptroller of her Houshold. From him descended Frederick Cornwallis of Broome, Esq; who was created a
Baronet May 4, 1627. He suffered much in the great
Rebellion, by the Sequestration of his Estate and Im-
prisonment of his Person. King Charles the II, at his
Restoration, in Testimony of the Esteem he had for
his Merit, not only made him Treasurer of his Houshold, Comptroller and Privy Councellor, but by Letters Patents bearing date April 20, 1661, created him
a Baron of this Realm by the Title of Lord Cornwallis of Eye, to him succeeded his Son Charles Lord
Cornwallis. He was one of the Lords of the Admiralty
in the Reign of King William III, and, Lord Lieutenant of the County of Suffolk, whose Son Charles
was Father of the present Lord Cornwallis.

BROCKFORD, a Hamlet of Wetheringsett.
BURGATE.
COTTON.
EYE. See Page 39.
FINNINGHAM. See Page 109.
GISSLINGHAM.
MELLIS.
MENDLESHAM. See Page 51.
OAKELY.
OCCOLD.
PALGRAVE.
REDLINGFIELD, memorable for a Monaste-
ry of Black Nuns or Benedictines, founded to the Ho-
nour of God and the Blessed Apostle St. Andrew,
(Mr. Speed says Virgin Mary) by Manasses Earl of
Guisnes and Emma his Wife, and endowed by them
with

with the Manour of this Parish. Their Deed of Settlement (says my Author) bears date Anno 1120. The Annual Revenues of this House at the Suppression was found to be 67 l. os. 1 ½ d. says Dugdale, but Speed and Leland say they were 81 l. 2 s. 5 ½ d.

THE Family of Beddingfield have long enjoyed this Monastery, if it was not granted to them at its Dissolution, and made it their Seat ; but it has lately been purchased by John Willis, Esq.

REDGRAVE, antiently the Lordship of the Abbot of Bury St. Edmund's ; but in these latter Ages it came into the Family of the Bacons, who had their Seat at Redgrave Hall. Sir Nicholas Bacon of this Place, Knt. was by King James I, created the first Baronet in England, May 22, 1611. That Family has now its Seat at Garboldisham in the County of Norfolk; for the late Sir Edmund Bacon of Redgrave Hall, Bart. sold this Noble old Mansion, and his Estate in these Parts to Sir John Holt, Knt. Lord Chief Justice of the King's Bench, in which Family it now remains, being at present vested in Rowland Holt, Esq.

IN or near this Parish is Lopham Gate, or Causeway, or Lopham Ford, remarkable for the Head of two large Navigable Rivers which arise one on one side of the Gate, and the other on the other, viz. The Waveny running Eastward empties itself into the Sea at Yarmouth, and the Little Ouse running Westward empties itself into the Ocean near Lynn. But the chief Spring Head of the Little Ouse is in or near Whattisfield, which joyns itself with the Ouse about a Mile West of Lopham Gate.

RICKINGALE Superior.

RISHANGLES.

STOAK-ASH.

STUSTON, Stuston Hall is a good old Seat and was for many Ages the Seat of the Knightly Family of the Castletons.

THORNDON.

THORNHAM Magna, at present of remark only for the Residence of Charles Kelligrew, Esq; who has beautified the Hall, and made it his Seat.

THORNHAM Parva.

THRANDISTON,

THRANDISTON, antiently a Market-Town, but not at prefent fo : Thomas de Moulton Lord Ergemout, 18 Edward I. obtained a Charter for a Market to be held here weekly on Tuefdays, and a Fair yearly on the Eve Day and Morrow after the Feaft of St. Mary Magdalen. How long this Market and Fair has been difcontinued we know not. Thrandifton Fair is now yearly on St. Margaret's Day, July 20. Thrandifton Hall is now the Seat of the Lord Chief Baron Reynolds, who married a Daughter of Thomas Smith, Efq; the former Poffeffor of it.

THWAITE. See Page 52.

WESTHORP. The Hall by the ruins now remaining befpeaks it to have been a very noble Structure. It was antiently the Seat of Charles Brandon, Duke of Suffolk; but for fome Ages it has been the Eftate of the Sheltons, and is now vefted in Thomas Taylor, Efq; who has his Seat at Wefthorp-Lodge in this Parifh.

NEAR Weftthorp Church is the Seat of John Ellis, Efq;

WETHERINGSETT

WICKHAM-SKYTH.

WYVERSTON, the Lordfhip of this Parifh did formely belong to the Dukes of Suffolk. It is now invefted in Thomas Barnardifton, Efq; who has his Seat there.

WORTHAM.

YAXLY, a Family of that Name lately refided at the Hall there, now extinct.

THIS Hundred contains 32 Parifhes, and Brockford Hamlet.

HOXNE Hundred

Is bounded on the South by the Hundreds of Loes and Plomefgate; on the Weft by the fame Hundred of Loes and the Hundred of Hartfmere; on the North by the River Waveny dividing it from Norfolk, and on the Eaft by the Hundreds of Wangford and Blithing. Its length is 15 Miles, its breadth 10 Miles, making the Circumference 41 Miles.

THERE being no Market Towns in this Hundred, the Villages are as followeth.

ATHELING.

BADDINGHAM

BADDINGHAM, where the Family of the Alexanders have long refided ; Waldgrave Alexander, Gent. now refides there. The Patronage of the Church is now vefted in the Reverend Barrington Blomfield, D.D. who has lately built a neat Manfion not far from the Church.

BEDDINGFIELD, of remark for a Family of that Name who were Lords of the Manour, and, as it was laid before, had their Seat at Redingfield Hall.

BEDFIELD.

BRUNDISH, where the Family of the Wyards have long refided in a Manfion near the Church, and is now vefted in the Perfon of James Wyard, Gent.

CARLETON.

DENHAM.

DENNIGTON, of Note for being the Burial Place of the Lord Bardoff who lies buried in this Church, and had his Seat at the Hall in this Parifh, which by the ruins appears to have been a fumptuous Building ; afterwards it defcended to the Wingfields, then to the Roufes, and now is vefted in Sir John Roufe, Bart. a Minor.

FRESSINGFIELD. See Page 46.

HORHAM.

HOXNE, giving Name to this Hundred : but more memorable for being the Place where the Danes cruelly Martyr'd Edmund King of the Eaft Angles. For here it was that, becaufe this moft Chriftian King would not renounce his Faith in Chrift, thefe barbarous Pagans bound him to a Tree and Shot his Body full of Arrows ; and to increafe his Pain and Torture made Wound upon Wound 'till their Darts gave Place to one another.

Our Poets have thus reflected upon his Death :

As Dennis by his Death adorned France,
So Edmund's Sufferings did our Land Advance ;
The Crown his Head, Sceptre his Hand renown'd ;
But he was greater by his Blood and Wounds.

His Death happened Anno 870. his Body fo flain was removed to Bury and there buried, of which fee
more

more in the Account of that Town. The Christians of those Times built a Monastry in this Town in Honour of that Saint-like King, and dedicated it to St. Edmund; what the Order or the Revenues thereof were does not appear. It is now the Seat of John Thurston, Esq.

HOXNE HALL, is a Noble Seat, and is now the Mansion of Thomas Maynard, Esq.

HERE is a considerable Fair Yearly for Cattle beginning November the 20th, being St. Edmund's Day.

KELSALE, KELLESAL or KELSAL, antiently the Demesne of John Duke of Norfolk which he had with the Countess Marshal as a Portion, till being attainted for siding with the House of York against Henry Duke of Richmond, this Manour and his other Estates being seized were given to John de Vere, Earl of Oxford, how long it remain'd in that Family we know not; the Manour of this Town is now vested in several Persons, but the Lodge has for many Years been in the Hobart's Family, and is now the Seat of
Hobart, Esq.

LAXFIELD is situate in a dirty Part of the County. Its Church and Steeple are very beautiful Edifices. It seems Laxfield was formerly of more remark than it is at present, there being still Two Fairs yearly, the one on May-Day, and the other October 13. The Family of Jacobs alias Bradilhagh have long had their Seat in this Parish, which is now vested in Nicholas Jacobs, Esq;

MENDHAM, a Parish situate on both sides of the River Waveny, taking into its bounds part of the Town of Harleston.

METFIELD.

MONK-SOHAM, so called, because the Monks of Bury were Patrons of the Rectory, and had probably the Manour here.

SAXTEAD.

SYLEHAM.

SOUTHOLT.

STRADBROOK is a considerable large well built Village, where the Generals and Spiritual Courts are held for that Part of the County.

TANNINGTON, where the Family of the Dades have long had their Seat in a good Manſion which now remains to that Family.

WETHERSDALE.

WEYBREAD.

WILBYE.

WINGFIELD, ſometime the Eſtate of Richard de Bruce, but more antiently belonged to a Family who took their Names from it, and were called De Wingfield, they were a Family of great Reputation here for many Ages; but they had their Habitation in after Times at Letheringham, as is mentioned under the Head of Loes Hundred. That Noble old Building called Wingfield Caſtle, which was the Seat of this Family before the Norman Conqueſt (as appears by an antient Pedigree now in that Family) whoſe ruinous Walls beſpeak its former Grandeur, has been a College or Chantry; of which we know no more than that the De la Poles Earls of Suffolk were Patrons of it, and that at the Suppreſſion of it, 36 Henry VIII. it was found worth 50 l. 3 s. 5 ½ d. per Annum, Weaver. But Mr. Speed and Leland give the value to be 69 l. 14 s. 5 d. per Annum.

To whom this College was granted at its Diſſolution we know not. It has for ſome Ages been veſted in the Family of Catalyne, and at preſent remains to the Lady of Sir Charles Turner, Bart. (She was the Relict of Sir Nevil Catalyne) after whoſe Death it deſcends to Thomas Leman of Wenhaſton, Eſq.

WORLINGWORTH.

This Hundred contains 26 Pariſhes.

LACKFORD Hundred

Is bounded on the North with the Little Ouſe dividing it from Norfolk; on the South by the Hundred of Risbridge; on the Eaſt by the Hundreds of Blackbourn and Thingoe, and on the Weſt by the River Cam in part, and a Brook in part, which has its riſe at or near Lidgate, and making its Courſe under Kentford Bridge, empties itſelf into the River Lark in or near Iſleham. This Hundred extends itſelf

in

in length 12 Miles, in breadth 11 Miles, making the Circumference 40 Miles, exclusive of the Parishes of New-Market St. Mary's, and Exning, which are part of this Hundred.

THE Towns and Villages in this Hundred are as followeth.

BARTON Mills, or BARTON Parva, to distinguish it from another Parish of this Name in the Hundred of Thedwestry.

BRANDON. See Page 75.

CAVENHAM, corruptly call'd Canham, antiently the Lordship and Demesne of Gilbert Earl of Clare; but now of Richard Webb, Esq.

DOWNHAM, very fitly called Sandy-Downham; the Sands often in windy Weather are blown off the Hills into the Valleys here, so as to render them unfruitfull. Mr. Hollingshead tells us that in October 1568, there were taken at the Bridge in this Village 17 Monstrous Fishes, some of them 27 Feet, others 24, and the least 20 Feet in length.

ELVEDON.

ERESWELL seems to have been larger than it is at present, as may be conjectur'd from the Ruins of a Church or Monastery at the North End of the Parish, towards Lakenheath.

EXNING or IXNING, a Village situate in the very utmost Limits of the County towards Cambridgeshire. It was formerly a Place of greater Note than now it is; for it was made famous of Old, (1) by the Birth of Etheldred the Daughter of Anna whom the Pope Canoniz'd for a Virgin though she had been Marry'd to two Husbands. (2) For the Conspiracy of Ralph Earl of the East Angles against William the Conqueror; which was formed at this Place upon his Wedding Day. (3) For the Way which Harvey the first Bishop of Ely made from Ely to this Place. But now the nearness to Newmarket, to which all Marketable Goods are carry'd in abundance, has render'd this Town inconsiderable. However it is now adorned with a beautifull Mansion, which is the Seat of Francis Sheppard, Esq.

FRECKINGHAM,

FRECKINGHAM, in this Parish Sir Robert Clark, Bart. has a Seat.

HERRINGSWELL.

HIGHAM GREEN, a Hamlet of Gaiefly.

ICKLINGHAM, confifts of two diftinct Parifhes, St. James and All-Saints, having two Parifh Churches. Near this Village there have been within the Memory of fome now (or very lately) living feveral Roman Coins dug up, which fhews the Antiquity of the Place, and that it probably enough has been a Roman Station.

LAKENHEATH, another large Village in this Hundred, fituate by the fide of the Fens in an unwholefome Air, at prefent of no great Remark, except it be for the Refidence of Sir Simeon Stewart, who has a Seat there.

MILDENHALL. See Page 77.

NEW-MARKET. See Page 78.

TUDDENHAM.

WANGFORD.

WORLINGTON.

THIS Hundred contains 16 Parifhes and one Hamlet

LOES Hundred

Is bounded on the North with the Hundred of Hoxne; on the Eaft with the Hundred of Plomefgate; on the South by the Hundred of Wilford, and on the Weft by the Hundreds of Bofmere and Claydon, Thredling, and Hartfmere. Its length is 15 miles, its breadth in fome Places 5, and in other Places not 3 Miles, making its Circumferences 40 Miles. The Towns and Villages in this Hundred are, viz.

BRANDESTON; this in the Conqueror's Time was the Lordfhip of Odo or Eudo de Campania, Earl of Holdernefs, whofe Pofterity granted it to the Burnells, from them it defcended to the Weylands; from the Weylands to the Tuddenhams; from the Tuddenhams to the Beddingfields, the laft of which Henry Beddingfield, Efq; was a cruel Jailor to the Princefs (afterwards Queen) Elizabeth in the Reign of her Sifter Queen Mary. Andrew Revet, Efq;

Efq; Anno Dom. 1548, purchafed the Manour of Bran-
defton and made the Hall is Seat. To him fucceeded
John Revet, Efq; hiseldeft Son ; to him Nicholas Rivet,
Efq; Son of the faid John; to him John Revet, Efq:
Son of the faid Nicholas; to him Thomas Revet, Efq;
Son of the faid John, and to him John Revet, Efq;
Son of the faid Thomas now living.

BUTLEY, the Church is in this, the Abbey in
Plomefgate Hundred, of which See Page 34.

CAMPSEY Afh, worthy of remark for a Nunnery,
firft of the Order of St. Auguftine, but afterwards that
of St. Clare, founded by Joan and Agnes de Voloines,
two Sifters, who dedicated it to the Honour of God and
the Bleffed Virgin Mary. This Monaftery was feated in
a fruitful and pleafant Valley on the Eaft of the River
Deben; on the North it had a large Mere or Pool of
Water; as the Water fupplied them with Fifh and Wild
Fowl, fo the Land afforded them almoft all the neceffaries
of Life. Maud de Lancafter, Countefs of Ulfter, who
afterwards married Ralph de Ufford, Chief Juftice of
Ireland, obtained a Licence of King Edward III. to
found a Chantry of 5 Chaplains, Secular Priefts, to
Pray and Sing Mafs in the Church of this Nunnery for
the Souls of William deBurgh, Ralph deUfford, and for
Elizabeth de Burgh and Maud de Ufford her Daughters, and for the good Eftate of herfelf and of Sir John
de Ufford, and Sir Thomas de Hereford, Knts. during
their Lives and for their Souls afterwards. Which
Chantry having remained there fome Years was removed by the faid Lady to the Manour of Rokehall in
Bruifyard. In the Window of the Parlour in the Abby
Houfe is a Piece of Glafs, now ftained with the Arms of
the de Ufford's, and in the Window in the Chamber
over it is the Effigies of a Lady ftain'd on a piece of
Glafs, with thefe Words underneath in old Roman
Capitals, GOVERNAS GRACE. This Monaftery was
valued at its Diffolution, the 35 Henry VIII. at 1821.9s.
5 d. per Annum, and granted by that King to Sir William Willoughby, who Sold it to John Lane, Gent. From
the Lanes it was purchafed by Frederick Scot, Gent.
who Sold it to Sir Henry Wood of Loudham, in whofe
Family it ftill remains, being now vefted in Charles
Wood,

Wood. Efq; In this Parifh of Campfey, is an old Seat which was formerly the Eftate of Theophilus Howard Earl of Suffolk. This was Purchafed by John Braham, or Brame. He was the Son of George Braham, Son of Sir John Braham of Braham's Hall, Kt. and fettled here, making it his Seat, but that Family failing of Iffue Male, it is now vefted in two Maiden Ladies of that Name. The high Houfe in Campfey Afh is a good Seat, and was built by John Glover, Efq; fometime Servant to Thomas Howard, Earl of Norfolk, whofe Succeffor removing to Froftendon in this County fold this Seat to John Sheppard, Gent. whofe Succeffor John Sheppard, Efq; now the prefent Poffeffor has made great Ad- ditions to it.

CHARSFIELD, formerly the Lordfhip of the Bed- ingsfields, and by them Sold to Sir John Leman, Knt. Alderman, and Lord Mayor of London. To him fuc- ceeded William Leman, Efq; the eldeft Son of John Leman, Efq; the eldeft Son of William Leman of Beccles, Efq; the eldeft Brother of Sir John Leman. To him fucceed John Leman, Efq; his eldeft Son, and to him his Son William Leman, Efq; whofe relict Eliza- beth (the only Daughter and Heir of Robert Ster- ling of this Parifh Gent.) now refides there.

CRETINGHAM.

DALLINGHOO, part in this and part in Wilford Hundred. Here was a handfome Seat built by William Churchil, Efq; who fome time refided here. He grant- ed it to his Son-in-Law Francis Negus, Efq; who rebuilt it, but it was unfortunately confumed by Fire. Anno Dom. 1729.

EARL-SOHAM. See Page 38.

EASTON, formerly the Lordfhip and Demefne of the antient Family of Knightly Degree in Kittleburgh, Sirnamed Charles; afterwards the Wingfields of Le- theringham, of like Degree, were Proprieteors of both, in which Family they continued a longer fpace of time than in the former. Anthony Wingfield, Efq; removing from Letheringham to Godyns in Hoo, was created a Baronet May 17, A D. 1627. He built the White Houfe in Eafton, and removing from Hoo thither, made it his Seat. To him fucceeded Sir Richard Wingfield, Bart. after him Sir Robert Wingfield, Bart. After him Sir Hen-

ry

ry Wingfield, Bart. And to him his eldeſt Son Sir Henry Wingfield, Bart. who ſold this Seat and the Remainder of the Wingfield's Eſtate in the Neighbourhood, to the Right Hon. William Zuile-ſtein, Lord of Zuileſtein, in the Province of Utrecht, Maſter of the Robes to King William III, created Baron of Enfield, Viſcount Tunbridge, and Earl of Rochford 10 May, 7 William III. William Henry Earl of Rochford, his eldeſt Son ſucceeded him in Honour and Eſtate ; he commanded the left Wing of the Engliſh Army under General Stanhope at Lerida, in the Plains of Balaguer in Spain, where valiantly Fighting for the Honour, tho' not for the Profit of his Country, he was ſlain July 14, 1710.

FREDERICK Earl of Rochford his Brother now living ſucceeded him in his Honour and Eſtate, and hath honoured his Pariſh with his Reſidence chiefly at the White Houſe.

EYKE.

FRAMLINGHAM. See Page 43.

HACHESTON. See Page 42.

HOO.

KITTLEBURGH, in this Pariſh is the Seat of Robert Sparrow Gent. King Henry III. Anno Dom. 1265, granted a Market and Fair to the Manour of Kittleburgh, but how long they have been diſuſed we know not.

KENTON, the Wareyns deſcended from Robert Wareyn D. D. Rector of Melford ejected 1641, have a Seat in this Pariſh wherein now reſides John Wareyn Gent.

LETHERINGHAM. See Page 37.

MARLSFORD, the Manour of which did antiently belong to the Sackviles; then to the Rokes; afterwards to the Druries ; lately to the Devereuxes, and now to Simon Dove of Barham, Eſq.

MONODEN or Monewden, at preſent of little remark.

RENDLESHAM. See Page. 31.

WOODBRIDGE. See Page 16.

This Hundred contains 19 Pariſhes.

LOTHING

LOTHING or LUTHING LAND Hundred

Probably took its Name from that Spacious Lake called by Mr. Cambden the Lake Luthing. It is reckoned, in refpect of the Civil Government of the County, but a Half Hundred; the other Half Hundred is called the Half Hundred of Mutford; and they are generally called the Half Hundreds of Lothingland and Mutford. But in the Map of this County, following the natural Divifion of them, That part of this Hundred on the North fide of the Lake Lothing which divides the two Half Hundreds, we have called Lothingland Hundred and That on the South fide, Mutford Hundred. The Hundred of Lothingland is bounded on the Eaft with the Ocean and the River Yar; on the Weft by the River Waveny dividing it from Norfolk; on the North by Bredon Water and the River Yar; and on the South by the Lake Lothing or Luthing. Its length from North to South is 8 Miles; Its breadth from Eaft to Weft 5 Miles, making the Circumference 21 Miles.

THE Towns and Villages in this Hundred are as followeth:

ASHBYE.
BELTON.
BLUNDESTON.
BRADWELL.
BURGH CASTLE. See Page 22.
CORTON.
FLIXTON.
FRITTON.
GORLESTON. See Page 24.
GUNTON.
HOPTON.
HERINGSFLEET, in which Parifh was a Priory, of which fee more Page 22.
LOUND.
LOWESTOFT. See Page 25.
OULTON.
SOMERLITON, now corruptly called Somerley, is of remark for a Beautiful old Seat called the Hall,

having

having for many Years been the Seat of the Knightly Family of Allen, who sometime had their Seat at Blundeston. Our Author informs us, that Thomas Allen, of Blundeston, Esq; was created a Baronet the 7th of February 1672, which Sir Thomas or his Successor, gave this Seat to his Nephew Anguish Esq. This Gentleman or his Successor Richard Anguish alias Allen of this Place, Esq; was created a Baronet December the 15, 1699. This Noble Seat is now vested in his Son Sir Thomas Allen Baronet.

This Hundred contains 16 Parishes, but besides these Parishes we observed divers Hamlets, as Brotherton, a Hamlet now consolidated to Hopton ; Browston, a Hamlet consolidated to Belton. Broston Hall is the Seat of Symonds Esq.

NORMANSTON, now corruptly called Nomans-Town, lies between Mutford Bridge and the Town of Lowestoft. It is now the Estate of Richard Jenkinson Gent. Adjoining to Yarmouth Bridge is an Hamlet called Westown, and nearer to Gorleston is another Hamlet called Southtown ; and these two viz. Westown and Southtown are called in old Writing Little Yarmouth.

MUTFORD Hundred

Is bounded on the East by the Ocean; on the North by the Lake Lothing ; on the West by the River Waveny, and on the South by the Hundred of Blithing. Its length from East to West is 4 Miles ; its breadth from North to South is 3 Miles, making the Circumference to be 15 Miles.

There is no Market Town sin this Hundred ; the Villages are as followeth,

BARNBY.

CARLTON Colvile.

GISLEHAM.

KESSINGLAND, formerly of more remark than it is as present, as may be conjectured from the Ruins of its old and once beautiful Church.

KIRKELY. The Church is now in Ruins.

MUTFORD

MUTFORD, giving Name to this Hundred.
PAKEFIELD. See Page 25.
RUSHMERE.
THIS Hundred contains 8 Parishes.

PLOMESGATE Hundred

Is bounded on the East with the Ocean; on the North with the Hundreds of Blithing and Hoxne; on the West with the Hundred of Loes, and on the South with the Hundred of Wilford. Its length is 12 Miles; its breath 9 Miles; making the Circumference 42 Miles

THE Towns and Villages in this Hundred are as followeth,

ALDEBURGH. See Page 35

BENHALL, of remark for a beautiful Seat, which for some time has been the Seat of the Knightly Family of the Dukes; Sir Edward Duke of this Place Knt. who built this delightful Mansion was created a Baronet July 17, 1661; to him succeeded in his Honour and Estate Sir John Duke Baronet; To Sir John succeeded Sir Edward Duke Baronet, who dying without Issue, the Honour is now extinct. But this Seat is now vested in Edmund Tyrell, Esq; the Sister's Son of the late Sir Edward, by Thomas Tyrell, Esq; of Gipping Hall.

BLAXHALL.

BRUISYARD, memorable for a College of Nunns founded by Matilde de Lancaster Countess of Ulster (at that time a Nunn in the Collegiate Church of Campsey) for five Chaplains, whose order of Government William Bishop of Norwich appointed in the Year 1354, which are too long to be here inserted. This College was dedicated to the Blessed Virgin Mary, and was valued at its dissolution at 56 l. 2 s. 1 d. per Annum. To whom this College was granted at its Suppression we know not. It has been for some time in the Family of the Rouse's, and is now vested in Sir John House Bart. a Minor.

BUTLEY. See Page 34.
CHILLESFORD.
CRANSFORD.

DUNNINGWORTH,

DUNNINGWORTH, now a Hamlet of Tunstal.

FARNHAM.

FRISTON antiently belonged to the Priory of Snape. Sir Henry Johnson, Knt. having purchased the said Priory and its Appendances, built Friston Hall and made it his Seat; whose only Daughter and Heiress marrying the Right Hon. Thomas the Earl of Strafford carried this delightful Seat and a plentiful Estate into that Noble Family.

GEDGRAVE.

GLEMHAM MAGNA or NORTH GLEMHAM, is of Note for the Family of Edgar, who have for many Generations had their Seat in this Parish. This Family was divided into three Branches, viz. This at Glemham of which is William Edgar, Esq; now living. The Second at Ipswich, of which is Devereux Edgar, Esq; of Ipswich; The Third at Eye now extinct, the Heiress of which Family at Eye married Arthur Jenny, late of Bredfield, Esq.

GLEMHAM Parva, famous for a Race of Gentlemen who took their Names from it, being called de Glemham. which Family flourished there for many Descents. In the last Century, we find Two of this Family bright Examples in Church and State; viz. Dr. Henry Glemham, who adhearing firmly to the Church of England was a great Sufferer in the late Times of Disorder; whom King Charles II; after his Restoration, created Bishop of St. Asaph. He died January 17, 1669, and was Buryed in the Vault belonging to his Family, in the Parish-Church of Little Glemham. Of like Eminence in the State was his Brother Sir Thomas Glemham, who was also a great Sufferer in those unhappy Times, undergoing great Troubles in the Service of his Royal Master; he, with his two worthy Countrymen, Colonel Gosnold of Otley, and Major Naunton of Letheringham, defended Carlisle with remarkable Circumstances of Courage, Industry, and Patience; at last, dying in Holland in the Year 1649, his Body was brought into England, and Buried in the aforesaid Vault belonging to this Family. The Glemham Family being reduced and failing of Male Issue, their pleasant

U 2

and

and noble Seat, with the reft of their Eftate, was purchafed by Dudley North, Efq; who added greatly to its Beauty. It is now vefted in his Son Dudley North, Efq.

HASLEWOOD, a Hamlet of Aldeburgh.

IKEN.

ORFORD. See Page 34.

PARHAM. See Page 42.

RENDHAM.

SAXMUNDHAM. See Page 18.

SNAPE. See Page 30.

STERNFIELD.

STATFORD St. Andrew.

SUDBOURNE, of remark for a noble Seat, for fome time the Refidence of the Vifcounts Hereford. It is now the Seat of the Hon. Price Devereux, Efq; Son and Heir Apparent to the Right Hon. the Lord Vifcount Hereford.

SWEFLING.

TUNSTALL.

WANTISDON.

This Hundred contains 23 Parifhes and 3 Hamlets.

RISBRIDGE Hundred

Is bounded on the Eaft with the Hundreds of Babergh, Thingoe and part of Lackford; on the Weft with Cambridgefhire; on the South with the River Stour dividing it from Effex, and on the North with the Hundred of Lackford. Its length is 15 Miles, its breadth 8 Miles, making the Circumference 45 Miles.

The Towns and Villages in this Hundred are as followeth.

BARNARDISTON, corruptly called BARNSON, of no great Note, but for giving Name to a Family whofe feveral Branches have their Seats at Kedington, Brightwell and Wyverfton in this County.

BRADLEY Magna. Here is a Fair yearly September 29.

BRADLEY Parva.

CLARE. See Page 81.

CHED-

CHEDBURGH.

CHILTON, a Hamlet of Clare. The Church (or Chapel) is now converted into a dwelling Houfe.

COOLING, corruptly called CULIDGE or COWLIDGE. In this Parifh is a good Seat called by the Name of Branches, which (with the Manour of this Town) was the Eftate of William Long-Efpee Earl of Salisbury and Somerfet, bafe Son to King Henry II, by Fair Rofamond. They are now vefted in Francis Dickins, Efq. In this Town are held two Fairs yearly, the one on July 20, the other on October 6.

DALHAM, anciently the Lordfhip and Demefne of William de Ufford Earl of Suffolk; afterwards it came into the Family of the Stutevills. It is now the Lordfhip and Seat of Gilbert Affleck, Efq.

DENHAM, anciently the Lordfhip of Margaret de Say; but now of the Right Hon. the Lord Lynn, Son and Heir Apparent to the Right Hon. the Lord Vifcount Townfend, who has his Seat at Denham-Hall.

DENSTON. In this Parifh is a beautiful Seat which now or late was the Manfion of the Hon. John Robinfon, Efq; Lieut. Col. in the Cold Stream Regiment of Foot Guards.

DEPDEN. The Hall did formerly belong to the Jermyns, afterwards to the Coels, and now is the Seat of Coel Thornhill, Efq.

GAZELY, or GAIESLY.

HAVERHILL. See Page 92.

HAWKEDON. In this Village is now the Manfion of   Hammond, Efq.

HUNDON.

KEDINGTON, or (as it is written in Domefday Book) KEDITVNE, now corruptly called KETTON, was then the Lordfhip and Demefne of Ralph Baynard; afterwards it belonged to the Earls of Clare. In later Times the Family of Barnardifton have had their Seat here. Sir Thomas Barnardifton of this Place Knt. was created a Baronet the 7th of April 1663, and Sir Samuel Barnardifton, Bart. now refides at Kedington Hall, a beautiful Seat. Kedington Fair is yearly July 29.

KENTFORD.

LIDGATE. See Page 100.

MOULTON.

OUESDON. In this Parifh is the Seat of Richard Mofely, Efq.

POSLINGFORD, or (as it is written in Domef-day Book) POSELINGWORD, was antiently (as Kedington) the Lordfhip of Ralph Baynard. Poflingford Hall is now the Seat of George Golding, Efq.

STANSFIELD. In this Parifh is the Seat of Robert Kedington Gent.

STOKE by Clare. See Page 91.

STRADDISHALL.

THURLOW Magna. The Hall in this Parifh is the Seat of James Vernon, Efq.

THURLOW Parva, in this Parifh we obferv'd a noble old Seat where the Family of Soame have long refided. It is now the Seat of Stephen Soame Efq.

WHIXOE.

WICKHAM-BROOK, now a Parifh of large Bounds, to which feveral Hamlets (or Parifhes) have been annexed, four of which appear in fome old Parchment Writings now in the Cuftody of Robert Edgar of Ipfwich, Efq; viz. the Hamlet or Parifh of Clopton (or Cloptune) The Tythes of which Hamlet did antiently belong to Stoke College. Badmondesfield, Alderisfield, and Nether-Attilton.

BADMONDESFIELD Hall was formerly the Poffeffion of Charles Somerfet Son and Heir of Sir George Somerfet, who was the fecond Son to Charles Earl of Worcefter. Since Sir Henry North's now Warner Efq.

GIFFORD's Hall once in Sir Hugh Francis, fince Thomas Heigham, Efq; afterwards Charles Owers Gent. now George Chinery Gent.

CROPTON, or WICKHAM HOUSE, was formerly the Habitation of Major Robert Sparrow, and now fometimes the Refidence of Devereux Edgar of Ipfwich, Efq.

WETHERSFIELD.

WRATTING Magna.

WRATTING Parva.

THIS Hundred contains 30 Parifhes and the aforefaid five Hamlets.   SAMFORD

SAMFORD Hundred

Is bounded on the South with the River Stour ; on the Weft with the Hundreds of Babergh and Cofford ; on the North and Eaft by the Hundred of Bofmere and Claydon, the Liberties of Ipfwich and the River Orwell. It's length from Eaft to Weft is 13 Miles, its breadth 7 Miles, making the Circumference to be 36 Miles. There being no Market Towns in this Hundred, the Villages are as followeth :

ARWERTON, a fmall Village, but of Note for the Seat of the antient Family of Parker. Our Author informs us that Philip Parker of Arwerton Hall, Efq; was created a Baronet July 16, 1661. The Honour and Eftate is now vefted in Sir Philip Parker Long Bart. He having lately taken the Sirname of Long.

BELSTEAD, of Note for being the Seat of the Family of Blois, and is now vefted in Tobias Blofs, Efq.

BENTLY, antiently the Seat of the Knightly now noble Family of Tallemach who had their Seat here, before they fettled at Helmingham. This Place is alfo memorable for a Monaftery there founded by the Duke of Norfolk, dedicated to St. Mary, and valued at its Diffolution at 42 l. 18 s. 8 ¼ d. per Annum, and is now called by the Name of Dodnafh, and was formerly the Eftate of the Earl of Dyfert's Progenitors; but fince it has been in the Family of the Dukes, and now remains to Robert Arbuthnot, Efq; who married an Heirefs of that Family. Our Author informs us alfo of a College in or near this Place called Denfton, valued at its fuppreffion at 22 l. 8 s. 9 ½ d. per Annum ; but whether there was any fuch College in this Place is uncertain.

BRANTHAM.

BURSTALL.

CAPELL St. Peter.

CHATTISHAM.

CHELMONDISTON, now corruptly called Chempton.

COPDOCK,

COPDOCK, in this Parish is the Seat of Thomas De Grey, Esq.

EASTBERGHOLT. See Page 97.

FRESTON.

HARKSTEAD.

HIGHAM.

HINTLESHAM, antiently the Lordship of the Talbot's, but for many Ages of the Timperley's, who had their Seat at the Hall there. But this beautiful Seat has been lately purchased by Richard Powis, Esq; and is now his Seat.

HOLBROOK, in this Parish is the Seat of Thomas Thurston, Esq.

HOLTON.

RAYDON.

SHELLY, 9 Edward II, was the Seat of John de Appleby, afterwards it was the Seat of the Tilneys, and now remains to Thomas Kerridge, Esq.

SHOTLEY, antiently called Kirketon.

SPROUGHTON, in this Parish we observed a very good new built Seat called the Chantry. This with some other Estates of considerable value were called the Chantry Lands, because they were given by Edmund Dandy of Ipswich, in the 6th Year of Henry VIII, 1514, for the establishing a Chantry at the Altar of St. Thomas the Martyr in St. Laurence Church in Ipswich, for two perpetual Secular Priests to sing Mass and pray for the King, and Queen Katherine, the said Edmund Daudy, William Dandy his Son, and Thomas Wulsey Clerk, Dean of Lincoln, during Life; and after, for their Souls; and for the Souls of Anne, his late Wife and of Robert Wulsey and Anne his Wife the Father and Mother of the said Thomas, and for the Souls of all their Ancestors and Benefactors. It is now the Mansion of Edward Ventris, Esq; near this is the Seat of Robert Harland, Esq; for many Years a Commander in his Majesty's Navy; and some other Gentlemen have Seats in this Parish.

STRATFORD. See Page 58.

STUTTON.

TATTINGSTON, in this Parish is a good old Seat
called

called the Place, which is now the Seat of Thomas Whight, Efq;

WASHBROOK.

WENHAM, Magna.

WENHAM Parva. Little Wenham Hall appears to have been a noble old Building. It was formerly the Seat of the Family of Bruce and now remains to Madam Thurfton.

WHERSTEAD. In this Parifh is the Seat of Ellis Brand, Efq. Commander of one of his Majefty's Ships of War.

WOOLVERSTON. In this Parifh is the Seat of Knox Ward Efq; Clarencieux King at Arms.

THIS Hundred contains 28 Parifhes.

STOW Hundred

IS bounded on the North by the Hundred of Hartfmere; on the Weft by the Hundreds of Blackbourne and Thedweftry; on the South and Eaft by the Hundreds of Cosford, and Boſmere and Claydon. Its greateft length is 8 Miles, its breadth 6 Miles, making the Circumference 21 Miles.

THE Towns and Villages in this Hundred are as followeth.

BUXHALL. This Village is rendred famous for the Birth of Sir William Coppinger. He was the Son of Walter Coppinger of this Place; and being bred a Fifhmonger in London became its Lord Mayor in the Year 1512. His Eftate (which was very large) at his Death he divided between God and Man, i. e. Half to the Poor and other pious Ufes, and Half to his Heirs and Kindred; another Zacheus in his Liberality, though of a better Profeffion. This good Man having fettled his Family in this Parifh, in very plentiful Circumftances, even to the Proverb of Living like the Coppingers, at this Day ufed in the neighbourhood, they have continued there ever fince in good Repute.

COMBS, was 43 Edward III the Lordfhip of Robert de Ufford, afterwards it came into the Family of Willoughbys Lords of Eresby; from them it de-

X   fcended

scended to Charles Brandon Duke of Suffolk, who married an Heiress of the Willoughby Family, but he dying, she marry'd Richard Bertue, Esq; and brought it into his Family. It has been for some time the Seat of the Bridgemans. Orlando Bridgeman, Esq; lately deceas'd, new built the Hall in a beautiful Manner, and left it to his Son William Bridgeman, Esq; now living. His Father, William Bridgeman, Esq; was Clerk of the Council in the Reigns of King Charles II, King James II, and King William and Queen Mary, Son of the Lord Bishop of Chester. Brother to Sir Orlando Bridgeman, Lord Keeper of the Great Seal in the time of King Charles II, who are both mentioned with Honour in Lord Clarendon's History. Madam Crowley has lately purchased this Seat.

CHILTON, now a Member or Hamlet of Stow-Market.

CREETING St. Peter, mentioned by mistake with the other Creetings in Bosmere and Claydon Hundred.

DAGWORTH, now a Hamlet of Newton.

FINBOROUGH Magna. In this Parish is a good old House, which is the Seat of William Wollaston, Esq. Member of Parliament for Ipswich.

FINBOROUGH Parva.

GIPPING, of remark for being the Residence of a Branch of the ancient Family of the Tyrells, some of which Family have enjoyed the Honour of Knighthood in a direct Line about 600 Years, and do still enjoy it. They are descended from Sir Walter Tyrell, Knt. who held at the general Survey of William the Conqueror, the Lordship of Langham in Essex. William Tyrell of Gipping was the second Son of Sir Walter Tyrell of Heron, who was the eighth Knight in a Lineal descent from Sir Walter first named. He was Father of James Tyrell, Captain of Guisnes in France in the Time of Henry VII, and from him is descended Thomas Tyrell, Esq; the present Proprietor of Gipping, who has his Seat there, where there is a very neat Chapel built by his Ancestors.

HALSTON.

HAUGHLLY, See Page 107.

NEW-

NEWTON.

ONEHOUSE.

STOW-MARKET. See Page 61.

STOW-UPLAND. See Page 61.

SHELLAND, where William Mordant, Efq; has a Seat.

WETHERDEN; of which See more in the Account of Haughley, Page 107.

THIS Hundred contains 14 Parifhes and 2 Hamlets.

THEDWESTRY or THEDWASTRY Hundred

Is bounded on the South with the Hundreds of Babergh and Cosford; on the Eaft by the Hundred of Stow; on the North and North Eaft by the Hundred of Blackbourn, and on the Weft with the Hundred of Thingoe. Its length is 12 Miles, its breadth 9 Miles, making the Circumference 37 Miles. There being no Market Town in this Hundred the Villages are as followeth,

AMPTON, antiently the Lordfhip of the Abbot of Bury St. Edmunds, to whom it was granted at the Diffolution of that Abbey we know not. The Calthropes have long refided at Ampton Hall, which is now vefted in James Calthrope, Efq.

BARTON (which we will call Barton Magna, to diftinguifh it from Barton Mills or Barton Parva near Mildenhall in the Hundred of Lackford) was anciently the Lordfhip of the Abbot of Bury St. Edmunds, but fince the Diffolution of that Abbey it has been the Eftate of the Family of Cotton, who had their Dwelling at Necton-Hall in this Parifh, which has been lately built in a beautifull manner by   Fowke, Efq; whofe Daughter and Heirefs being married to Sir Thomas Hanmer Bart. carry'd it into his Family.

BEYTON.

BRADFIELD Combuft.

BRADFIELD St. Clare.

BRADFIELD St. George.

DRINKSTON,

X 2

FEL-

FELSHAM. In this Parish is a neat Mansion, being now the Seat of John Reynolds, Esq; and a considerable Fair for Lambs Yearly, beginning August the 5th.

FORNHAM St. Genoveve. In this Parish is the Seat of Samuel Kent, Esq. Member of Parliament for Ipswich.

FORNHAM St. Martin. In this Parish is the Seat of Francis Hutcheston, Esq.

GEDDING In this Parish is the Seat of Buckenham, Esq.

HESSET, antiently written Hedgesset or Hegset was the Lordship of the Abbot of Bury St. Edmunds. To whom it was granted at the dissolution of that Abbey we know not. Michael Le Heup, Esq; has a Seat here.

LIVERMERE Magna.

PAKENHAM, is of remark, First, for being the place where the Family of the Springs have long had their Seat, originally descended from Thomas Spring of Lavenham commonly called the Rich Clothier; who, if not born at Lavenham, yet got his Wealth by the Trade of it. He was a great Benefactor to that beautiful Church and Chancel, and dying Anno 1510 was buried there under a Monument of his own Erection. From him descended William Spring of Pakenham, Esq; who was created a Baronet August the 11th, Anno 1641, which Honour is now vested in Sir William Spring Baronet. Secondly, for the Family of the Ashfields, who formerly had their Seat at Nether-Hall in this Parish. John Ashfield of this Place, Esq; 17 Queen Elizabeth was the first High Sheriff of Suffolk, separate from Norfolk, as is mentioned in Page 3. From him descended Sir John Ashfield of Nether-Hall Knt. who was created a Baronet July 27, 1626; which Family being extinct, this Seat is now vested in Thomas Bright, Esq. Thirdly, for the Family of Le Strange, who had also their Seat in this Parish, which has lately been purchased by   Curwin, Esq; who now resides there.

RATTLESDEN.

ROUGHAM. In this Parish is one Seat called the Place, lately the Seat of Sir Robert Davers Bart. but

now

now of John Corrance, Efq. Another good Manfion being the Seat of John Cooke, Efq: and another where the ancient Family of the Heigham's have long refided.

RUSHBROOKE a Manour belonging to the Abbey of Bury St. Edmunds, but fince the diffolution has been famous for the Noble Family of Jermyn who for many Ages had their Seat at Rufhbrook-Hall. John Jermyn of this Place, Efq; was High Sheriff of this County and of Norfolk 29 Henry VI. afterwards this Family produced divers Perfons who were eminent in the State, as Sir Thomas Jermyn who was Privy Counfellor and Vice Chamberlain to King Charles I. His fecond Son Sir Henry Jermyn Knt. was Treafurer of the Houfhold to that King and Mafter of the Horfe to his Queen. He was for his wife Conduct and faithful Services in thofe unhappy Times by King Charles I created Lord Jermyn of St. Edmunds Bury, the 8th of Sept. 1644. And at Breda in Brabant the 27th of April Anno Dom. 1660, was by King Charles II created Earl of St. Albans. He died unmarried Jan. 2. 1663, and Thomas his Elder Brother being then dead, this Honour (being limited to the two Brothers) became extinct. But Henry Jermyn, Efq; fecond Son of Thomas, was by King James II created Baron of Dover May 13, 1686, and died without Iffue in April 1708. This Family concluded in Heirs general, the eldeft of which was married to Sir Robert Davers, Bart. (fo created May 12, 1682) by which means the Eftate and Seat here were brought into his Family, and are now vefted in Sir Jermyn Davers, Bart. a Reprefentative in Parliament for this County of Suffolk.

TOSTOCK, anciently the Lordfhip of the Abbot of Bury St. Edmunds, afterwards it came into the noble Family of the Lords North and Grey, who had their Seat at Toftock Place, which now is vefted in Richard Mofely, Efq.

TIMWORTH.
WELNETHAM Magna.
WELNETHAM Parva.
WOOLPIT. See Page 62.

THIS Hundred contains 24 Parifhes.

THINGOE

THINGOE Hundred

Is bounded on the East with the Hundred of Thedwestry; on the South with the Hundreds of Babergh and Risbridge; on the West with the Hundreds of Risbridge and Lackford, and on the North with the Hundred of Blackbourne, extending itself in length 10 Miles, in breadth 6 Miles, making the Circumference 28 Miles.

THE Towns and Villages in this Hundred are as followeth.

BARROW, anciently the Lordship and Seat of the Counteis of Gloucester; afterwards it belonged to the Lord Badlesmere, who adhering to the Earl of Lancaster against King Edward IV, was taken Prisoner at Barrowbridge and hanged. The Ruins of their Seat a little South of the Church bespeak it to have been a noble Building. It is now vested in the Right Hon. the Earl of Bristol.

BROCKLEY.

BURY St. Edmunds. See Page 63.

CHEVINGTON.

FLEMPTON.

FORNHAM All-Saints. In this Parish is the Seat of   Pooley, Esq.

HARDWICK House, reserved as a Seat for the eldest Son and Heir of the Family of the Cullums.

HARGRAVE.

HAWSTEAD, in the 9 Edward II was the Lordship and Estate of Thomas Fitz-Eustace; but in these latter Times, of the Family of the Drurys, who had their Seat at the Manour House called Hawstead-Place. This Family of Drurys produced many famous Men, the greatest of which was Sir William Drury of this Place, who atchieved great Things in Ireland, mentioned by Mr. Cambden in the Life of Queen Elizabeth. The Cullums are now in Possession of this Manour and Seat. The Founder of their Family was Sir Thomas Cullum, Citizen and Sheriff of London 22 Charles I. His Son Thomas Cullum of this Place, Esq; was created a Baronet June

18,

18, 1660. To him fucceeded Sir Dudley, and to Sir Dudley fucceeded Sir Jafper now living.

HENGRAVE, anciently the Lordfhip of Edmund de Hengrave in the Reign of Edward I; but in later Times of the Family of the Kitfons who built Hengrave Hall (a noble old Houfe) and made it their Seat. It has for fome defcents been in the Family of the Gages; for George Gage of Hengrave Hall, Efq; was created a Baronet July 15, 1662. The Honour and Eftate is now vefted in Sir Thomas Gage, Bart.

HORNINGSHERTH. Thomas Davers Efq; has built very beautiful Seat in this Parifh. Horfecroft in this Parifh is the Seat of John Turnor Efq; and perhaps is that Horningfherth Parva mentioned in fome Authors. Horningfherth Fair is Yearly on St. Bartholomew's Day.

ICKWORTH. This Parifh is now converted into a noble Park, in which is the Seat of the Right Hon. the Earl of Briftol.

LACKFORD.

NOWTON.

REED. In this Parifh is a Manfion called Dowings, the Inheritance of the ancient Family of Sparrow.

RISBY.

SAXHAM Magna is of note for having been for many Years the Seat of the Family of Eldred. Our Author informs us that Revet Eldred of this Place, Efq; was created a Baronet Jan. 29, 1641. But the Honour is now extinct; yet the Eftate and their Seat at the Hall is now vefted in a Gentleman of that Name, which is John Eldred, Efq.

SAXHAM Parva, is alfo of Note for being for fome Ages the Seat of the Family of Crofts, one of which viz. William Crofts, Efq; was by King Charles II, at Bruffels in Brabant, created Lord Crofts of Saxham; but he leaving no Male Iffue, that Honour was extinct at his Death. The Hall and Eftate there now remain to a Gentleman of that Family which is Crofts, Efq.

WESTLY.

WHEPSTEAD.

SOUTHWELL, alias South-Park, is a Hamlet of Hargrave..

This Hundred contains 20 Parishes and 2 Hamlets.

THREDLING Hundred

Is bounded on the East with the Hundred of Loes; on the North with the Hundred of Hartsmere, and on the West and South with the Hundred of Bosmere and Claydon. Its length is four Miles, and near the same in breadth, making its Circumference 14 Miles. The Towns and Villages in this Hundred are as followeth,

ASHFIELD, the Church now in ruins.

DEBENHAM. See Page 54.

FRAMSDEN, where there is a Fair Yearly on Ascension Day.

PETTAUGH.

THORP, a Hamlet of Ashfield.

WINSTON.

This Hundred contains 5 Parishes and one Hamlet.

WANGFORD Hundred

Is bounded on the East. with the Hundreds of Mutford and Blithing ; on the North with the River Waveny dividing it from Norfolk; on the West with the Hundred of Hoxne, and on the South with the aforesaid Hundred of Blithing, extending its self in length about 11 Miles, and 6 in breadth, making the Circumference 36 Miles.

This Hundred is divided into three Parts, the nine Parishes, the seven Parishes, and the remaining Part of the Hundred about Beccles.

The nine Parishes are as followeth.

ALL-SAINTS Southelmham.

St. MARY FLIXTON, (the chief of the nine Parishes, which probably took it Name from Felix the first Bishop of Dunwich) was memorable for a Nunnery there founded by Margery de Creke, Daughter to Jeffery Hauvile, and Widow of Bartholomew de Creke, about the Time of King Henry III. It was of the Order of St. Augustine, and valued at its Dissolution

at

at 23 l. 4 s. 1 ¾ d. The said Foundress gave the Manour of Flixton to this House, and it is probable the Manours of all these nine Parishes belonged to this House, the Lordships of which Parishes for many Years have been vested in the Family of the Tasburghs, and is now, with the Nunnery, vested in George Tasburgh, Esq; who lives at Flixton-Hall, a noble old Seat the antient Mansion of his Ancestors.

St. GEGRGE Southelmham.
St. MARY Homersfield.
St. JAMES Southelmham.
St. MARGARET Southelmham.
St. MICHAEL Southelmham.
St. NICHOLAS Southelmham, whose Church is so entirely demolished, that hardly any Rubbish of it is to be found.
St. PETER Southelmham.
THE seven Parishes are as followeth,
St. ANDREW Ilketshall.
St. MARY } BUNGAY, two Parishes. See Page
TRINITY }   69.
St. JOHN Ilketshall.
St. LAURENCE Ilketshall.
St. MARGARET Ilketshall.
ALL-SAINTS Mettingham. See Page 71.
THE remaining Parishes in this Hundred are,
BARSHAM.
BECCLES. See Page 21.
ELLOUGH.
HULVERSTREET, now a Hamlet of Henstead.
INGATE, the Church wholly in ruins. See more Page 21.
NORTH COVE.
REDDISHAM.
RINGSFIELD.
SATTERLY is worthy of remark for the Family of Playters, a very ancient Family, having had their Seat at Satterly Hall ever since the Reign of King Edward II. This Family were very early in the List of Baronets, for Sir Thomas Playters of Sattlerly Knight was created a Baronet August 13, 1623, which Honour is now vested in Sir John Playters Bart.

Y   SHAD-

SHADDINGFIELD.

SHIPMEADOW.

WESTON. In this Parifh is the Seat of Suckling Leman Gent. and alfo that of Capt   Barry.

WILLINGHAM. The Church wholly in ruins.

WORLINGHAM. The Hall is a neat Manfion, and is now the Seat of Sir Thomas Robinfon Bart. of whom fee more in the Account of Melford, Page 84.

THIS Hundred contains 29 Parifhes and one Hamlet.

WILFORD Hundred

Is bounded on the Eaft by the Ocean; on the North and North Eaft by the Hundreds of Plomefgate and Loes; on the North Weft by the Hundreds of Loes and Carlford, the River Deben dividing it from the faid Hundreds and from the Hundreds of Colnes, on the South Weft. This Hundred extends itfelf in length 13 Miles, in breadth in fome Places 6, in other fome not above three Miles, making the Circumference 37 Miles.

THE Towns and Villages in this Hundred are as followeth,

ALDERTON, formerly of remark for being the refidence of the antient Family of the Nauntons, who were Lords of this Manour and Patrons of the Church. This Family removing to Letheringham, who fucceeded them in this Manour we know not. It is now vefted in Dr. Chamber'len.

BAUDSEY. See Page 33.

BING, a Hamlet of Petiftree.

BOULDGE.

BREDFIELD. In this Parifh is a pleafant Seat, where the late Arthur Jenny, Efq; refided. It now remains to his Son Edmund Jenny, Efq.

BOYTON.

BROOMSWELL.

CAPELL, a Hamlet of Butley.

DALLINGHOO, Part in this and Part in Loes Hundred, of which fee more in the Account of that Hundred.

DEBACH.   HOL-

HOLLESLEY.

LOUDHAM or LUDHAM, is a Hamlet of Petiftree, and took its Name from the Ludhams, an antient Family who had their Seat at Loudham or Ludham-Hall; from the Ludhams it defcended to the Blenerhayfetts, who had alfo their Seats there; from the Blenerhayfetts it defcended to Sir Henry Wood, and is now vefted in Charles Wood, Efq.

MELTON.

PETISTREE, where the Family of the Wyards have for fome time refided.

RAMSHOLT.

SHOTTISHAM.

SUTTON.

UFFORD. At prefent of no great remark, but formerly was, for giving Name to the Noble Family of the De Uffords, originally defcended from the Peytons of Peyton Hall in Boxford, as is mentioned Page 93. They were a Family of vaft Poffeffions in this County, having been Lords and Proprietors of the Caftles of Orford, Eye, Framlingham, Bungay, Mettingham and Haughley. They had their Seat in this Parifh, about two Furlongs North of the Church, where a Farm Houfe now ftands appropriated to Charitable Ufes in Framlingham.

THERE is in this Parifh the Ruins of a Chapel; for the Ground whereon it ftood the Rector of Ufford pays an annual Rent to the Crown of 20 s. on the Weft of which is a Piece of Land in the form of a Rectangled Parallelogram containing about three Acres. There ftill appears a Ditch or Moat furrounding it; in which Piece of Land, it is reported, there ftood a Caftle, anciently the Seat of the De Uffords Earls of Suffolk, but I could never meet with any Perfon that ever dug up or heard there was dug up any ruinous Walls; fo perhaps this is only Conjecture; however I have followed the vulgar Report in inferting this Caftle in my Map.

THE Family of the Hammonds had their Seat in this Parifh, which is now vefted in Samuel Thompfon, Gent.

THIS

THIS Parish furnished London with a Lord Mayor, which was William Oatley, Son of Roger Oatley of this Place. He was Lord Mayor Anno Dom. 1434.

WICKHAM-MARKET. See Page 17.

THIS Hundred contains 16 Parishes, and 3 Hamlets.

The two following Roads, not being inserted in their proper Places, are as followeth.

The Road from the Market Crofs in Bury, to Finningham White Horfe Inn.

PASS out at the Eaft-Gate through the Eaft-Gate-Street, at the end of which avoid the right hand Way leading to Stow-Market; here take the left hand Way (being the Road before treated of from Bury to Ixworth) leaving Barton Church clofe on the left. At 3 m. $4\frac{1}{4}$ f. leave the Road right forward being the Ixworth Road, take the right hand Way. At 4 m. is Capt. Curwin's Manfion a little on the right. At 4 m. 5 f. the right goes to Bradfield Manger Inn, the left to Ixworth. At 5 m. $\frac{1}{4}$ f. the left goes to Ixworth; here turn on the right through Pakenham Village. At 5 m. 1 f. is Pakenham Bell Inn on the left; the Road right forward goes to Norton, therefore turn on the left, leaving Pakenham Church a little on the right. At 6 m. $6\frac{1}{3}$ f. the right goes through Norton to Stow-Market, the left through Ixworth to Thetford, both which are before treated of. At 7 m. $1\frac{1}{2}$ f. is Stowlangtoft Church clofe on the left. At 8 m. $1\frac{1}{3}$ f. is Hunfdon Boarding School clofe on the left, the Church a little on the right. At 8 m. 7 f. is a Windmill a little on the left, where the right (called the lower Way) goes through Afhfield to Finningham, but we keep the Road right forward, being the common Coach Road. At 9 m. $2\frac{1}{4}$ f. is

Badwell-

Badwell-Afh Church ciofe on the left, the Road right forward goes to Walfham, therefore turn on the right, leaving Afhfield Church about 3 f. on the right. At 10 m. 1 ½ f. the aforefaid lower Road comes in on the right. At 11 m. 5 f. enter in at a Gate by Cutting's-Hole. At 12 m. 1 ½ f, the right goes to Bacton, the left to the Manfion of Thomas Barnardifton, Efq. leave Wyverfton Pond clofe on the left. At 12 m. 7 f. Wyverfton Church clofe on the left. At 13 m. 3 ½ f. is a Gate on the right, which leads to the Manfion of Baron Prettyman, Efq. At 13 m. 7 f. Wefthrop Hall a little on the left, and at 14 m. 6 ½ f. is Finningham White Horfe Inn.

From Bury Market-Crofs to Finning- ┐
ham White Horfe is —————————————— ┌ 14 m. 6 ½ f.

The Road from Wickham-Market to Aldeburgh, viz.

FROM the Crown Inn in Wickham-Market, pafs along in the Saxmundham Road. At 1 m. at the 5 Crofs Ways, take the fecond turning on the right. A 1 m. 2 ½ f. the right to Campfey-Afh, the left to Hachefton. At 1 m. 5 f. a Brick Kiln clofe on the left. At 1 m. 6 ¾ f. the right forward goes to Tunftall. At 2 m. is the Well Houfe; where the right goes to Campfey-Afh, the left to Marlsford. At 2 m. 5 f. is Black Stock Water; the left acute backward goes to Marlsford. At 3 m. ¼ f. enter Blaxhall Lane. At 4 m. is Blaxhall Church, a little on the left. At 4 m. 4 f. leave Blaxhall Lane; the left acute backward goes to Glemham Parva. At 4 m. 5 ¼ f. left to Langham Bridge. At 5 m. 7 f. Dunningworth Hall clofe on the left. Pafs along over Snape Bridge in the Road before mentioned, from Leifton to Melton. At 8 m. 2 ¼ f. Polsborough Gate. Take the right hand Way as beforementioned. At 11 m. 4 f. Aldeburgh Crofs.

From Wickham-Market to Aldeburgh 11 m. 4 f.

A N

A N
INDEX
Of the Roads in this Treatife.

To

Through Bures and Neyland to Stratford Swan Inn,
Page 94.

4. The Roads from Woodbridge.

To Aldeburgh begins Page 35
To Baudfey-Ferry, Page 32.
To Landguard-Fort, Page 50.
To Orford, Page 33.

5. The Roads from Wickham-Market.

To Aldeburgh begins Page 165.
To Eye, Page 37.
To Harlefton in Norfolk Page 41.
To Needham by Way of Catts-Hills, Page 40.

6. The Roads from Lavenham.

To Bildefton begins Page 99.
To Sudbury, Page 89.

7. The Road from Bungay,

To Halfeworth begins Page 102.

8. The Roads from Halefworth.

To Beccles begins Page 105.
To Harlefton in Norfolk, Page 106.
To Loweftoft, Page 105.
To Southwould, Page 104.
To Yoxford, Page 103.

9. The Roads from Stow-Market.

Through Haughley to Botefdale, begins Page 107.
Through Ixworth to Thetford, Page 109.
Through Bildefton and Hadleigh to Stratford Swan,
Inn, Page 111.

10. The

The Alphabetical Table at the end of this Treatife, fupplies the want of any further Index, as for

EXAMPLE.

Suppofe it is defired to find Dunwich; in the Alphabetical Table under D is Dunwich in Blithing Hundred, which being turn'd to, you are there referred to Page 27 for a further Account, and fo of the reft.

A General TABLE.

IT having been thought proper to publish an Alphabetical Table of all the Parishes and Hamlets in the County, and to shew what Hundred and Deanry every one is in ; I have in order to make it the more useful, added the Name of the Saint to whom each Church was dedicated ; shewn whether the Benefice be a Rectory, Vicarage or Impropriation ; given the best Account I could get of the Patrons, and of the Religious Houses which the Impropriations formerly belonged to. It must be acknowledged that herein great use has been made of Mr. Brown Willis's Parochiale; my Friends have supplied some defects, and corrected some mistakes in that Laborious Gentleman's Performance; and I shall be thankful to those who will help me to make this more perfect, by sending a Letter directed to me at Wickham Market,

Z

Places.	Saints to whom the Church dedicated.	Hundred,	Deanry.	Rec. Vica. or Imp.	Patrons Names.	Religious Houfes to which Impropriated.
A						
Acton	All-Saints	Baber.	Sudb.	V	Mr. Drew	Priory of Hatfield Peverell.
Akenhenham	St. Mary	Bof.&Clay.	Clay.	R	Mr. Drury	
ALDEBURGH	St. Peter and St. Paul	Plomfgate	Orford	V	Earl of Strafford	Abbey of St. John's at Colchefter.
Alderton	St. Bartholom.	Wilford	Wilf.	R	Dr. Chamberlen turns, Bifhop of Norwich one.	
Aldham	S. Mary	Cosford	Sudb.	R	Lord Lovell	
Aldringham	St. Andrew	Blithing	Dunw.	Imp.	Lady Anne Harvey	Leifton Abby.
Alpheton		Baber.	Sudb.	R	Mr. Martin	
All Saints in Southelmham	All-Saints	Wangfor.	Southel	R	Mr. Briton	
AltftonChurch down	St. John	Colnes	Coln.	R *		
Ampton	St. Peter	Thed w.	Thedw.	R	James Calthorp Efq.	
Arwarton, vid Erwarton						

	St. John Bapt.	Loes	Loes.	R	Mr. Carew	
Afh by Campfey	St. John Bapt.	Loes		R	Mr. Carew	⎰ Priory of Chrift
Afh-bocking	All Saints	Bot.&Clay	Bofm.	V	The Crown	⎱ Church Canterbury
Afhby alias Haskeby	St. Mary	Lothingl.	Loth.	R	Sir Thomas Allin	Priory of Butley
Afhfield Church down	St. Mary	Thredl.	Clay.	Imp.	Mr. Pitt's Heirs	Priory of Ixworth
Afhfield Great	All Saints	Blackb.	Blackb	Imp.	Mrs. Smyth	Priory of Butley
Afpall		Hartf.	Hartfm.	Imp.	Clem. Chevalier Efq.	⎰ Priory of Hatfield
Affington	St. Edmund	Baber.	Sudb.	V	John Gurdon Efq.	⎱ Peverell
Athelington alias Allington	⎰ St. Peter	Hoxne	Hoxne	R	The Crown	
Aye vid. Eye	⎱					
B						
Bacton	S.Ma.Affumpt.	Hartf.	Hartf.	R		
Baddingham	St. John Bapt.	Hoxne	Hoxne	R	Dr. Blomfield	
Badly	St. Mary	Bof&Clay.	Bolm.	Imp.	Mrs. Crowley	Knights Templars
Badwell-Afh	St. Mary	Blackb.	Blackb.	Imp.	Mr. Clough	Priory of Ixworth
Bardwell	⎰ St. Peter and St. Paul	Blackb.	Blackb.	R *	St. John's Col. Oxon	

* Note, That Bardwell was formerly a Vicarage, and the great Tythes were impropriated to the Priory of Broomholme in Norfolk, but given to the Vicarage by Mrs. Goulfton. Vid. Kennet's Augm. of Vic. p. 228.

Place	Church	Deanery		R/V	Patron	
Barham	St. Mary	Bof.&Clay	Clay.	R	Nicholas Bacon Esq.	
Barking	St. Mary	Bof.&Clay	Bofm.	R	Mrs. Crowley	
Barnardiston	All Saints	Risbr.	Clare	R	Sir Sam. Barnardiston	
Barnby alias Barneby	St. John Bapt	Mutford	Loth.	R	*	
Barnham	{ St. Gregory / St. Martin }	Blackb,	Blackb.	R	Duke of Grafton	
Barningham	St. Andrew	Blackb.	Blackb.	R	Thomas Evans Gent.	
Barrow	All Saints	Thingo	Thingo	R	St. John's Col. Camb.	
Barham	Holy Trinity	Wang.	Wang.	R	Denz. Suckling Esq.	
Barton Great	H. Innocents	Thedw.	Thedw	V	Sir Thomas Hanmer	Abby of Bury
Barton Little alias Barton Mills	St. Mary	Lack.	Fordh.	R	The Crown	Col. Stoke by Clare
Battisford	St. Mary	Bof.&Clay	Bofm.	V	Sir William Barker	
Bawdley	St. Mary	Wilford	Wilfd.	V	The Crown	{ Priories of Campley and Butley.
Baylham	St. Peter	Bof.&Clay	Bofm.	R	William Acton Esq.	
Bealing Great	St. Mary	Carlford	Carlf.	R	Mr. Pitt's Heirs	
Bealings Little	All Saints	Carlford	Carlf.	R	Mrs. Atkinson	
BECCLES	St. Michael	Wang.	Wang.	R	Mr. Yallop's Heirs	
Bedingfield	St. Mary	Hoxne	Hoxne	R	‡ Char. Bedingfield Esq.	

* Consoliated to Mutford.
‡ This was formerly a Vicarage, and impropriated to the Priory of Snape.

Parish	Dedication			Patron	Notes
Bedfield	St. Nicholas	Hoxne	Hoxne R	Sir John Rous	
Deyton or Beighton		Thedw.	Thedw. R	The Crown	Trinity Priory in Ipfwich.
Belftead	St. Mary	Samford	Samf. R	Tobias Blofs Efq.	
Belton	All Saints	Loth.	Loth. R	Bifhop of Norwich	
Benacre	St. Michael	Blith.	Dunw. R	Tho. Carthew Efq.	
Benhall	St. Mary	Plomfgate	Orford V	Edm. Tyrell Efq.	
Bentley	St. Mary	Samford	Samfd. V	Mrs. Morgan	
BILDESTON	St. James	Cosford	Sudb. R	Bartholo. Beale Efq.	
Bing		Wilford *			
Bixley		Carlford.	Carlf. † R		
Blakenham Great or upon the Water.	St. Mary	Bof.&Clay	Bofm. R	Eaton College	
Blakenham Little or upon the Hill	St. Mary	Bof.&Clay	Bofm. R	John Milner Efq.	
Blaxhall	St. Peter	Plomfgate	Orford R	Mr. Eade	
Blundefton	St. Mary	Loth.	Loth. R	Sir Thomas Allin	
Blythborough	Holy Trinity	Blith.	Dunw. Imp	Sir Charles Blois	Priory of Blythborough.
Blythford	All Saints	Blith.	Dunw. Imp	Sir Charles Blois	
BOTESDALE	St. Botolph	Hartf.	Hartf ‡	Charles Wood Efq.	

* A Hamlet of Petiftree.   † adjoyning to Rufhmer.
‡ A Chapel to Kedgrave.

Place	Dedication	Hundred	Deanery		Patron	Impropriator
Bouldge or Boulge	St. Michael	Wilford	Wilfd.	R	Sir Thomas Hanmer	
Boxford	St. Mary	Babergh	Sudb.	R	The Crown	
Boxstead		Babergh	Sudb. *			
Boyton	St. Andrew	Wilford	Wilfd.	R	Mrs. Warner	
Bradfield Burnt		Thedw.	Thed.	R	} Mr. Youngs	
Bradfield Clare	St. Clare	Thedw.	Thed.	R	}	
Bradfield Monks	St. George	Thedw.	Thed.	R		
Bradley Great	St. Mary	Risbr.	Clare	R	Sir Jermyn Davers	
Bradley Little	All Saints:	Risbr.	Clare	R	Mr. Brooksbank	
Bradwell	St. Nicholas	Loth.	Loth.	R	Francis Dickens Esq.	
Bramfield	St. Andrew	Blithing	Dunw.	V	Sir Thomas Allin	Priory of Blithboro.
Bramford	St. Mary	Bosf.&Clay	Bosm.	V	The Crown	Abby of Battle.
Brampton	St. Peter	Blithing	Dunw.	R	Chapter of Canterbury	
Brandeston	All Saints	Loes	Loes	V	Robert Leman Esq.	Priory of Woodbridge
Brandon	{ St. Peter and St. Paul	Lackford	Fordh.	R	{ Mess. Eales, Scot, and Elicot. / Row. Holt Esq.	
Brantham	St. Michael	Samford	Samf.	R	Sir Henry Hankey	
Bredfield	St. Andrew	Wilford	Wilt.	V ‡	The Crown	{ Priories of Campsey and Butley.
Braiesworth or Briesworth	{	Hartf.	Hartf.	R	Lord Cornwallis	

* A Hamlet to Hartest.   ‡ Bredfield Vicarage is endowed with the great Tythes.

Parish	Dedication	Hundred	Deanery	V/R	Patron	Religious House
Brent-Ely	St. Mary	Babergh	Sudb.	V	Edward Colman Esq.	Abby of S. Osith's
Bretenham	St. Mary	Cosford	Sudb.	R	The Crown	
Brightwell	St. John Bapt.	Carlford	Carlf.	Impr	Ar. Barnardiston Esq.	Trinity Priory in Ipswich.
Bricet Great	St. Mary	Bof.&Clay	Bosm.	Impr	King's Col. Cambridg.	Priory of Bricet
Bricet Little the Church down		Bof.&Clay	Bosm.	R *		
Brockford		Hartf. †				
Brockley	St. Andrew	Thingo.	Thing.	R	Heirs of Mr. Gibbs	
Brome	St. Mary	Hartimere	Hartf.	R	Lord Cornwallis	
Bromfwell	St. Edmund	Wilford	Wilfd.	R	Earl of Suffolk	
Brooks Hamlet ‡						
Brotherton		Lothing 3				
Bruifyard or Bruſyard	St. Peter	Plomgate	Orford	Impr	Sir John Rous	Nunnery of Bruſyard
Browston		Lothing ¶				
Brundish	St. Andrew	Hoxne ||	Hoxne ||	R	Philip Broke Esq.	
Bucklefham	St. Mary	Colnes	Colnes	V	Henry Benyan Esq.	
Buers or Bures	St. Mary	Babergh	Sudb.			Col. Stoke by Clare.

* Confolidated to Offton.　† A Hamlet of Wetheringfet.　‡ Adjoyning to St. Clement's Parifh in Ipfwich.　3 A Hamlet of Hopton.　¶ A Hamlet to Belton.　|| Chapel to Tattington alias Tannington.　§ Bures Vicarage was and is endowed with a Penfion of 40 l. a Year by the Will of William Martin Efq. Vid. Kennet's Augmentation of Vicarages, p. 340.

(176)

Place	Church	Hundred		Type	Patron	Religious house
* BUNGAY	{ St. Mary { Holy Trinity	Wangford	Wang.	§Im V	John Anstis Esq. Bishop of Ely	{ Priory of Bungay { Priory of Barlings
Burgate	St. Mary	Hartf.	Hartf.	R	Rowl. Holt Esq.	
Burgh	St. Botolph	Carlford	Carlf.	R	Thomas Betts, Esq.	
Burgh Castle	St. Peter	Lothing	Loth.	R	The Crown	
Burstall	St. Mary	Samford	Samf. ‡			
Bulcamp or Bulkeham		Blithing †				
BURY St. ED-MUNDS	{ St. James { St. Mary }	Thingo	Thing.	Impr	Corporation of Bury	Abby of Bury.
Butley	St. John Bapt.	{ Loes & { Plomf.	Wilf.	Impr	George Wright, Esq.	Priory of Butley
Buxhall	St. Mary	Stow	Stow	R	Mrs. Coppinger	
Buxlow Church down	St. Peter	Blithing	Dunw.	R ‖		
C						
Campsey, vid. Ash by Campsey }	{ St. Andrew	Wilford	Wilfd.	Imp§		
Capell Church down	St. Mary	Samford	Samfd.	R	Mr. Hingeston	
Capell	St. Peter	Hoxne	Hoxne	R	Consolidated to Kelsale.	
Carelton						

* The two Parishes in Bungay are often called Bungay Borough and Bungay Boyscot. ‡ Is a Chapel to Bramford. † A Hamlet of Blithborough. ‖ Consolidated to Knoddishhall. § Annexed to Butley.

Parish	Church	Hundred	Deanery	R/V	Patron	Impropriation
Carlton Colvile	St. Peter	Mutford	Loth.	{ R Im	Sir Thomas Allin Mediety Impr. to	Broomholme Priory.
Cattiwade Chap. down		Samford *				
Cavendish	St. Mary	Baberg	Sudb.	R	Jesus College Cambr.	
Cavenham	St. Andrew	Lack.	Ford.	V	The Crown	Col. Stoke by Clare
Charsfield	St. Peter	Loes	Loes	Impr	Mr. William Naunton	Priory of Letheringh.
Chattisham-	All Saints	Samford	Samf.	V	Eaton College	Eaton College
Chedburgh	All Saints	Risbr.	Clare	R	Earl of Bristol	
Cheddiston or Cheston	St. Mary	Blithing	Dunw.	V	Walter Plumer Esq.	Priory of Pentney
Chelmondeston or Chempton	St. Andrew	Samford	Samf.	R	The Crown	
Chelsworth	All Saints	Cosford	Sudb.	R	The Crown	
Chepenall or Chebenhall‑		Hoxne †				
Chevington	All Saints	Thingo	Thing.	R	{ Mess. Turner and Risby	
Chickering Chapel down	St. Mary	Hoxne	Hoxne‡			
Chillesford	St. Michael	Plomesgate	Orford	R	Mr. Reg. Eade	

A a

* A Hamlet of Brantham. † A Hamlet of Frefingfield. ‡ A Hamlet of Wingfield or Stradbrooke.

		Babergh / Stow / Risbr.	Sudb. / Stow / Clare			
Chilton		Babergh	Sudb.			
Chilton		Stow	Stow		Sir John Woodhouse	
Chinley or Chibley †		Risbr.	Clare	R		*
CLARE	{ St. Peter and St. Paul	Risbr.	Clare	V	The Crown	Col. Stoke by Clare
Claydon	St. Peter	Bof.&Clay	Clay.	R	Mr. George Drury	
Clopton	St. Mary	Carlford	Carlf.	R	Mr. Folkard	
Cockfield	St. Peter	Babergh	Sudb.	R	St. John's Col. Camb.	
Cockfield-Hall p. 19						
Coddenham	St. Mary	Bof. Clay	Bofm.	V	Nicholas Bacon Esq.	Priory of Royston
Combs	St. Mary	Stow	Stow	R	Mrs. Crowley	
Cony-Weston or Countston	} All Saints	Blackb.	Blackb.	R	Mau. Shelton Esq.	
Cookley	St. Michal	Blithing	Dunw.	R	Lord Lovel	
Copdock or Coppedhooke	} St. Peter	Samford	Samf.	R	{ Thomas de Grey Esq.	
Cornearth or Cornerd Great	} St. Andrew	Babergh	Sudb.	V	John Eldred Esq.	Abby of Malling
Cornerd or Cornearth Little	} All Saints	Babergh	Sudb.	R	Mr. Newman	

* A Hmlet of Stow † Called also Chilton, a Hamlet of Clare.

Town	Church	Hundred	Deanery	R/V	Patron	Appropriator
Corton	St. Bartholom.	Loth.	Loth.	V	The Crown	Abby of Leiston
Cotton	St. Andrew	Hartfmere	Hartf.	R	Baron Prettyman Esq.	
Covehith vid. Northales	}					
Cove North	St. Botolph	Wangford	Wang.	R	The Crown	
Cove South	St. Lawrence	Blithing	Dunw.	R	The Crown	
Cooling, Cowling, Culidge or Cowlidge	St. Andrew or St. Margaret	Risb.	Clare	Impr	Trinity Hall Cambr.	Trinity Hall
Cranley *	St. Peter	Hartfmere	Hartf.	V †	Dr. Blomfield	
Cransford	St. Mary	Plomfgate	Orford	V ‡	Lord Lovel	
Cratfield	All Saints	Blithing	Dunw.	R	Mr. Bridgeman	Sibton Abby
Creeting	St. Mary	Stow	Stow	R	Eaton College	Priory of St. Neot's
Creeting East	St. Olaves ||	Bof&Clay.	Bofm.	R	Mr. Bridgeman	
Creeting Churchdown	St. Peter	Bof&Clay.	Bofm		Mr. Bridgeman	{ Priory of St. Peter
Creeting West	St. Andrew	Stow	Stow	R	Mr. Ferneley	{ in Ipswich
Cretingham	All Saints	Loes	Loes	V	The Crown	
Crowfield §		Bof&Clay.	Bofm.			
Culford	All Saints	Blackb.	Blackb.	R	Lord Cornwallis	

* Hamlet of Eye. † Cransford Vicarage is endowed with the great Tythes by the Will of Mr. Da-
mant. ‡ Cratfield Vicarage is endowed with the great Tythes by the Gift of Mr. John Laney Anno
Dom. 1635. || Consolidated to Creeting All Saints. § A Chapel to Coddenham.

	St. Botolph	Carlford	Carlf.	Impr	Sir Charles Blois	Leiston Abby
Culpho						
D						
Dagworth *						
Balham	St. Mary	Stow Risb.	Stow Clare	R	Gilbert Affleck Esq.	
Dallingho	St. Mary	{ Loes & Wilford	Wilf.	R	Earl of Rochford	
Darmsden or Dornsden	St. Andrew	Bos.&Clay. Bosm. †				{ Priory of Mary's in Thetford
Darsham	All Saints	Blithing	Dunw.	V	Sir John Rous	
Debach	All Saints	Wilford	Wilf.	R	Sir Thomas Hanmer	
DEBENHAM	St. Mary	Thredl.	Clayd.	V	Mr. Pitt's Heirs	Priory of Butley
Denham	St. John Bapt.	Hoxne	Hoxne	V	Will. Maynard Esq.	Priory of Norwich
Denham		Risb.	Clare	Impr	Lord Lynn	Priory of St. Osith's
Dennington	St. Mary	Hoxne	Hoxne	R	Sir John Rous	
Denston		Risb.	Clare	Impr	Mr. Robinson	
Depden	St. Mary	Risb.	Clare	R	Coel Thornhill Esq.	Priory of Tunbridge
Dodnash vid. p. 151.						
Downham	St. Mary	Samford	Samf.	Impr	Mr. Wright	
Drinkston	All Saints	Lackford Thedw.	Fordh. Thed.	R	George Gooday Esq.	Priory of Ixworth

* Hamlet of Haughley.   † A Chapel to Barking.

		Colnes	Colnes*			
Dunham Bridge						
Dunningworth }	St. Mary	Plomsgate	Orford	R ‡		
Church down }	All Saints	Blithing	Dunw.	Impr	Sir George Downing	Priory of Eye
DUNWICH						
E						
Earl Soham vulgo }	St. Andrew	Loes	Loes	R	The Hon. Pryce Devereux Esq. }	
Earlesham }					Pembroke Hall Camb.	
Earl Stonham	St. Mary	Bosm.&Clay	Bosm.	R		
Eastbergholt	St. Mary	Samford	Samf.	†		
Easton	All Saints	Loes	Loes	R	Earl of Rochford	
Easton Bavent Church down }	St. Nicholas	Blithing	Dunw.	R	Thomas Carthew Esq.	
Edwardston }	St. Mary	Babergh	Sudb.	V	Sir Robert Kemp	
Ellough }	All Saints	Wangford	Vang.	R	Sir John Players	
Elmset or Helmset	St. Peter	Cosford	udb.	R	Clare Hall Cambridge	
Elmswell	St. John Evang.	Blackb.	Blackb	R	Charles Wood Esq.	
Elvedon or Elden	St. Andrew	Lackford	Fordh.	R	Smith Esq.	
Endgate or Ingate }	St. Mary	Wang.	Wang	R	The Crown	Priory of Colne
Church down }						

* Extraparochial, as 'tis faid.   ‡ Goes along with Tunftal.   † A Chapel to Brantham.

Parish	Church	Hundred	Deanery		Patron	
Erefwell, Erifwell or Earfwell }	St. Laurence	Lackford	Fordh.	R	Edward Owen Efq.	
Erwarton	St. Andrew	Samford	Samf.	R	Sir Philip Parker	
Efham Chaple down	Holy Trinity	Hoxne	Hoxn.†		Duke of Grafton	
Euston or Ewfton	St. Genoveve	Blackb.	Black.	R	Thomas Burdus Efq.	
EYE	{ St. Peter and St. Paul	Hartfmere	Hartl.	V	Mr. Boad	Priory of Eye
Eyke	All Saints	Loes	Loes	R	Chapter of Canterbury	Abby of Battel
Exning	St. Martin	Lackfrd	Ford.	V		
F						
Fakenham Great	St. Peter	Blackb.	Black.	R	Duke of Grafton	
Fakenham Little	St. Andrew	Blackb.	Black.	R	Duke of Grafton	
Faulkenham or Falkenham }	* St. Ethelbert	Colnes	Colnes	V	The Crown	Priory of Dodnafh
Farnham	St. Mary	Plomfgate	Orford	Impr	Dudly North Efq.	Priory of Butley
Felixftow	{ St. Peter and St. Paul	Colnes	Colnes	V	Mrs. Atkinfon	Priory of Felixftow
Felfham	St. Peter	Thedw.	Thed.	R	Higham Risby Efq.	
Finningham or Feningham }	{ St. Bartholom.	Hartfmere	Hartf.	R	Edward Frere Efq.	

† Hamlet of Wingfield   * Omitted in the Account of Colnes Hundred.

Parish	Dedication	Hundred	Deanery		Patron	Religious House
Finborough Great	St. Andrew	Stow	Stow	V	Bishop of Ely	Priory of Butley
Finborough Little	All Saints	Stow	Stow	V	King's Col. Cambridge	Priory of Bricet
Flempton	St. Catharine	Thingo	Thing.	R	Sir Thomas Gage	
Flixton Church down	St. Andrew	Loth.	Loth.	R *		
Flixton	St. Mary	Wangford	Southel	V		Priory of Flixton
Flowton	St. Andrew	Bof.&Clay	Bofme.	R	Mr. Will. Peppen	
Fordley Church down	Holy Trinity	Blithing	Dunw.	R	Mrs. Martin's Heirs	
Fornham	All Saints	Thingo	Thingo	R	Mr. Warren	
Fornham	St. Genoveve	Thedw.	Thed.	R	Mr. Harrington	
Fornham	St. Martin	Thedw.	Thed.	R	Sir Thomas Gage	
Foxhall Church down	All Saints	Carlf.	Carlf.	Im. †		Trinity Priory in Ipswich
FRAMLINGHAM	St. Michael	Loes	Loes	R	Pembroke Hall Cambr.	Priory of Minories in London
Framsden	St. Mary	Thredl.	Clayd.	V	Earl of Dysert	Peculiar to the Bishop of Rochester
Freckingham or Frekenham	St. Andrew	Lackford	Fordh.	R	Mrs. Sotherton	
Fresingfield	St. Peter and St. Paul	Hoxne	Hoxne	V	Eman. Col. Cambridge	College in the Fields Norwich
Freston	St. Peter	Samford	Samf.	R	Mr. Wright	
Friston	St. Mary	Plomsgate	Orford	V	Earl of Strafford	Snape Abby

* Consolidated to Blundeston.   † Goes along with Brightwell.

Parish	Church	Hundred	Deanery		Patron	
Fritton	St. Edmund	Loth.	Loth.	R.	Mrs. Carter	
Froftendon	All Saints	Blithing	Dunw.	R.	Mr. Glover	
G						
Gazely	All Saints	Risbr.	Clare	V	Trinity Hall Cambr.	Col. Stoke by Clare
Gedding		Thedw.	Thedw	R	Corporation of Ipfwich	
Gedgrave		Plomfgate	Orfd *			
Gipping		Stow	Stow		Thomas Tyrell Efq †	
Giffleham	Holy Trinity	Mutford	Loth.	R	The Crown	
Gillingham	St. Mary	Hartfmere	Hartl.	R	Char. Bedingfield Efq.	
Glemham Great or North Glemham	All Saints	Plomfgate	Orford	Impr or V	Will. Edgar. Efq.	Priory of Burley
Glemham Little or South Glemham	St. Andrew	Plomigate	Orford	R	Dudley North Efq.	
Glemsford	St. Mary	Babergh	Sudb.	R	Bifhop of Ely	
Gorlefton	St. Andrew	Lothing	Loth	V	Chriftopher Beding- field Efq.	Priory of St. Bartholomew London
Gosbeck	St. Mary	Bof.&Clay.	Bofm.	R	Mr. Crompton	
Groton	St. Bartholom.	Babergh	Sudb.	R	Thomas Waring Efq.	

* A Hamlet of Sudborn.   † A Hamlet of Stow; Mr. Tyrell procures a Minifter to Preach every Fortnight.

Parish	Dedication	Carlford Loth.	Carlfd. Loth.	R	Patron	
Grundisburgh	St. Mary				Trinity Col. Cambr.	
Gunton	St. Peter				Mr. Lufon	
H						
HADLEIGH	St. Mary	Cosford	Sudb.	R	Archb. of Canterbury	Peculiar to Archb.
HALESWORTH	St. Mary	Blithing	Dunw.	R	Thomas Betts, Efq.	
Halftead or Hawftead	All Saints	Thingo	Thingo	R	Sir Jafper Cullum	
Hardwick Houfe		Thingo *				
Hargrave		Thingo	Thingo	R	⎰ Meff. Turner and ⎱ Risby	
Harkftead	.St Mary	Samford	Samf.	R	Mr. Coxe	
Parlefton		Stow	Stow	R	Mr. Gage	
Hartest	All Saints	Babergh	Sudb.	R	The Crown	
Hasketon	St. Andrew	Carlford	Carlf.	R	Mr. Folkard	
Haflwood Chap.down	St. Mary	Plomfgate ‡				
Hachefton	All Saints	Loes	Loes	V	John Corrance Efq.	Priory of Hickling
HAVERHILL	St. Mary	Risb.	Clare	V	George Coldham Efq.	Priory of Caftleacre
Haughley	St. Mary	Stow	Stow	V	Mr. Needham	Abby of Hales
Hawkedon		Risbr.	Clare	R	Mrs. Maltyward	
Heflet or Hedgeffet	St. Ethelbert	Thedw.	Thed.	R	Mich. le Heup Efq.	

* Extraparochial.   ‡ A Hamlet of Aldeburgh.

Parish	Church	Deanery	Archd.	R/V	Patron	Formerly
Hemingham	St. Mary	Bof.&Clay.	Clay.	R	The Crown	
Hemly	All Saints	Colnes	Colnes	R	The Crown	
Hemingston	St. Gregory	Bof.&Clay.	Bofm.	R	Mr. Chrif. Grove	
Hengrave		Thingo *				
Henham	St. Peter	Blithing	Dun. ‡	V	Chapter of Norwich.	Priory of Norwich.
Henly	St. Mary	Bof.&Clay.	Clay.	R	{ Emanuel College { Cambr. for 3 Turns.	
Henftead		Blithing	Dunw.	R	Mr. Rye	
Hepworth	St. Peter	Blackb.	Black.	R		
Heringfleet	St. Margaret	Loth.	Loth.	Impr	Hill Muffenden Efq.	Priory of St. Olave:
Heringfwell	St. Elthelbert	Lackford	Fordh.	R	Mr. Wright.	
Havenningham or Hevenningham	St. Margaret	Blithing	Dunw.	R	The Crown	
Higham	St. Mary	Samford	Samf.	V	{ Truftees of Impro- { priation.	{ Trinity Priory in { Ipfwich.
Higham Green		Lackford †				
Hindercley	St. Mary	Blackb.	Black	R	Rowland Holt Efq.	
Hintlefham	St. Nicholas	Samford	Samf.	R	Richard Powis Efq.	
Hinton -		Blithing ‖				
Hitcham or Hecham	All Saints	Cosford	Sudb.	R	The Crown	

* Confolidated to Flempton.   ‡ A Hamlet of Wangford.   † A Hamlet of Gazely.   ‖ A Hamlet of Blithburgh.

Place	Church	Hundred	Hund.		Patron	Notes
Holbrook	All Saints	Samford	Samf.	R	Mr. Thurlow	
Hollefly	All Saints	Wilford	Wilf.	R	Charles Wood Efq.	
Holton	St. Peter	Blithing	Dunw.	R	The Crown	
Holton	St. Mary	Samford	Samf.	R	Sir John Williams	
Homersfield	St. Mary	Wangford	Southel	R	Mr. Britton	
Honnington or Honiton	All Saints	Blackb.	Black.	R	The Crown	} Priory of Letheringham
Hoo	{ St. Andr, & St. Euftache	Loes	Loes	Impr	Robert Nauaton Efq.	
Hopton or Hepton	All Saints	Blackb.	Black.	R	The Crown	
Hopton	St. Margaret	Loth.	Loth.	Impr	Chapter of Norwich	Priory of Norwich.
Horham	St. Mary	Hoxne	Hoxne	R	Lord Lovell	Priory of Norwich.
Horningsheath Gr. or Horninger Lit.	St. Leonard	Thingo * Thingo	Thingo	R	Sir Jermyn Davers.	Confolidated
Horse Croft	{ St. Peter and St. Paul	Thingo	Thingo	R		
Hoxne		Hoxne	Hoxne	V	Will. Maynard Efq.	Priory of Norwich.
Hulverstreet		Blithing ‡				
Hundon	All Saints	Risbr.	Clare	V	Jefus Col. Cambridge	Stoke College.
Hunston	St. Michael	Blackb.	Black.	Impr	Mr. Larkin	Priory of Ixworth
Huntingfield	St. Mary	Blithing	Dunw.	R	Lord Lovell.	

* Vid. Page 159 in the Account of Horningfheath.   ‡ A Hamlet of Henftead.

I

Icklingham	All Saints	Lackford	Fordh.	R	Earl of Effex	
Icklingham	St. James	Lackford	Fordh.	R	Gwilt Efq;	
Ickworth		Thingo	Thing.	R	*	
Iken	St. Botolph	Plomefgate	Orford	R	Earl of Rochford	
Ilketfhal	St. Andrew	Wangford	Wang.	V	Mr. Hen. Williams	Priory of Bungay
Ilketfhal	St. John	Wangford	Wang.	R	The Crown	
Ilketfhal	St. Laurence	Wangford	Wang.	Imp	Mr. Styles	Priory of Bungay
Ilketfhal	St. Margaret	Wangfo rd	Wang.	V	John Anftis Efq;	
Ingham	St. Bartholo.	Blackbourn	Black.	R	Meff. Sidey and Lyng	
	St. Clement			R	Phillip Broke, Efq.	
	S. Hellen			R	Mr. R. Hingefton	
	St. Laurence			Imp	The Parifhioners	
IPSWICH	St. Margaret			Imp	Tho. Fonncreau Efq.	Trinity Priory in Ipf- wich.
	St. Mary Tower			Imp	The Parifhioners	
	St. Mary Key			Imp	The Parifhioners	
	St. Mary at Elms			Imp	The Parifhioners	St. Peter's Pri. Ipfwich
	St. Mary Stoke			R	Chapter of Ely	Trinity Pri. Ipfwich.

* Confolidated to Chedburgh.

		Deanery		Patron / Owner	Former Priory
IPSWICH	St. Matthew		R *	The Crown	Trinity Pri. Ipswich
	St. Nicholas		Impr	The Parishioners	St. Peter's Priory in Ipswich
	St. Peter		Impr	Tho. Fonnereau Esq.	
	St. Stephen		R	Tho. Fonnereau Esq.	
IXWORTH	St. Mary	Blackb.	Impr	Thomas Norton Esq.	Priory of Ixworth
Ixworth Thorp vid. Thorp					
K					
Kedington alias Ketton	St. Peter and St. Paul	Risbr.	R	Sir Samuel Barnardiston	
Kelsale	St. Mary	Hoxne	R	Alexander Bence Esq.	
Kenbrooke		Colnes ‡			
Kentford	St. Mary	Risbr. †			
Kenton	All Saints	Loes	V	Mr. Pitt's Heirs	Priory of Butley
Kersey	St. Mary	Cosford	Impr	King's Col. Cambr.	Priory of Kersey
Kesgrave		Carlford	Inpr	Ar. Barnardiston Esq.	Priory of Butley
Kessingland	St. Edmund	Mutford	V ||	Bishop of Norwich	Priory of Minories in London
Kettlebarston	St. Mary	Cosford	R	Madam Leman	

* N. B. That St. Matthew's is always called a Rectory. But Trinity Priory formerly, and the Owners of Christ Church Estate now have the great Tythes, and the Rector only some Glebe Lands, and Subscriptions. ‡ A Hamlet of Bucklesham. † A Chapel to Gazely. || Kessingland Vicarage is endowed now with almost all the great Tythes.

Parish	Dedication	Deanery		Patron	Notes
Kettleburgh	St. Andrew	Loes *	R	Mr. Sparrow	
Kirkely Church down	All Saints	Loth.	R	Richm. Garneys Esq.	
Kirton or Kirkton	St. Martin	Colnes	R	The Crown	
Knettishall or Knadishall	All Saints	Blackb.	R	Mrs. Read	
Knoddishall	St. Laurence	Blithing	R	Robert Jenny Esq.	
L					
Lackford	St. Laurence	Thingo	R	Mr. Holman	
Lakenheath	St. Mary	Fordh.	V	Chapter of Ely	Priory of Ely.
Langerston		Colnes ‡			
Langham	St. Mary	Blackb.	R	The Crown	
LAVENHAM	St. Peter and St. Paul	Babergh	R	Gonvile and Caius College Cambridge	
Lawshall	All Saints	Babergh	R	Tho. Lee Esq.	
Laxfield	All Saints	Hoxne	V	Lord Lovell	Priory of Eye.
Layham	St. Andrew	Cosford	R	St. John's Col. Cambr.	
Leiston or Layston	St. Margaret	Dunw.	Impr	Haberdashers Company in London.	Abby of Leiston.
Letheringham	St. Mary	Loes	Impr	Robert Naunton Esq.	Letheringham Priory.

* Kettleburgh is some times said to be in Wilford Deanery; but being at a distance from all the other parts of it, I have placed it (as it is commonly taken to be) in Loes. ‡ In Felixstow Parish.

Levington	St. Peter	Colnes	Colnes R	Mr. Stebbing	
Lidgate	St. Peter	Risbr.	Clare R	Sir Jermyn Davers	
Lindsey		Cosford	Sudb. Impr	King's Col. Cambridg.	King's College.
Linstead Great	St. Peter }	Blithing	Dunw. Impr	Mr. Freston	Mendham Priory.
Linstead Little	St. Margret }				
Livermore Great	St. Peter }	Thedw.	Thedw R }	Baptist Lee Esq.	
Livermore Little	S.Pet. & S.Paul }	Blackb.	Blackb. R }		
Lound	St. John Bapt.	Loth.	Loth. R	Sir Thomas Allin	
Loudham Chur. down		Wilford*			
LOWESTOFT	St. Margaret	Loth.	Loth. V ‡	Bishop of Norwich	{ Priory of St. Bartholomews London. }
M					
Marlesford	St. Andrew	Loes	Loes R	Mr. Williams	
Martlesham	St. Mary	Carlford	Carlf. R	Mrs. Goodwyn	
Melford or Long- }	Holy Trinity	Babergh	Sudb. R	Sir Cord. Firebrace	
Melford					
Mellis	St. Mary	Hartsmere	Hartf. R	The Crown	
Melton	St. Andrew	Wilford	Wilf. R	Chapter of Ely	
Mells Chapel down	St. Margaret	Blithing †			

* A Hamlet of Petistree.   ‡ The great Tythes of this Parish are brought in for the Benefit of the Vicar, but the Purchate Money must first be paid by the Yearly Produce.   † A Hamlet of Wenhaston.

Mendham	All Saints	Hoxne	Hoxne	V	Mr. Whitaker	⎰One Mediety to the Priory of Mendham ⎱other Trin. Pri. Ipf.
MENDLESHAM	St. Mary	Hartsmere	Hartf.	V *	Mr. Chilton	Abby of Battel
Metfield ‡	St. John Bapt.	Hoxne	Hoxne	Impr	The Parishioners	Mendham Priory
Merringham	All Saints	Wangford	Wang.	V	Tobias Hunt Esq.	Bungay Priory
Mickfield	St. Andrew	Bos. & Clay.	Bofm.	R	Lord Hobart	
Middleton	St. Mary	Blithing	Dunw.	Impr	⎰The Church is served by the Rector of Fordley	Leiston Abby
MILDENHALL	St. Mary	Lackford	Ford.	V	Mrs. King	
Milden or Milding		Babergh	Sudb.	R		Abby of Bury
Monedon or Monewden	St. Mary	Loes	Loes	R	John Sheppard Esq.	
Monks Ely or Monks Illeigh		Babergh	Sudb.	R	⎰Archbishop of Canterbury	⎰Peculiar to the Arch Bishop of Canterb.
Monks Soham	St. Peter	Hoxne	Hoxne	R	Mrs. Morgan	
Moulton	St. Peter	Risbr.	Clare		Mr. Bradford	Peculiar to A. B. Can.
Mutford	St. Andrew	Mutford	Loth.	V	⎰Gonvile and Caius College Cambridge	⎰Gonvile and Caius College Cambridge

* A Vicarage endowed with a third Part of the Great Tythes, paying 40 s. a Year to the Dean and Chapter of Chichester. ‡ This is said to be anciently a Chapel and Hamlet to Mendham. How generously the Minister's Salary was augmented by Mr. Chapman, See Kennet's Aug. of Vic. Page 329.

N

Parish	Dedication	Hundred	Deanery		Patron	Note
Nacton	St. Martin	Colnes	Colnes	R	Philip Broke Esq,	
Naughton or Nawton	St. Mary	Cosford	Sudb.	R	Mr. Stubbing	
NEYLAND or } Nayland	St. James	Babergh	Sudb. *	R	Richard Philips Esq.	
Nedging or Nedding						
NEEDHAM ‡	St. John Bapt.	Bof&Clayd.	Sudb.	R		
Nettlestead	St. Mary	Bos.&Clayd.	Bosm.	R	Mr. Bradley	
Newbourn	St. Mary	Carlford	Carlf.	R	Mrs. Western	
NEWMARKET	St. Mary	Lack.	Fordh.	R	Duke of Somerset.	
Newton	St. Mary	Stow	Stow	V	Samuel Clark Esq.	
Newton	All Saints	Babergh	Sudb.	R	Mr. Alston	Abby of St. Oath
Nomanstown †						
Nowton or Nolton	St Peter	Thingo	Thingo	R	Sir Jermyn Davers	
Northales or Covehithe	St. Andrew	Blithing	Dunw.	V	Thomas Carthew Esq.	Priory of Bungay
Norton	St. Andrew	Blackb.	Blackb.	R	St. Peter's Col. Camb.	

O

Parish	Dedication	Hundred	Deanery		Patron
Oakely	St. Nicholas	Hartsmere	Hartf.	R.	Lord Cornwallis
Occold	St. Michael	Hartsmere	Hartf.	R	Mr. Malyn

* A Chapel and Hamlet to Stoke. ‡ A Chapel and Hamlet to Barking.

Lowestoff; Vid. Page 145. † A Hamlet to

Cc

Offton or Offa's Town	St. Mary	Bos. & Clayd	Bosm.	V	Mr. Sparrow	Priory of Monks in Thetford
Onehouse	St. John Bapt.	Stow	Stow	R	Mr. Pettiward	
ORFORD	St. Bartholom.	Plomsgate	Orfor.*			
Otley	St. Mary	Carlford	Carlf.	R	Lord Abergavenny	
Oulton	St. Michael	Lothing	Loth.	R	Mr. Vanheythnyssen	
Ousdun or Owelden	St. Peter	Risbr.	Clare	R	Richard Mosely Esq.	
P						
Pakefield	All Saints	Mutford	Loth.	R / R	Sir John Playters / Mr. Proctor	Two Medieties
Pakenham	St. Mary	Thedw.	Thed.	V	Sir William Spring	Abby of Bury
Palgrave	St. Peter	Hartsmere	Hartf.	R	Lord Cornwallis	
Parham	St. Mary	Plomesgate	Orford	V	John Corrance Esq.	Priory of Hickling
Peasenhall	St. Michael	Blithing	Dunw‡			
Pettaugh	St. Catherine	Thred.	Clayd.	R	Mrs. Hallum	
Pettistree	St. Pet. & Paul	Wilford	Wilfor.	V	The Crown	Priory of Campsey
Playford	St. Mary	Carlford	Carlf.	Impr	Earl of Bristol	Priory of Eye
Polstead	St. Mary	Babergh	Sudb.	R	Mr. Sindrey	
Poslingford	St. Mary	Risbr.	Sudb.	V	George Golding Esq.	Priory of Dunmow

* A Chapel to Sudborn.　　‡ A Chapel to Sibton.

	St. Mary	Babergh Coines	Sudb.	R	Emanuel Col. Cambr.	
Preston Purdis * R	St. Mary				Emanuel Col. Cambr.	
Ramsholt	All Saints	Wilford	Wilf.	Impr	Mr. Martin	Priory of Butley.
Rattlesden	St. Nicholas	Thedw.	Thed.	R	George Gooday Esq.	
Raydon	St. Margaret	Blithing	Dunw.	V	Sir John Rous	Priory of Wangford
Reed or Rede	All Saints	Thingoe	Thing.	R	The Crown	
Redgrave	St. Mary	Hartmere	Hartl.	R	Rowland Holt Esq.	
Redisham Great	St. Peter	Wangford	Wang.	Impr	Mr. Yallop's Heirs	Priory of Butley
Redisham Little Church down	St. James	Wangford	Wang.	R ‡		
Redlingfield		Hartmere	Hartl.	Impr	John Willes Esq.	Redlingfield Priory
Rendham	St. Michael	Plomgate	Orford	V	Mrs. Powel	Sibton Abby
Rendlesham	St. Gregory	Loes	Loes	R	The Crown	
Rickingale or Rickenhale Upper	St. Mary	Hartmere	Hartl.	R	} Rowland Holt Esq.	
Rickinghale or						
Rickenhale Lower	St. Mary	Blackb.	Black.	R		

* Propably a Corruption of St. Parnel, who had a Chapel there abouts.   ‡ Consolidated to Ringsfield.

Parish	Dedication	Hundred		Patron	Priory
Ringsfield	All Saints	Wangford	Wang. R	Mr. Prime	
Ringshall or Ringsale		Bof. & Clay	Bosm. R	Mr. Peppen	
Risby	St. Giles	Thingo	Thingo R	Mr. Lurkin	
Rishangles	St. Margaret	Hartimere	Hartf. R	Mr. Vernon	
Rougham	St. Mary	Thedw.	Thedw R	John Corrance Esq.	
Roydon	St. Mary	Samford	Samf. R	Mr. Guibbon	
Rumburgh	St. Michael	Blithing	Dunw. Impr	William Godbolt	Rumburgh Priory
Rushbrook	St. Nicholas	Thedw.	Thedw R	Sir Jermyn Davers	
Rushmere	St. Andrew	Carlford	Carlf, V	Ar. Barnardiston Esq.	Trinity Priory Ipswich
Rushmere	St. Michael	Mutford	Loth. R	Richn. Garneys Esq	
S					
Sancroft	St. George	Wangford	Southel. R	Duke of Grafton	
Sapiston	St. Andrew	Blackb.	Blackb R	Sir John Playters	Ixworth Priory
Satterly	St. Margaret	Wangford	Wongf. R	Mr. Carter	
Saxham Great	St. Andrew	Thingo	Thingo R	Mr. Crofts.	
Saxham Little	St. Nicholas	Thingo	Thingo R	Charles Long Esq.	
SAXMUNDHAM	St. John Bapt.	Plomesgate	Orford R		
Saxstead	All Saints	Hoxne	Hoxne*		
Sackford ‡					

* Consolidated to Framlingham. ‡ A Hamlet situate between Woodbridge, Great Bealings and Martlesham; but reckoned as a Hamlet of Great Bealings.

Parish	Dedication	Hundred	Deanery	R/V	Patron	Abbey
Semer or Seamer	All Saints	Cosford	Sudb.	R	Mr. Cooke	
Shaddingfield	St. John Bapt.	Wangford	Wang	R	Earl of Suffolk	
Shelland		Stow	Stow	Impr		
Shelly	All Saints	Samford	Samf.	Impr	ThomasKerridge Esq.	Abby of Hales
Shimpling or Shimpling Thorn	St. George	Babergh	Sudb.	R	Mr. Fiske	Priory of Butley
Shipmeadow	St. Bartholom.	Wangford	Wang	R	Denz. Suckling Esq.	
Shottisham	St. Margaret	Wilford	Wilf.	R	Mr. Kell	
Shotley or Kirton	St. Mary	Samford	Samf.	R	Earl of Bristol	
Sibton	St. Peter	Blithing	Dunw.	V	Mrs. Baker	Sibton Abby
Sizewell Chapel down	St. Nicholas	Blithing*				
Snailbridge ‡						
Snape	St. John Bapt.	Plomsgate	Orfor	V	Earl of Strafford	Snape Abby
SonamEarl&Monk. vid. Earl & Monk's						
Somerlyton	St. Mary	Loth.	Loth.	R	Sir Thomas Allin	
Somersham	St. Mary	Bos.& Clay	Bofm	R	Mr. Glanvile	
Somerton		Babergh	Sudb	R	Blundevile	
Sotherton	St Andrew	Blithing	Dunw	R	Sir John Rous	

* A Hamlet of Leiston.   ‡ A Hamlet of Bures, vid. Page 95.

	Church	Hundred			Patron	
Southelmam	All Saints	Wangford	Southel	R	Mr. Kerridge	
	St. James	Wangford	Southel	R	Mr. Godbolt.	
	St. Margaret	Wangford	Southel	R		
	St. Michael	Wangford	Southe.	Impr		
	St. Nicholas	Wangford	South.	R		
	St. Peter	Wangford	Southe	R ‡		
	St. Margaret	Hoxne	Hoxne†			
Southolt						
South Park						
South Town		Thingo ‖				
Church down						
SOUTHWOULD or Southwold	St. Nicholas	Loth.	Loth. 5			
Spexhall	St. Edmund	Blithing	Dunw¶	R	The Crown	
Sproughton	St. Peter	Blithing	Dunw.	R	Earl of Briſtol	
Stanningfield	All Saints	Samford	Samf.	R	Sir Jermyn Davers	
Stansfield	St. Nicholas	Thedw.	Thed.	R	The Crown	
Stanſtead	All Saints	Risbr	Clare	R		
Stanton	St. James	Babergh	Sudb.	R		
Stanton	St. John ⎰	Blackb.	Blackb.	R	Mr. Bugg	
Stanton	All Saints ⎱					
Sternfield	St. Mary	Plomesgate	Orford	R	Dudley North Eſq.	Rumburgh Priory

* The Church down and Conſolidated to All Saints.   ‡ Conſolidated to St. Margarets.   † A Chapel to Worlingworth.   ‖ A Hamlet of Hargrave.   5 Conſolidated to Gorleſton.   ¶ A Chapel to Raydon.

Place	Dedication	Hundred	Deanery		Patron	Religious House
Stoke Afh	All Saints	Hartfmere	Hartf.	R	T.Tyr.BokenhamEfq	
Stoke by Neyland	St. Mary	Babergh	Sudbur.	V	Sir John Williams	Priory of Prittlewell
Stoke by Clare	St. Auftin	Risbr.	Clare	V	Sir Harvey Elwes	Stoke Priory
Stonham Afpall	St. Mary	Bof. & Clay	Bofm.	R	Earl of Effex	
Stonham Earl vid. Earl Stonham	}					
Stonham Little	St. Mary	Bof. & Clay.	Bofm.	R	Mr. Alexander	
Stoven	St. Margaret	Blithing	Dunw.	Impr	Mr. Paine	Priory of Wangford
Stowlangtoft	St. George	Blackb.	Blackb	R		
STOW-MARKET	St. Peter	Stow	Stow	V	Mr, Blackerby	Priory of St. Ofith
Stowupland Church down	St. Mary † }					
Stradbrook	All Saints	Hoxne	Hoxne	V	Bifhop of Ely	Wingfield College
Straddifhal	St. Margaret	Risbr.	Clare	R	Duke of Devonfhire	
Stratford	St. Mary	Samford	Samf.	R	The Crown	
Stratford or Stretford	St. Andrew	Plomefgate	Orford	R	The Crown	
Stratton Church down	}	Colnes *				
Stufton	All Saints	Hartfmere	Hartf.	R	Lord Cornwallis	
Sutton	St. Peter	Samford	Samf.	R	Mr. White	
Sudbourn	All Saints	Plomefgate	Orford	R	The Crown	

† Confolidated to St. Peter.   * Looked upon as Extraparocial.

SUDBURY	All Saints	Babergh	Sudb.	V	Mr. Littell	Abby of St. Albans
	St. Gregory *	Babergh	Sudb.	Impr.	Mr. Sands	Sudbury College
	St. Peter *					
Sutton	All Saints	Wilford	Wilf.	V	Sir John Rous	Bruisyard Priory
Swefling	St. Mary	Plomesgate	Orford	R	Mr. Jenkenson	
Swilland or Swillond	St. Mary	Bof. & Clay	Clayd.	V ‡	Bishop of Ely	Priory of Wikes
Syleham	St. Margaret	Hoxne	Hoxne†	Impr†	Mr. Barry	Wingfield College
T						
Tannington or Tadington	St. Etlebert	Hoxne	Hoxne	V	Bishop of Rochester	Priory of Eye
Tadgiton	St. Mary	Samford	Samf.	R	Mr.	
Thebberton or Theberton	St. Peter	Blithing	Dunw.	R	The Crown	
Thelnetham	St. Nicholas	Blackb.	Blackb.	R	Thomas Tyrel, Esq.	
THETFORD	St. Mary ǁ	Lackford		Impr	Corporation of Thetford	Priory of Monks Thetford
Thorington	St. Peter	Blithing	Dunw.	R	Alexander Bence Esq.	
Thorndon	All Saints	Hartsmere	Hartf.	R	Mr. Howes	

* A Chapel to St. Gregory's.   ‡ This Vicarage is now endowed with all the Great Tythes-
the Tythes of Syleham are given to the Minister by Mr. Barry. Vid. Kennet's Augmentation of Vicar-
ages Page 325.   ǁ Vid. Page 74.   † All
rages Page 74.

Thornham Great	St. Mary	Hartf.	R	Cha. Killegrew Esq.	
Thornham Little			R		
Thorp Morieux	St. Mary	Costford	R	Higham Risby Esq.	
Thorp	St. Peter	Thred.		Sudb.	
Thorp Chapel down	St. Mary	Blithing ‡		Clay. *	
Thorp by Ixworth	All Saints	Blackb.	Blackb. Impr	Tho. Crofts Read Esq.	Ixworth Priory
Thrandeston	St. Margaret	Hartfmere	Hartf. R	Lord Cornwallis	
Thurlston †					
Thurlow Great	All Saints	Risbr.	Clare R	James Vernon Esq.	
Thurlow Little	St. Peter	Risbr.	Clare R	Stephen Soame Esq.	
Thurston	St. Peter	Thedw.	Thedw V	Thomas Bright Esq.	Blithburgh Priory
Thwaite	St. George	Hartfmere	Hartf. R	John Sheppard Esq.	
Timworth	St. Andrew	Thedw.	Thedw R	Lord Cornwallis	
Toftock	St. Andrew	Thedw.	Thedw V	Richard Mosely Esq.	Bury Abby
Trimly	St. Martin	Colnes	Colnes R	Sir John Barker	
Trimly	St. Mary	Colnes	Colnes R	The Crown	
Troston	St. Mary	Blackb.	Blackb. R	The Crown	
Tuddenham	St. Mary	Lackford	Ford. R	Earl of Bristol	
Tuddenham	St. Martin	Carlford	Carlf. V	Tho. Fonnereau Esq.	Trinity Priory Ipswich
Tunstal	St. Michael	Plomesgate	Orford R	Mr. Philip Carter	

* A Chapel and Hamlet to Ashfield. ‡ A Hamlet to Aldringham. † A Chapel now used for a
Barn. It is joyned to Whitton.

D d

		Hundred	Deanery		Patron	Impropriator / Priory
U						
Ubbeston	St. Peter	Blithing	Dunw.	V*	Sir Robert Kemp	
Ufford	St. Mary	Wilford	Wilf.	R	Charles Wood Esq.	
Uggeshall	St. Mary	Blithing	Dunw.	R	Sir John Rous	Priory of St. Neot
W						
Walderswick	St Andrew	Blithing	Dunw.‡	R	Clare Hall Cambridge	
Waldingfield Great	St. Laurence	Babergh	Sudb.	R	Mrs. Jackson	Priory of Colne
Waldingfield Little	St. Laurence	Babergh	Sudb.	V	Ar. Barnardiston Esq.	
Waldringfield	All Saints	Colnes	Colnes	R	Mrs. Forward	Redlingfield Priory
Waipole	St. Mary	Blithing	Dunw.	Impr	Mrs. Hunt	
Walsham in the Willows	St. Mary	Blackb.	Blackb.	Impr	Mrs. Atkinson	Priory of Ixworth
Walton	St. Mary.	Colnes	Colnes	V	Rowland Holt Esq.	Priory of Felixslow
Wangford	St. Dennis	Ford.	Ford.	R	Sir John Rous	
Wangford	St. Pet. & Paul	Lackford	Dunw.	Impr	Charles Wood Esq.	Wangford Priory
Wantiden	St. John Bapt.	Plomesgate	Orford	Impr		Burley Priory
Washbrook or Great Belstead	St. Mary	Samford	Samf.	V†	Thomas De Grey Esq.	Priory of Dartford

*N.B. The Great Tythes of Ubbeston were given to the Vicarage about 1685, by the Will of Mrs. Sone. ‡A Chapel and Hamlet to Blithburgh. †This Vicarage is endowed with the Great Tythes of all, except the Copyhold Lands.

Parish	Church	Hundred	Deanery	R/V	Patron	Appropriated to
Wattisham	St Nicholas	Cosford	Sudb.	Impr	King's Col. Cambridg	Bricet Priory
Whattisfield, Wattisfield or Watchfield	St Margaret	Blackb.	Blackb.	R	Mrs. Baker	
Welnetham Great	St. Mary Mag.	Thedw.	Thedw.	R		
Welnetham Little	St. John	Thedw.	Thedw.	R		
Wenham Great		Samford	Samf.	R *	Sir Jermyn Davers	
Wenham Little		Samford	Samf.	R	Sir Philip Parker	
Wenhaston	St. Peter	Blithing	Dunw.	V	Mr. Hingeston	
Westerfield	St. Mary	Bof. & Clay	Clayd.	R	The Crown as thought	Priory of Blithburgh
Westhall	St. Andrew	Blithing	Dunw.	V	Bishop of Ely	
Westleton	St. Peter	Blithing	Dunw.	V	Chapter of Norwich	{ Chauntry near Norwich Cathedral; Priory of Blithburgh
Westhorpe	St. Margaret	Hartfmere	Hartf.	R	Mr. Ever. Woods	
Westley	St. Tho. Becket	Thingo	Thingo	R	Mr. Sparrow	
Weston	St. Peter	Wangford	Wang.	R	The Crown	
Weston Coney, vid. Cony Weston						
Weston Market	St. Mary	Blackb.	Blackb.	R	{ Thomas Tyrell Bokenham, Esq.	

* This was formerly a Vicarage, one half of it was Impropriated to the Priory of Ely, and the other to the Priory of Lewes.

		Hundred	Deanery	R	Patron	
West Stow	St. Mary	Thedw. *	*Thedw	R	Mr. Progers	
Westwood	St. Mary	Bithing	Stow	R	The Crown	
Wetherden	All Saints	Stow	Hartf.	R	Edmund Jenny Esq	
Wetheringset	St. Mary	Harttmere	Hoxne	V	Mr. Colman	Butley Priory
Weybread		Hoxne				
Whattesfield, Whatfield, or Wheatfield		Cosford	Sudb.	R		
Whepstead		Thingo	Thingo	R		
Wherstead	St. Mary	Samford	Samf.	V	The Crown	Trinity College in Ipswich.
Whitton	St. Thomas	Bof. & Clay.	Clayd.	R ‡	Bishop of Ely	Pipewell Priory
Wickham Brook †	All Saints	Risbr.	Clare	V	The Crown	Campsey Priory
Wickham Market	All Saints	Wilford	Wilf.	V	The Crown	Abby of St. John's in Colchester.
Wickham Skyth	St. Andrew	Hartsmere	Hartf.	V	Sir Edmund Bacon	
Wilbye	St. Mary	Hoxne	Hoxne	R	Earl of Rochford	
Willingham	St. Mary	Wangford	Wang.	R	The Crown ||	
Willisham	St. Mary	Bof. & Clay.	Bosm.	Impr	Mrs. Brownrigg!	Trinity Priory Ipswich
Wingfield	St. Andrew	Hoxne	Hoxne	Impr	Bishop of Norwich.	Wingfield College

* A Hamlet of Blithburgh. ‡ Formerly holden of St. Buttolls. † Wickham Brook consists of divers Hamlets, of which see Page 150. || Church down, and now goes with Ellough, if not Consolidated thereto.

Parish	Dedication	Hundred	Deanery		Patron	Priory / Appropriation
Winston	St. Andrew	Thred.	Clayd.	V	Chapter of Ely	Priory of Ely.
Wissett	St. Andrew	Blithing	Dunw.	Impr	Mr. Fleetwood Smith	Rumburgh Priory.
Wilton	St. Mary	Babergh	Sudb.	V	The Crown	Harkesly Priory.
Wetherdale or Witherdale	St. Mary Mag	Hoxne	Hoxne	R	Emanuel Col. Cambr.	
Wethersfield or Withersfield, Wittingham *	St. Mary	Risbr.	Clare	R	Sir John Jacobs	
Witnesham	St. Mary	Carlford	Carlf.	R	Mr. Beaumont	
Wixo, Whixoe or Wickeshoe		Risbr.	Clare	R	Henry Berkely Esq.	
Wulpit	S. Mary	Thedw.	Thedw	R	Charles Wood Esq.	
Wolverston	St. Mary	Samford	Samf.	R	Knox Ward Esq.	
WOODBRIDGE	St. Mary	Loes	Loes	‡Impr	Thomas Carthew Esq.	Woodbridge Priory
Wordwell	All Saints	Blackb.	Blackb.	R	Earl of Bristol	
Worlingham	St. Mary	Wangford	Wang.	R	The Crown	
Worlingron	All Saints	Lack.	Ford.	R	Samuel Sandys Esq.	
Worlingworth	St. Mary	Hoxne	Hoxne	V	Edward Barker Esq.	
Wortham	St. Mary	Hartsmere	Hartf.	R †		Bury Abby.
Wrating Great	St. Mary	Risbr.	Clare	R	Sir Sam. Barnardiston	

* A Hamlet of Fresingfield. ‡ The Tythes of this Parish are given to the Minister. Vid. Kennet's Augmentation Page 280. † Two Rectorys or Medietys of a Rectory, one presented by Rowland Holt, Esq. the other by Nathaniel Acton, Esq.

Wratting Little	St. Nicholas	Risbr.	Clare	R	Vernon Esq.
Wrentham	St. George	Blithing	Dunw.	R	Hump. Brewster Esq.
Wyverston		Hartfmere	Hartf.	R	Tho. Barnardiston Esq.

Y

Yaxley	St. Mary	Hartfmere	Hartf.	R	The Crown
Yoxford	St. Peter	Blithing	Dunw.	V	Sir John Rous

Containing Parish Churches now standing wherein Divine Service is celebrated, to the } 507

Number of Parishes or Hamlets wherein there have been Churches or Chapels dedicated to God's Service, but now in Ruins to the Number of } 59

Besides the four Hamlets or Parishes mentioned Page 150, and now annexed to Wick-ham Brook, whose Churches or Chapels are also now in Ruins } 4

The whole Number of Parishes and Hamlets in the County is } 570

(Priory of Monks in Thetford)

F I N I S.

E R R A T A.

PAGE 8. l. 18. r. South side p. 33. l. 29. for 5m; 3 ¾ f. r. 1 m. 3 ¾ f. p. 44. l. 12. for Francis r. William. p. 65. l. 18. after Foundation r. no. p. 68. l. 27. for Saturdays r. Wednesdays. p. 93. l. 10. for September r. December. p. 109. l. 13. for Edmund r. Edward. p. 126. l. 24. after Times r. It is now in Nicholas Bacon and Miles on Edgar, Esqrs. Nathaniel Action Esq. has a Seat here formerly call ed Style, it having been built by a Family of that Name now extinct. p. 158. l. 24. for Pooley Esq. r. Richard Gooday Esq. p. 166. l. 17. for 83. r. 80. p. 187. Horse Croft, vid. p. 159. p. 199 l. penult. for Sutton read Stutton.

Index to the Hundreds in Both Editions of
The Suffolk Traveller

The Hundred in which a parish or town occurs can usually be found by looking up the later page in the following index and comparing it with this table. E.g. Alderton (162) must be in WILFORD (162).

Hundreds	1735	1764
BABERGH	113	254
BLACKBOURN	116	230
BLYTHING	120	128
BOSMERE and CLAYDON	124	199
CARLFORD	128	72
COLNEIS	130	72
COSFORD	131	269
HARTISMERE	132	172
HOXNE	135	164
IPSWICH and the Liberties	5	7
LACKFORD	138	238
LOES	140	95
LOTHINGLAND	144	150
MUTFORD	145	149
PLOMESGATE	146	118
RISBRIDGE	148	246
SAMFORD	151	61
STOW	153	186
THEDWASTRE	155	222
THINGOE	158	211
THREDLING	160	184
WANGFORD	160	155
WILFORD	162	109

Index of Towns and Parishes in
The Suffolk Traveller 1735

Modern spelling is used throughout

Appendix A

ALPHABETICAL DIRECTORY OF
THE NOBILITY, CLERGY AND GENTRY
compiled from the 1735 *Suffolk Traveller* and
the 1736 map, giving owners and tenants of estates,
and indicating those whose arms are shown on the map

The 129 coats of arms, prefixed A, are numbered serially in their order on the map.
P = seat in park shown enclosed on the map; R = rector; V = vicar; pc = perpetual
curate.

	Acton, Nathaniel, Esq.	Hemingstone
	Acton, William, Esq.	Bramford
A32, P	Affleck, Gilbert, Esq.	Dalham
A33	Alexander, Waldegrave, Esq.	Badingham
A30, P	Allin, Sir Thomas, 2nd Bart	Somerleyton
A34	Alston, Joseph, Esq.	Edwardstone Priory
	Alston, William, Esq.	Bildeston
	Arbuthnot, Robert, Esq.	Bentley
A11	Bacon, Sir Edmund, 6th Bart	Garboldisham and Gillingham, Norfolk
	Bacon, Nicholas, Esq.	Shrubland Hall, Barham
A35	Bacon, Philip, Esq.	Battisford
	Baker, Samuel, Esq.	Giffard's in Wattisfield
A13, P	Barker, Sir John, 6th Bart	Grimston Hall, Sproughton and Trimley
A25	Barker, Sir William, 2nd Bart	Bocking Hall, Essex and Ringshall
	Barker, Francis, Esq.	Yoxford
A36	Barlow, Lewis, Esq.	
A37, P	Barnardiston, Arthur, Esq.	Brightwell
A23	Barnardiston, Sir Samuel, 5th Bart	Kedington d.s.p. 1736
	Barnardiston, Thomas, Esq.	Wyverstone
	Barry, Anthony, Capt.	Weston and Syleham
	Bedingfield, Charles, Esq.	Thornham Parva
	Bedingfield, Henry, Esq.	Stoke Ash
A38	Bence, Alexander, Esq.	Thorington
	Bence, Robert, Gent.	Henstead
	Bennet, Thomas, Esq.	Coddenham Hall, Boxford
	Benyon, Henry, Esq.	Boxford
A39	Betts, Thomas, Esq.	Halesworth, Spexhall
	Birch, Joseph, Esq.	Brandon
A40	Bishop, Thomas, DD	Ipswich, St Mary-le-Tower, pc
A28	Blois, Sir Charles, 1st Bart	Grundisburgh and Yoxford, Cockfield Hall
A41	Blomfield, The Revd Dr Barrington	Badingham & Cransford, R
	Blomfield, Samuel, Esq.	Four Elms, Stonham Parva
	Bloss, Tobias, Esq.	Belstead
	Bohun, Edmund, Esq.	Westhall
A42	Bohun, William, MD	Beccles
	Bokenham, Thomas, Esq.	Gedding

A43	Bond, Henry Jermyn, Esq.	Bury St Edmunds
	Braham or Brame, The Misses	Campsey Ash
	Brand, Capt. Ellis	Wherstead
	Brand, Jacob, Esq.	Polstead
	Brewster, Humphrey, Esq.	Wrentham
A44	Brewster, Philip, Esq.	Wrentham
P	Bridgeman, Orlando, Esq.	Combs
	Bright, Thomas, Esq.	Pakenham
A45	Broke, Philip, Esq.	Nacton
A46	Bryan, William, Esq.	possibly Whelnetham Magna
	Burch, Joseph, Esq.	Brandon
A47	Burward, Anthony, Esq.	Melton
A9	Butts, The Right Revd Robert	Lord Bishop of Norwich
	Calthorpe, James, Esq.	Ampton
A48	Canham, John, Esq.	Milden Hall
A50	Carter, James, AM	North Cove, R
A49	Carter, John, AM	Wilby, R and Sibton, Peasenhall, V
A51	Carthew, Thomas, Esq.	Benacre, Easton Bavants and Woodbridge Priory
	Chamberlen, Dr	Alderton
	Chevallier, Clement, Esq.	Aspal
A52	Chilton, Jacob, AM	Mendlesham and Ufford, V
	Chinery, George, Gent.	Gifford's Hall, Wickhambrook
	Clarke, Sir Robert, 2nd Bart	Freckenham and Snailwell
	Cocksedge, Henry, Esq.	Drinkstone
P	Coke, Thomas, baron Lovel	Holkham, Cratfield and Huntingfield
	Colman, Edward, Esq.	Brent Eleigh
	Colman, Philip, Esq.	Weybread
A53	Cook, Roger, Esq.	?Bardwell
	Cooke, John, Esq.	Rougham
	Coppinger, George, Esq.	Buxhall
	Corbould, Mr William, 'a wealthy Quaker'	Rumburgh
A7, PP	Cornwallis, Charles, 5th baron	Brome Hall, Culford Hall and Ingham
A54	Corrance, John, Esq.	Rougham
A55	Cotton, Frederick, Gent.	Marlesford
P	Crofts, William, Esq.	Saxham Parva
	Crowley, Ambrose, Esq.	Barking
P	Crowley, Mrs	Badley and Combs
A18, P	Cullum, Sir Jasper, 4th Bart	Hawstead
	Cullum, John, Esq.	Hardwick
	Curwin, John, Esq.	Pakenham
	Dade, Mr John	Tannington
A56, P	Dashwood, George, Esq.	Heveningham and Peyton Hall, Boxford
A27, P	Davers, Sir Jermyn, 4th Bart	Rushbrooke, Villa Sicklesmere
A57	Davers, Thomas, Esq.	Horningsheath
A6	Devereux, Price, 9th viscount Hereford	Christchurch (until autumn 1735)
P	Devereux, the Honble Price	Sudbourne (succ. 1740 as 10th visct)
	Dickins, Francis, Esq.	Cowling
A59	Discipline, Thomas, Esq.	Bury St Edmunds
	Dove, Simon, Esq.	Barham and Marlesford
	Downing, Sir George, 3rd Bart	Dunwich
A58	D'Oyley, James, AM	Layham
	Driver, Thomas, Esq.	Earl Stonham
P	Duke, Lady	Redisham
A60	Eachard, Christopher, AM	Debach and Cransford, V

	Edgar, Devereux, Esq.	Clopton House, Wickhambrook
A61	Edgar, William, Esq.	Glemham Magna
A62	Edgar, Robert, Esq.	Ipswich, Grimston House
A63	Edgar, Mileson, Esq.	The Red House and Westerfield
A64	Eldred, John, Esq.	Saxham Magna
A65	Ellis, John, Esq.	Westhorpe
A19	Elwes, Sir Hervey, 2nd Bart	Stoke-by-Clare
A66	Eure, Edward, Esq.	
	Ewen, John, Gent.	Raydon
A67	Fairfax, Blackerby, Gent.	Woodbridge
A29	Firebrace, Sir Cordell, 3rd Bart	Melford Hall
A1, PP	Fitzroy, Charles, 2nd duke of Grafton	Euston Hall, Barningham Park and Barnham
A68	Fonnereau, Thomas, Esq.	Christchurch, Ipswich (from autumn 1735)
A31	Fowke, Sir Sydenham, Kt	West Stow
	Fox, Capt. Simon	Stradbroke
A69	Frere, Edward, Esq.	Finningham
A22, P	Gage, Sir Thomas, 3rd Bart	Hengrave Hall
	Gibson, Barnaby, Esq.	Stonham Parva
	Gibson, Capt.	Mendlesham
	Glover, John, Esq.	Frostenden and High House, Campsey Ash
A70	Godbold, Richard, AM	Sudbury All Saints, V
A71	Golding, George, Esq.	Poslingford
	Gooch, The Revd Sir Thomas, 2nd Bart, DD	Benacre Hall (later bishop)
	Gooday, George, Esq.	Fornham All Saints
A72	Goodrich, John, Gent.	Ipswich
	Gurdon, The Revd Mr Brampton, AM	Archdeacon of Sudbury
	Gurdon, John, Esq.	Assington
A73	Hamby, Robert, Gent.	Ipswich
	Hammond, Philip, Esq.	Hawkedon
A74	Hankey, Sir Henry or Joseph, Esq.	East Bergholt
A12	Hanmer, Sir Thomas, 4th Bart	Mildenhall and Great Barton
	Harland, Capt. Robert	Sproughton
	Harvey, Lady Anne	Leiston
	Harvey, Mrs	Cockfield
	Harwood, Henry, Esq.	Crowfield
A75	Heigham, John, Esq.	Hunston
A76	Heigham, Arthur, Esq.	Hunston and Rougham
A4, P	Hervey, John, 1st earl of Bristol	Ickworth, Barrow, Bealings, Shotley and Wordwell
	Hobart, Capt.	Kelsale Lodge
A78	Hodges, Thomas, Esq.	Ipswich, St Matthew's
A77	Holt, Rowland, Esq.	Redgrave
A79	Hunt, Tobias, Esq. (now Mrs)	Walsham le Willows
	Hutcheson, Francis, Esq.	Fornham St Martin
	Jacob, J., Gent.	Yaxley
	Jacobs *alias* Bradlaugh, Nicholas, Esq.	Laxfield
	Jenkinson, Richard, Gent.	Normanton nr Lowestoft
	Jennens, William, Esq.	Acton
A80	Jenny, Robert, Esq.	Knodishall
A81	Jenny, Edmund, Esq.	Bredfield
A82	Johnston, Henry, LLD	Stowmarket and Monk Soham, R
A83	Kedington, Ambrose, Esq.	Acton

	Kedington, Robert, Esq.	Stansfield
A84	Kedington, Roger, Gent.	Waldingfield Magna
A85	Kelligrew, Charles, Esq.	Thornham Magna
A17	Kemp, Sir John, 4th Bart	Ubbeston
A86	Kent, Samuel, Esq.	Fornham St Genevieve
	Kerridge, Thomas, Esq.	Shelley
A87	Knapp, Thomas, Gent.	Battisford
	Knipe, Charles, Esq.	Haughley
	Lathum, A., Esq.	Badwell Ash
A88, P	Lee, Baptist, Esq.	Livermere Parva
	Le Heup, Michael, Esq.	Hessett
	Leman, Robert, Esq.	Brampton
A89	Leman, Suckling, Esq.	Weston
	Leman, Thomas	Wenhaston and Wingfield
A90	Leman, Mrs, widow of William	Charsfield
A91	Leybourn, Robert, DD	Pluralist, Suffolk links untraced
A92	Lloyd, Richard, Esq. (recte Sir)	Hintlesham
A93	Long, Charles, Esq.	Hurts Hall, Saxmundham
A21	Long, Sir Philip Parker, 4th Bart	Erwarton Hall
	Luck, Thomas, Esq.	Herringswell
	Macro, Cox, DD	Norton
	Maddocks, Robert, Esq.	Troston
P	Major, Sir John, 1st Bart	Worlingworth Hall
A15	Mannock, Sir Francis, 4th Bart	Gifford's Hall, Stoke by Nayland
A24	Martin, Sir Roger, 2nd Bart	Melford Place
A94	Martin, Thomas, Gent.	Palgrave
	Maynard, Thomas, Esq.	Hoxne Hall
	Meadows, Daniel, Gent.	Witnesham
A95	Moore, John, Esq.	Kentwell Hall, Long Melford
	Mordant, William, Esq.	Shelland
A96	Mosely, Richard, Esq.	Tostock
	Mussenden, Hill, Esq.	Herringfleet
A97	Naunton, William, Esq.	Letheringham
A98	North, Dudley, Esq.	Glemham Parva and Hurts Hall
A99	Norton, Thomas, Esq.	Ixworth and Stowlangtoft
A100	Pitt, George, Esq.	Crows Hall, Debenham
A101	Plampin, Robert, Esq.	Chadacre Hall, Shimpling
	Plampin, William, Esq.	Shimpling
A14	Playters, Sir John, 7th Bart	Sotterley
A102	Plumer, Walter, Esq.	Chediston and Akenham
	Poley, J., Esq.	Boxted Hall
	Pooley, ——, Esq.	Fornham All Saints
A103, P	Powys, Richard, Esq.	Hintlesham
A104, P	Pretyman, Baron, Esq.	Bacton
	Pretyman, Dr	Laxfield
A105	Prime, Samuel, Esq.	Bury St Edmunds
	Purvis, George, Esq.	Darsham
	Rabett, Reginald, Esq.	Bramfield
A106	Radclyffe, Hugh, Gent.	Glevering Hall
	Ray, Richard, Esq.	Shelland, Wetherden
	Read, Thomas Crofts, Esq.	Bardwell
	Revett, John, Esq.	Brandeston
A107	Rewse, William, Esq.	
A10	Reynolds, Lord Chief Baron James	Thrandeston
	Reynolds, John, Esq.	Felsham
	Risby, H., Esq.	Thorpe Morieux

	Robinson, the Hon. John	Denston
A26	Robinson, Sir Thomas, 3rd Bart	Worlingham, formerly Melford
A20, P	Rous, Sir John, 1st Bart	Henham, Bruisyard, Darsham and Dennington
	Sancroft, William, Gent.	Fressingfield
A108	Sayer, John, BD	Wickham Market, V [elected not admitted]
A109	Scrivener, Charles, Esq.	Sibton
	Shelton, Maurice, Esq.	Barningham Hall and Westhorpe
	Sheppard, Francis, Esq.	Exning
P	Sheppard, John, Esq.	Brockford
	Sheppard, Thomas, Esq.	Tunstall
A110	Smyth, Charles, Esq.	
A111	Smyth, Samuel, Gent.	
A112, P	Soame, Stephen, Esq.	Thurlow Parva
	Sparhauke, H., Gent.	Leiston
	Sparrow, R., Gent.	Kettleburgh
	Spencer, Miss Anne	Rendlesham
A16	Spring, Sir William, 4th Bart	Pakenham
	Stewart, Sir Simeon, 2nd Bart	Lakenheath
A113	Sturgeon, James, Gent.	Bury St Edmunds
P	Sulyard, Edward, Esq.	Haughley
A114	Syer, Dey, Gent.	Waldingfield Parva
	Symonds, Thomas, Esq.	Browston Hall, Belton
P	Tasburgh, George, Esq.	Flixton Hall
A115	Tasburgh, Richard, Esq.	South Elmham St Peter
	Taylor, Thomas, Esq.	Westhorpe
	Thompson, Samuel, Esq.	Bredfield and Ufford
	Thornhill, Colonel	Depden Hall
	Thurston, Mrs	Wenham Parva
P	Thurston, John, Esq.	Hoxne
	Thurston, Thomas	Holbrook
	Tisser, Mr John, AM	Kedington, R
A5, P	Tollemache, Lionel, 4th earl of Dysart	Helmingham
A8	Townsend, Charles, 3rd baron Lynn	Denham
	Turner, John, Esq.	Langham and Horsecroft, Horringer
	Turner, Lady	Wingfield College
A116, P	Tyrell, Edmund, Esq.	Benhall
	Tyrell, Sir John, 5th Bart	Elveden
	Tyrell, Thomas, Esq.	Gipping
	Tyrell, Thomas, Esq. junior	Weston Market
A117	Van Heythuysen, Gerard, Esq.	Oulton
	Ventris, Edward, Esq.	Sproughton
A121	Vere, Thomas, Esq.	Henley
A118	Vernon, Edward, Esq.	Nacton
	Vernon, James, Esq.	Thurlow Magna
P	Ward, Knox, Esq.	Woolverstone
	Ward, Neal, Gent.	Bramfield
A119	Wareyn, John, Gent.	Kenton
	Warner, Samuel, Esq.	Waldingfield Parva and Badmondesfield Hall, Wickhambrook
	Warren Thomas, Esq.	Groton
	Watts, ——, Esq.	perhaps Walpole
A120	Webb, Richard, Esq.	Cavenham
	Wentworth, Anne, baroness	Nettlestead

A3	Wentworth, Thomas, 3rd earl of Strafford	Friston and Snape
	Wenyeve, John, Esq.	Brettenham
A124	Wild, John, Gent.	probably Lowestoft
A122	Wilkins, The Revd Dr David	Hadleigh, V and Archdeacon of Suffolk
A123	Wilkinson, William, Gent.	perhaps Walsham-le-Willows
P	Williams, Sir John	Tendryng Hall, Stoke by Nayland
	Willis, John, Esq.	Cranly Hall Redlingfield
	Wingfield, the late John MA ⎫	
A125	Wingfield, Thomas, Gent. ⎭	Broughton Hall, Stonham Aspal
	Wodehouse, Sir Armine, 4th Bart	Chilton Hall
A126	Wollaston, William, Esq.	Finborough
	Wood, Charles, Esq.	Blythford, Campsey Ash and Elmswell and Loudham
A127	Woodroffe, John, Gent.	Bury St Edmunds
	Wright, Thomas, Esq.	Tattingstone
A128	Wyard, Hunn, Gent.	Pettistree
A129	Wyard, James, Gent.	Brundish
A2, P	Zuylestein, Frederick Nassau de, 3rd earl of Rochford	Letheringham Lodge

Appendix B

ALPHABETICAL DIRECTORY OF THE NOBILITY, CLERGY AND GENTRY
compiled from the 1764 *Suffolk Traveller* and the 1766 map, giving owners and tenants of estates, indicating those whose arms are shown on the map

The two-year difference between book and map may account for changed names. Places of residence are usually placed before manorial holdings.

The 124 coats of arms, prefixed B, are numbered serially in their order on the map. P = seat in park shown enclosed on the map; R = rector; V = vicar; pc = perpetual curate. Names in the subscribers' list to the 1764 *Suffolk Traveller* have, where they occur, been compared with names in its text and on the map.

B23 P	Acton, Nathaniel, Esq.	Bramford Hall, Claydon
P	Adair, William, Esq.	Flixton
B24 P	Affleck, John, Esq.	Dalham
	Aldham, ——, Esq.	Abbots Hall, Lavenham
	Aldrich, The Revd Mr William, AB	Stowmarket (unbeneficed)
	Allen, The Revd Mr Ashurst	Blundeston and Flixton, R succ. 3rd Bart
P	Allin, Sir Thomas, 2nd Bart	Somerleyton, Belton, Corton etc.
	Alpes, Mr ——	Brokes Hall, Ipswich
B25	Alston, Edward, Esq.	Edwardstone Priory
	Alston, William, Esq.	Bildeston, Edwardstone
	Arnold, Sampson, Esq.	Beccles
	Arrow, The Revd Mr John, AB	Lowestoft and Kessingland, V
	Arrowsmith, Thomas, Gent.	Bungay
	Ashburnham, George, 2nd earl of Ashburnham	Barking
	Ashby, George, Esq.	Thornham Parva
	Aspin, The Revd Mr Harvey, AM	Hartest and Boxted, R
	Atkinson, Mr Jonathan	Seckford Hall, Bealings Magna
B26 P	Bacon, Nicholas, Esq.	Shrubland Hall, Barham
	Bacon, The Revd Mr Nicholas, AM	Baylham, Coddenham, V and Barham, R
	Bacon, Philip, Esq	Battisford Hall
B12	Barker, Sir John Fytch, 7th Bart	Sproughton, Levington and Trimley d.s.p. 1766
P	Barne, Miles, Esq.	Sotterley
	Barnwell, The Revd Mr Frederic, AB	Lawshall and Brockley, R
	Barry, Capt.	Weston
	Barry, Lambe, Esq.	Syleham
	Beachcroft, Sir William, Kt	Preston Hall, Kettlebaston
B27	Beaumont The Revd Mr Robert, AB	Witnesham (unbeneficed)
	Beddingfield, Charles, Esq.	Gislingham
	Benet, The Revd Mr James, AM	Aldeburgh and Snape, V
	Bennet, Thomas, Esq.	Coddenham Hall, Boxford
	Benyon, Revd Mr George	Boxford, R

B28	Berners, William, Esq.	later Woolverstone Park
	Betts,The Revd Mr George, LLB	Wortham; Bressingham, R
B29	Bishop, The Revd Mr Thomas, AM	Ipswich St Mary-le-Tower, pc
B30	Blake, Patrick, Esq.	Langham Hall
B16	Blois, Sir John, 5th Bart, High Sheriff	Cockfield Hall, Grundisburgh, Kelsale Lodge, Culpho
B31	Blomefield, Samuel, Esq.	Four Elms, Stonham Parva
	Bohun, Edmund, Esq.	Westhall
	Bokenham, Thomas, Esq.	Gedding
	Bowers, The late Thomas, Esq.	Crows Hall, Stutton
	Boyce, James, Esq.	Stonham Parva
	Boyfield, John, Esq.	Earl Soham Lodge
	Braham, The Misses	Campsey Ash
B32	Brand, William Beal, Esq.	Belstead, Polstead and Bildeston
	Brewster, Philip, Esq.	Wrentham Hall
	Bridges, George, Esq.	Great Bealings Hall
	Bridges, James, Esq.	Crows Hall, Debenham
B33	Broke, Philip, Esq.	Broke Hall at Nacton
	Broke, The Revd Mr John, LLB	Nacton, minor canon of Norwich
	Brome, The Revd Mr Richard, AM	Ipswich
B34	Brooke, Francis, Esq.	Ufford Place
	Brown, The Revd Mr James	Died Ipswich 1763, Nedging and Baylham, R
	Brundish, Mrs	Troston
B15	Bunbury, Sir Thomas Charles, 6th Bart	Mildenhall and Barton Magna succ.1764
	Bunbury, Revd Sir William, DD, 5th Bart	Mildenhall, V. Barton Magna d.1764
	Burch, Joseph, Esq.	Brandon, Barham
B35	Burrell, John, Gent.	Ipswich
	Burton, The Revd Mr George, AM	Elveden and Herringswell, R
B36	Burward, Jonathan, Esq.	Woodbridge
	Buxton, The Revd Mr Robert, AM	Darsham, R
P	Calthorpe, James, Esq.	Ampton Hall
B37	Calvert, Turner, Esq.	Brundish Lodge
P	Campbell, William Henry, Esq.	Melford Hall, Fellow of Pembroke, Cambridge
B38	Canham, John, Esq.	Milden Hall
B39	Canning, The Revd Mr Richard, AM	Ipswich St Lawrence pc *inter alia*
	Capell, Edward, Esq.	Troston and the Stantons
B41	Carter, The Revd Mr James, AM	North Cove, R. Sibton and Peasenhall, V
B40	Carter, The Revd Mr Philip	Tunstall and Bromeswell, R
B42	Carthew, The Revd Mr Thomas, AM	Woodbridge Priory
	Chapman, The Revd Dr John	Archdeacon of Sudbury (otherwise not beneficed in Suffolk)
B43 P	Chapman, William, Esq.	Loudham Hall, Bromeswell, Eyke, Wantisden, Campsey Ash etc.
	Chedworth, Dowager Lady	Erwarton Hall
	Chevallier, The Revd Mr Temple, AM	Aspall, pc
	Chilton, The Revd Mr Jacob, AM	Ufford, R
	Chilton, The Revd Mr Richard, AB	Mendlesham, V
	Chinery, George, Esq.	Giffards Hall, Wickhambrook
	Chinery, Mr John	Chilton Hall, Sudbury
	Church, The Revd Mr John, AM	Boxford, R
	Clarke, Sir Robert, 4th Bart	Freckenham
	Clarke, T., Esq.	Melton
	Clubbe, The Revd Mr John, AB	Whatfield, R

	Clutterbuck, Thomas, Esq.	Grove Park, Yoxford
	Cocksedge, Ambrose, Esq.	Drinkstone
	Cocksedge, The Revd Mr Roger, AM	Bury St Edmunds
B44	Coggeshall, Thomas, Esq.	Shaddingfield
B45	Collett, Anthony, Esq.	Eyke
B46	Collett, Henry, Esq. Atty at Law	Ipswich
B47	Colville, Richard, Esq.	Hemingstone
	Cooke, The Revd Mr Thomas, AM	Semer, R
	Cooper, John, Esq.	Burgh Castle
B6 PP	Cornwallis, Charles, 2nd earl Cornwallis	Culford Hall and Brome Hall, Wordwell
	Cornwallis, The Revd Mr William	Ipswich and Chelmondiston, R
	Corrance, The late John, Esq.	Rougham Place
	Couperthwaite, The Revd Mr William, AB	Clopton, R, formerly St Helen, Ipswich
	Courtney, The Hon. Elizabeth	Leiston
	Coyte, Dr William, MB	Ipswich
	Coyte, The Revd Mr Wm, B, MB	Ipswich
	Craske, The Revd Mr Walter, AB	Bury St Edmunds, Minister St Mary's
	Crofts, William, Esq.	Saxham Parva
	Crossman, The Revd Mr Henry, AM	Sudbury, Cornard Parva, R
B49	Crespigny, Philip Champion, Esq.	Broughton Hall in Stonham Aspal and Creetings
B48	Cuddon, Thomas, Esq.	Shaddingfield
	Cullum, Sir John, 5th Bart	Hardwick House
	Cullum, The Revd Mr John Cullum	Hawstead, R
	Cullum, Mr Thomas Gery, Surgeon	Bury St Edmunds
	Curry, ——, Esq.	Monewden
B50	Dade, John, Esq.	Tannington
	Dalton, Isham, Gent.	Bury St Edmunds
	Daniels, Mrs	Frostenden
	Dashwood, George, Esq.	Peyton Hall, Boxford, Wood Hall, Sudbury
B67	Dashwood, Henry, Esq.	perhaps the late, succ. by George
P	Davers, Sir Charles, 5th Bart	Villa Sicklesmere, Rushbrooke, and Whelnetham Parva
	Davers, The Revd Mr Thomas	Whelnetham Parva, R. Stowlangtoft, V
B51	Davy, Eleazar, Esq.	perhaps already tenant at Ubbeston Hall
	Dawson, John, Esq.	Groton
B53	D'Eye, Francis, Gent.	
	D'Eye, Nathaniel, Gent.	Bungay
B52	D'Eye, The Revd Mr Thomas	Palgrave R
	De Grey, Thomas, Esq.	Washbrook
B54	Dickins, Ambrose, Esq.	Braunches Hall, Cowlinge
B55	Dove, Thomas, Esq.	
B56	Dove, The Revd Mr Fynn, AM	Marlesford (not beneficed)
	Downing, Lady	Dunwich
	D'Oyley, The Revd Sir Hadley, 5th Bart	Ipswich, Felixstowe, R
	D'Oyley, Peregrine, Esq.	Layham
B57	Drury, The Revd Mr George, AM	Claydon and Akenham, R. Wherstead, V
	D'Urban, John MD	Halesworth
B58 P	Edgar, Mileson, Esq. of Red House	Ipswich and Sibton, Occold
B59	Edgar, Robert, Esq.	Ipswich, Grimston House and Wickham House, Wickhambrook
	Edgar, William, Esq.	Sutton Hall
	Edge, The Revd Mr Peter, AM	Drinkstone, pc
	Elwes, Harvey, Esq.	Stoke by Clare

	Evans, The Revd Mr	Wortham
	Evans, ——, Esq.	Brandon
	Ewer, The Rt Revd Dr Bishop John of Llandaff	
	Farrell, ——, Esq.	Wickham Skeith
	Fenn, Thomas, Esq.	Sudbury
	Firebrace, Dowager Lady	Melford Hall
B1 P	Fitzroy, Augustus Henry, 3rd duke of Grafton	Euston Hall, Barningham Park, Honington
B60 P	Fonnereau, Thomas, Esq., MP	Christchurch, Ipswich
	Forster, The Revd Mr Thomas, AM	Halesworth, R
	Fowke, Sir Sydenham, Kt	West Stow Hall
	Fowler, The Revd Mr Richard, AB	Framlingham Dallinghoo and Easton, R
B61	Freeman, John, Gent.	Rickinghall Superior
	French, The Revd Mr John, AM	Bury St Edmunds, Saxham Magna and Horningsheath, R
	French, William, Gent.	Edwardstone
	Frere, Edward, Esq.	Finningham
B62	Frere, Sheppard, Esq.	Bacton
	Freston, Cook, Esq.	Mendham
B14 P	Gage, Sir William, 4th Bart	Hengrave Hall, Flempton
	Gallaway, The Revd Mr John Cole, AM	Botesdale Master of the Grammar School
	Glanville, R. G., Esq.	Elmsett
	Glover, John, Esq.	Frostenden
	Goate, Edward, Esq.	Brent Eleigh Hall; Wells Hall, Milden
B63	Golding, George, Esq.	New House, Poslingford, Kelsale
B17	Gooch, Sir Thomas, 3rd Bart	Benacre
	Gooch, James, Gent.	Brundish
	Goodall, The Revd Dr Henry	Mildenhall, R and Archdeacon of Suffolk
	Goodwin, The late John, Esq.	Martlesham
	Gordon, The Revd Dr William	Tacket Street Meeting House, Ipswich
	Grant, The Revd Mr Andrew, AB	Foxearth, Sudbury All Saints, pc
B64	Grigby, Joshua, Esq.	Horningsheath, Whepstead, Bury, Woolpit and Drinkstone
	Gurdon, Nathaniel, Esq.	Assington Hall
	Gwynn, Dr Nicholas, MD	Ipswich, Tacket Street
	Haddick, The Revd Mr	Brandon
	Hall, Samuel, Esq.	Fritton
B116	Hallum, Thomas, Esq.	Ipswich
B65	Hamby, Robert, Esq.	Ipswich
P	Hamilton, Elizabeth, widow of the 6th duke of Hamilton and Brandon	Easton Park, Rendlesham
B68	Hamilton, William, Esq.	Sparrowes Nest, Thurleston
	Hammond, Philip, Esq.	Hawkedon
	Hankey, Sir Joseph, Kt	East Bergholt
B66	Hanmer, Walden, Esq.	Waldingfield Parva
B69 P	Harland, Robert, Esq.	Sproughton and Belstead
	Harvey, Lady Anne	Leiston
	Harvey, The Revd Dr Charles	Cockfield, R. Prebendary of Ely
	Haynes, The Revd Mr Hopton, AM	Ipswich, Elmsett and Stansfield, R
	Hayward, John, Gent.	Mettingham Castle
	Heigham, The Revd Mr John	Walsham-le-Willows
	Heigham, Arthur, Esq.	Hunston
B70	Heigham, Pell, Esq.	Maltywards, Rougham
	Heigham, John S., Esq.	Hunston Hall
B21	Herbert, Hon. Nicholas	Great Glemham

B4 P	Hervey, George William, 2nd earl of Bristol	Ickworth and Shotley
	Hewett, The Revd Mr Thomas	Bucklesham, R
B71	Hill, The Revd Dr Henry	Buxhall pc
	Hingeston, The Revd Mr Peter, AM	Capel St Mary, R Wenham Parva, V
	Hodges, Thomas, Esq.	Ipswich
	Holden, John, Esq.	Herringswell
	Hollingsworth, William, Esq.	Pakenham
	Holmes, John, Gent.	Bungay
B72 P	Holt, Rowland, Esq., Knight of the Shire	Redgrave Hall, Rickinghall inferior
	Hudson, The Revd Mr Robert	Ipswich St Nicholas, pc
	Hunt, Miss	Walsham-le-Willows
	Ingham, Mr John, Attorney at Law	Grove Park, Yoxford
	Jeaffreson, The Revd Mr Christopher, AB	Melton, Butley, pc
	Jennens, William, Esq.	Acton and Charsfield
B73	Jenney, Edmund, Esq.	Bredfield and Knodishall
	Jessup, Mr Samuel	Leiston Abbey and Rumburgh
	Johnson, The Revd Mr Thomas, AM	Wickham Market, R
	Johnson, ——, Esq.	Cavenham
	Kedington, Ambrose, Esq.	Acton
B75	Kedington, Robert, Gent.	Stansfield
B74	Kedington, Roger, Esq.	Waldingfield Magna
	Kemp, Sir John, 4th Bart	Ubbeston Hall
	Kent, Samuel, Esq.	Fornham St Martin, St Genovieve and Denston
	Kilderbee, Mr Samuel, Attorney at Law	Ipswich
	Kirby, Mr William	Witnesham Hall
	Lathbury, The Revd Mr Peter, AM	Westerfield, R
	Lawrence, The Revd Mr Philip	Akenham, Henley and Ashbocking, V
	Layton, The Revd Mr Andrew, AM	Ipswich St Matthew, V
B76	Leake, Seymour, Esq.	Yaxley
B77	Leake, John, AM	Willisham
P	Lee, Baptist, Esq.	Livermere Parva, Magna and Lawshall
	Leeds, The Revd Mr John, AM	Woodbridge, Ramsholt and Sutton, V. Shottisham, R
B78	Le Heup, Michael, Esq.	Hessett
	Leman, The Revd Mr John, AM	Wenhaston (and Norfolk livings)
	Leman, The Revd Mr Robert, AB	Ellough
	Leman, The Revd Mr Robert, AM	Debenham, Mendham, V. Pakefield, R
	Leman, Robert, Esq.	Wickham Market, Brampton
	Leman, Thomas, Esq.	Wingfield Castle
	Leman, William, Esq.	Letheringham, Kettleburgh and Weston
	Lewin, The Revd Mr	Debenham
B80 P	Lloyd, Richard Savage, Esq., MP for Totnes	Hintlesham Hall
	Long, The late Sir Philip Parker, 4th Bart	Erwarton Hall
B79	Long, Charles, Esq.	Hurts Hall, Saxmundham
	Long, Mrs	Parham Hall
B81	Lord, The Revd Mr Thomas, AM	Whelnetham Magna, R
	Lumpkin, The Revd Mr John	Grundisburgh
	Luson, Robert, Esq.	Blundeston
	Lynch, William, Esq.	Ipswich and Abbot's Hall, Stowmarket
	Macro, The Revd Dr Cox	Norton
B19 P	Major, Sir John, 1st Bart	Thornham Magna

	Mandevile, The Revd Mr Charles, AM	Hardwick House, Woolpit and Beyton, R
	Manning, Thomas, Esq.	Bungay
	Mannock, Sir William, 5th Bart	Gifford's Hall, Stoke-by-Nayland d.1764
	Martin, The late Sir Roger, 3rd Bart	Melford Place [Sir Mordaunt succ.1762]
B9 P	Maynard, Charles, 1st viscount Maynard	Hoxne Hall, Denham near Eye
	Meadows, Daniel, Esq.	Botesdale and Witnesham
B108	Merest, John, Esq.	Bury or Wortham
B82 P	Middleton, William, Esq.	Crowfield
	Mills, The Revd Dr Bernard	Bury St Edmunds, Lecturer St Mary's
	Milner, Robert, Esq.	Ipswich, Seckford House
	Montgomerie, George, Esq.	Worlington
B83	Moore, Henry, Esq.	Glemsford
	Moore, John, Esq.	Kentwell Hall
	Moore, Richard, Esq.	Long Melford
	More, R., Esq.	Stonham Parva
B84	Mosely, Richard, Esq.	Ousden Hall, Rattlesden
	Mosely, Thomas, Esq.	Tostock Place, Fornham All Saints
	Mulliner, Thomas, Attorney at Law	Stratford St Andrew
	Mumbee, Valentine, Esq.	Horningsheath
	Mure, Hutchinson, Esq.	Saxham Magna, Depden
	Mussenden, Henry Hill, Esq.	Herringfleet
	Myers, The Revd Mr William	Walton
B20 P	Nassau, Hon. Richard Savage	Easton
	Naunton, William, Esq.	Letheringham Abbey
B85	Neden, The Revd Dr Gervase	Rougham Hall
	Negus, Henry, Gent.	Bungay
B99	Negus, William, Esq.	Dallinghoo
B86	Newcome, P., Esq.	Hobbetts, Layham
	Newcomen, The Revd Mr	Ipswich
	Newman, The Revd Mr John, AM	Sudbury, Cornard Parva, R
B87	Newton, R., Esq.	Leiston Hall
P	North, Dudley, Esq.	Glemham Parva
B88	Norton, Richard, Esq.	Ipswich and Ixworth Priory
	Nun, The Revd Mr Martin, AB	Holbrook and Hepworth, R
	Nunn, The Revd Mr Robert, AB	Pakenham, V
	Ord, Mrs	Fornham St Martin
	Parish, Robert, Esq.	Ipswich
	Parmenter, Mr William	Playford Hall
	Pawsey, The Revd Mr James, AB	Stuston and Mellis, R
B7	Perceval, John, 2nd earl of Egmont	Perhaps tenant Erwarton Hall
B121	Peyton, J., Esq.	
B89	Philips, Giles, Esq.	Ipswich
	Pickering, Samuel, Notary Publick	Ipswich
B90	Plampin, John, Esq.	Chadacre Hall, Shimpling
	Plumer, William, Esq.	Rice Hall, Akenham, Halesworth and Sweffling
B91	Pocklington, Robert, Esq.	Chelsworth and Whatfield
B92	Poley, George Weller, Esq.	Boxted Hall
	Powell, Mr Seth	Rendham Priory
B93	Preston, The Revd Mr Thos Dymock, AM	Waldingfield, Polstead and Wratting Parva, R
	Pretyman, The late Baron, Esq.	Bacton
B94	Pretyman, George, Gent.	but a Robert of Wingfield
	Primatt, The Revd Mr Humphry, AM	Higham, V
	Prime, Lady	Thwaite
	Punchard, The Revd Mr Henry, AM	Gazeley (unbeneficed)

B115	Purvis, Rear-Admiral George Wager, Esq.	Harwich
	Rabett, Reginald, Esq.	Bramfield
B95	Rant, Humphrey, Esq.	Ipswich
B22	Rawlinson, Sir Thomas, Kt	Stowlangtoft
B96	Ray, Richard, Esq.	Haughley, Shelland
	Read, Thomas Crofts, Esq.	Bardwell, Ixworth Thorpe
B97	Reilly, John, Esq.	Westhorpe, Coney Weston
B98	Revett, John, Esq.	Brandeston Hall, Cretingham
	Rich, Sir Robert	Roos Hall, Beccles
	Risby, The late H., Esq.	Thorpe Morieux
	Rookwood, Edward, Esq.	Coldham Hall, Stanningfield
	Robinson, Lt Col. John	Denston Hall
B13 P	Rous, Sir John, 1st Bart	Henham
P	Rowley, Admiral Sir William, KB	Tendryng Hall, Stoke by Nayland
B100 P	Rush, John, Esq.	Benhall
B101	Rush, Samuel, Esq. crescent	Shelley and Raydon
B102	Rushbrooke, Barham, Esq.	Mildenhall
	Rustat, The Revd Mr Tobias, AM	Stutton, R
	Safford, John, Gent.	Bungay
	Sancroft, James, Esq.	Fressingfield Hall
	Saunders, Vice Adml Sir Charles, KB	Gunton
B103	Sayer, John P., Esq.	Cretingham
	Scott, The Revd Mr	Ipswich
	Scott, J. M., MD	Felsham Hall
B104	Scrivener, John Friston, Esq.	Sibton
B5 P	Seymour-Conway, Francis, 16th earl of Hertford	Sudbourne Hall, Iken
	Sharp, The Revd Mr James	Bury St Edmunds
	Sheldon, Mr ——	Edwardstone Priory
P	Sheppard, John, Esq.	High House, Campsey Ash, Thwaite
	Smith, ——	The Lee, Ashfield
	Smyth, William, Esq.	Leiston
B105 P	Soame, Stephen, Esq.	Little Thurlow Hall
	Sparrow, Robert, Esq.	Worlingham Hall, Kettleburgh
	Stane, William, Esq.	Kenton
B106 P	Staunton, Thomas, Esq., MP	Pykenham's House, Ipswich, Holbrook and Harkstead
	Stebbing, The Revd Mr Titus, AM	Tattingstone, R
	Steggall, The Revd Mr William, AM	Wyverstone, R
	Stewart, Sir Simeon, 3rd Bart	Lakenheath, Hawkedon
B107	Stisted, Thomas, Esq.	Ipswich
B109	Strudwick, Edmund, Esq.	Ipswich
	Suckling, William, Esq.	Barsham
B110	Sulyard, Edward, Esq.	Haughley or Wetherden
B111	Syer, The Revd Mr Dey, AM	Waldingfield Parva,V. Badingham, R
B112	Symonds, John, Esq.	Ixworth
	Symonds, Mrs	Whelnetham Parva
B113	Tanner, The Revd Dr Thomas	Hadleigh, V and Dean of Bocking
	Tash, Colonel	Haverhill
B114	Thirkle, Michael, Esq.	Ipswich
B117	Thomas, George, Esq.	Kesgrave, Ramsholt, Brockley and Ipswich
	Thompson, John, Gent.	Southwold
	Thorrowgood, Sir Thomas, Kt	Kersey, Sampsons Hall
	Thruston, John, MD (Mott before 1744)	Market Weston

Thurston, Thomas, Esq.	Little Wenham Hall
P Tollemache, Lionel, 4th earl of Dysart	Helmingham, Stutton
Townshend, George, 4th viscount Townshend	Denham
Trigg, The Revd Mr Thomas, AM	Leiston, R
Trotman, William, Esq.	Ipswich
Turner, Mr Benjamin	Horsecroft, Horningsheath
B118 Tyrell, Edmund, Esq.	Gipping Hall and Redisham
Tyrell, Edmund, Esq.	Stowmarket
Tyrell, Sir John, Bart	Elveden
Tyrell, Thomas Bokenham, Esq.	Stowmarket
B120 Uvedale, Samuel, Esq.	Barking
Uvedale, The Revd Dr Samuel, LLD	Barking and Combs, R
Van Heythuysen, G., Esq.	Oulton
B18 P Vanneck, Sir Joshua, 1st Bart	Heveningham, Huntingfield and Aldham
Venn, Dr Edward	Ipswich
Ventris, The Revd Mr Edward, AM	Burgate, R, buried St Nicholas Ipswich 1764
B10 P Vernon, Francis, baron Orwell of Newry	Orwell Park, Nacton and Levington
Vernon, Henry, Esq.	Great Thurlow Hall
B119 Vesey, The late B.W., Gent.	Whatfield
P Ward, Knox, Esq.	Woolverstone
Wareyn, John, Esq.	Kenton
Waring, Thomas, Esq.	Groton Hall
B122 Warner, Mrs	Waldingfield Parva
Warner, The late Nathaniel, Esq.	Badmondesfield Hall, Wickhambrook
Warren, The Revd Mr Thomas, AB	Chattisham, V
Watson, Jonathan (or William), Esq.	Ringshall Hall
Watts, ——, Esq.	Walpole
Wayth, Daniel, Esq.	Glemham Magna
Wayth, Mr Daniel	Flowton
B3 Wentworth, William, 4th earl of Strafford	Friston and Aldeburgh
Wenyeve, Edward, Esq.	Brettenham
Whimper, Mr Thomas	Glevering Hall
Whitaker, The Revd Mr Thomas, AM	Mendham, V
P White, Robert, Esq.	Tattingstone Place
Whitmore, Edward, Esq.	Bury St Edmunds
Whittington, The Revd Mr John	Orford, Sudbourne and Theberton, R
Wilkinson, The Revd Mr	Brome
Willis, John or Henry, Esq.	Redlingfield
Wilson, Thomas, Esq.	Botesdale
B11 Wodehouse, Sir Armine, 5th Bart	Chilton
Wollaston, The Revd Mr Frederick, LLB	Bury St Edmunds, Lecturer St James
B123 P Wollaston, William, Esq.	Finborough
Wright, George, Esq.	Butley Priory
B124 Wright, Thomas, Esq.	Santon Downham
B8 Yonge, The Rt Revd Philip, Lord Bishop of Norwich	
B2 P Zuylestein, William Henry Nassau de, 4th earl of Rochford	Easton

Appendix C

John Kirby's Geometrical Accuracy

A year into his survey of the county, in the announcement of August 1733 (see page xv), Kirby was warning his subscribers not to expect absolute accuracy: 'We dare not say that it is mathematically true (for if so it must not vary the thousandth part of an inch).' However, he was still claiming a great deal for his methods, as an extract from his 287-word sentence shows. We can examine his claims in detail for the triangle of churches at which he began:

> The beginning of the said survey was on Tunstall-heath, by taking (on a plain parcel of land) a measured distance of fifty chains, or five furlongs, by help of which the true distance was found between Tunstall church and Wantisden church; and likewise between the said churches and that of Wickham-market, having thus completed a triangle by gaining all its sides and angles, (which upon proof was true, according to the rules of geometry, having its three angles equal to 180 degrees), from thence the calculations have been carried on hitherto (and it may be said without boasting) with great exactness, for as it is undeniably true, that, if two or three lines concur in one point, the work cannot be erroneous, . . .

Kirby is here guilty of a truism: he would be hard put to it to draw a triangle whose three angles did *not* add up to two right angles. It is a simple matter to trace the Tunstall (T), Wantisden (W), Wickham Market (M) triangle from a modern OS map, and to compare its sides and angles with the same triangle on the 1736 map. The angles can be measured with a protractor, but one must accept Kirby's engraved scale of miles to estimate his distances. Fig. 4 shows what Kirby's triangle looks like.

Table 1. Distances and bearings in Kirby's first triangle of churches

	Distances in metres			Angles in degrees		
	TW	WM	MT	<TWM	<WMT	<MTW
OS	1900	6500	6050	69	17	94
Kirby	1900	6920	6310	66	17	97
% error	0	6.5	4.2			

Kirby seems to have been able to lay out his measuring chain along the whole length of the straight line joining Tunstall and Wantisden churches to obtain an accurate distance. With just one distance measured correctly, he could in theory have progressed round the whole county provided that his bearings were reliable. Bearings from the tops of church towers should have been straightforward using a theodolite, and he did obtain the correct 17-degree angle between the two distant churches from Wickham. However, the 3-degree error in the other two angles of that triangle led to errors in its other two sides. Kirby's triangle drawn on the OS map moves Wickham church some 300 metres to the north of its true position. To test his claim (pages

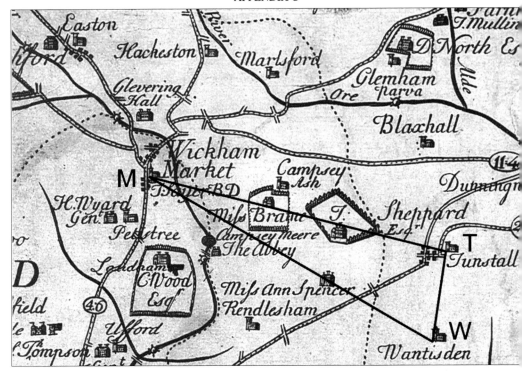

Fig. 4. Detail of the 1736 map showing the Tunstall, Wantisden, Wickham Market triangle where Kirby began his survey. (Full size)

17–18) that fifty churches were visible from Wickham tower, and in the hope that he took particularly careful bearings from it, a 'star' of bearing lines to other churches on his map was laid over the modern map (using the correct Wantisden and Tunstall bearings to anchor it). The results are mixed; no other church is on exactly the right bearing, and Chillesford, for example, which should lie outside the W/T angle, lies inside.

Was it to help Kirby that Tom Martin listed the churches visible from his house and church at Palgrave? The heading is: 'From Palgrave Steple 3 April 1735 *we saw*', which may imply that Kirby was with him. He claimed to see a total of forty churches and Brome Hall.[1] From the roof of his Palgrave house he made a rough plot of thirty-three churches and Brome Hall, which 'may be seen'. There is a small drawing of his house near the middle.

Kirby's advertisement of December 1733 gave more hostages to fortune in supplying the 'true horizontal distances of the several towns under-named, from the Market Cross of the town of Ipswich' because measurements made on modern maps show them all to be too long. If the percentage errors were consistent it might indicate that Kirby was using a different mile to the modern standard, for until the Act for the Uniformity of Measures in 1824 several different measures were current. However, Kirby's figures, given in the second column of Table 2 and converted from furlongs to

---

[1] BL, Add.MS 7102, fol. 28 has the drawing and the list.

decimals, show that the errors fluctuate wildly. It will be wise therefore to look for other advantages than geometrical accuracy in Kirby's maps.

Table 2. Distance from Ipswich of fourteen towns in Suffolk and Norfolk

Distances in miles from Ipswich to:	OS	Kirby	% error
Diss	17.6	22.5	28
Eye	15.4	18.3	19
Debenham	10.75	11.9	11
Harleston	22.1	24.75	12
Yarmouth	43.9	45.7	4
Halesworth	22.1	24.75	12
Framlingham	13.1	14.0	7
Lowestoft	38.25	38.4	0.4
Southwold	27.25	29.0	6
Wickham-market	10.4	11.0	6
Woodbridge	7.0	7.25	4
Aldeburgh	18.8	20.0	6
Orford	15.5	16.4	6
Harwich	9.4	10.0	6

If any further demonstration is needed, the road leading from Sudbourne to Orford Quay on the modern OS map runs approximately south-east. On Kirby's map the roads in the centre of the town are neatly aligned north–south and east–west. Furthermore, Butley church is shown north-north-east of the priory whereas it is to the north-north-west, continuing the 45-degree misalignment in the area (see Fig. 5).

Appendix D

Selected Features on the Large-Scale Maps

Windmills and water mills

Since the 1766 map is little more than a tracing of the 1736 map onto new copper plates, differences between them may be intentional or inadvertent, and it is rarely possible to be certain which. This is most easily demonstrated by listing the wind- and water mills which are shown (see Table 3).

Table 3. Windmills and watermills shown on the maps of 1736 and 1786

Parish Map:	windmills 1736	windmills 1766	water mills 1736	water mills 1766
Aldeburgh	1	1		
Alderton	1	1		
Aldham			1	1
Barnhams	1	1	1	1
Barton Mills			1	1
Battisford	1	1	1	1
Bealings Magna			1	1
Bealings Parva			1	1
Beccles	1	1		
Benhall	1	1	1	1
Blakenham Magna			1	1
Blakenham Parva			1	1
Blythford			1	
Boxford			1	1
Bradley Parva	1	1		
Bradwell	1	1		
Bramford			1	1
Brampton	1	1		
Brandon	1	1		
Brent Eleigh			1	1
Bungay	1	1		
Bures			1	1
Bury St Edmunds			1	1
Campsey Ash			1	1
Capel St Andrew			1	1
Cavendish			1	1
Chelsworth			1	1
Chillesford	1	1	1	1
Clare	1	1	1	1
Cornard Magna			1	1
Cornard Parva			1	1
Creeting St Peter			2	2

Parish Map:	windmills 1736	windmills 1766	water mills 1736	water mills 1766
Darmsden			1	1
Darsham	1	1		
Debenham	1	1	1	1
Diss (Norfolk)	2	2		
Easton			1	1
Flempton			1	1
Flixton St Mary			1	1
Framlingham	2	2		
Glemham Parva			1	1
Hacheston			1	1
Hadleigh			1	1
Halesworth	1	1		
Harwich (Essex)	1			
Haughley				
Holbrook			1	1
Holton St Mary			1	1
Holton St Peter	1	1		
Homersfield				1
Hoxne	1	1	1	
Hulver Street	1	1		
Icklingham			1	1
Ipswich	4	4	2	2
Ixworth			2	2
Lackford			1	1
Layham			1	1
Laxfield	1	1		
Letheringham			1	1
Long Melford	1		1	1
Lowestoft	2	2		
Melton			1	1
Mendham			1	1
Monks Eleigh			1	1
Nayland			3	3
Needham Market			2	2
Newbourne			2	2
Normanston	1	1		
Oakley	1	1		
Orford	1	1		
Pakenham				
Ringshall	1	1		
Sapiston	1	1	1	1
Semer			2	2
Shottisham			1	1
Sibton	1	1		
South Elmham St George			1	1
Southwold	1	1		
Sproughton			1	1
Stoke by Nayland				1

Parish	Map:	windmills 1736	windmills 1766	water mills 1736	water mills 1766
Stowmarket					2
Sudbury					2
Syleham				1	1
Tattingstone				1	1
Thelnetham					1
Thetford				2	2
Thornham Magna		1	1		
Thurston		1	1		
Trimleys				1	
Ufford				1	1
Uggeshall		1	1		
Walpole		1	1		
Wangford St Denis		1	1		
Westleton		1	1		
West Stow				2	2
Weybread		1	1		
Wissington				1	1
Wixoe				2	2
Woodbridge		2			
Woolpit		3	2		
Wrentham		1	1		
Yarmouth (Norfolk)		5	5		
Totals		57	52	72	76

Had five windmills been demolished in thirty years, two at Woodbridge and one each at Long Melford, Woolpit and Harwich? It seems unlikely. Had four watermills been built? It is easy to point to omissions of both types. Mill experts list early mills ignored by Kirby and his revisors.[1] However, some are mentioned in the *Traveller* which do not feature on the map. For example, at page 61 'turn on the right over Combs Ford. Pass between Stow Windmills, and at 3m, 4½f, is Stowmarket Cross.' The Stow mills were in fact first recorded 'south of the town' on a map of 1675. At Coldfair-Green (page 30) Kirby records 'a Windmill a little on the right' between Leiston and Snape, but fails to mark it on the map. As records here only go back to 1836, Kirby confirms that it stood here a century earlier. Seven other windmills not noticed by Kirby pre-date his survey. They were surely in existence, but were mostly on roads he did not take on his journeys. They are, or were, at Barrow (on a map of 1730), Combs (a map of 1736), Drinkstone (on a map of 1689 and still standing), Leiston (a monastic mill in the town pre-1603 and only demolished in 1870), two windmills at Stradbroke (map of 1688, demolished 1941; and map of 1704, demolished 1940, respectively) and one at Shotley. Kirby's own overshot mill at Erwarton is totally ignored by his survey.

To show that Kirby's recording and mapping of windmills was incomplete and unreliable one need only consider the mills of Woodbridge. He showed two on the 1736 map, but they were not transferred to the 1766 edition. Hodskinson (1789) marked three, but there were four on Mill Hills at some time, three pre-1819, one still there in 1866, and three more on Theatre Street, Drybridge Hill and Victoria road in 1825, one of them still there in 1930, and two remain, Trickers and Butrams which are both earlier than 1820.

---

[1] Brian Flint, *Suffolk Windmills*, Woodbridge 1979.

Other Features

Castles

Kirby's castles are very varied in their true or probable nature: they are here arranged in approximate date order:

Burgh: Roman fort
Clare: Norman motte and bailey with remains of a masonry shell-keep.
Haughley: Norman motte and bailey; footings suggest that it had a stone keep.
Framlingham: stone castle, twelfth century.
Orford: stone castle, twelfth century.
Walton 'Stone': presumably Roman fort reused in twelfth century as a Bigod castle.
Lidgate: Earthwork probably twelfth–thirteenth century; isolated stone wall in churchyard is probably part of a wall flanking the approach to the to the castle gate.
Mettingham: stone castle, fourteenth century.
Wingfield: stone castle, fourteenth century.
Landguard Fort: Henrician and later fort (what survives is 1744 and later).
Bredfield: just a moated site, apparently locally known as 'Oliver's Ditches' and now ploughed flat.
Ipswich: the castle at Ipswich is a complete enigma as to site and type, but Kirby (1735 *Traveller*, pp. 5–6) gives his own theories.

Monasteries, working from north to south

Burgh (in both editions of the *Traveller*).
Eriswell (ruins are of a parish church).
Flixton St Mary.
Eye (1736 only).
Hoxne (1736 only; 1735 *Traveller*, p. 137 has useful discussion).
Wangford.
Mendham.
Blythburgh (1766 only).
Snape.
Leiston (and earlier site).
Campsey Ash (and mere).
Butley.
Walton (1736 only).
Kersey.
Edwardstone.

Ferries between

Yarmouth and Gorleston.
Woodbridge and Sutton (1766 map only).
Bawdsey and Felixstowe.
Landguard and Harwich.

Rivers named

Waveny (*sic*); Alde, Ore, Stour, Brett, Ouse, Lark, Mildenhall Drain.

Estuaries named

Woodbridge Haven, Orwell Haven, Stour Haven, Minsmere Haven.

Bridges[2]

On the maps
Mutford bridge crossing between Oulton Broad and Lake Lothing.
Latimer Bridge over the Hundred River between Kessingland and Benacre.
Potters Bridge inland from Easton Broad.
Woolsey (*sic*) bridge over a tributary of the Blyth west of Southwold.
East Bridge over the Minsmere River at Theberton.
Snape Bridge over River Alde/Ore at Snape.
Wilford Bridge over the Deben at Melton.
Bourn (*sic*) Bridge over Belstead Brook south of Ipswich.
Two Cattawade Bridges over the Stour between Brantham and Manningtree.

Bridges mentioned in Traveller *but not on Maps*

At Martlesham a bridge over the Finn.
At Wickham a bridge over the Deben.
Dymers bridge over the Ore.
Langham bridge over the Alde.
Haddiscoe Dam over the Waveney.
At Yarmouth a bridge at the town end of Breydon Water.
At Southwold a bridge over Buss Creek.
At Claydon a bridge over the Gipping.
At Scole a bridge over the Waveney.
At Glevering a bridge over the Deben.
Durrance bridge on road from Framlingham to Badingham.
Froizly bridge at Dennington.
At Bramford a bridge over the Gipping.
Handford bridge over the Gipping.
Stratford bridge over the Stour.
Stoke bridge over the Orwell.

Lights at Lowestoft and Orford Ness.

Decoys, with what remains of them today

Fritton: Decoy woods and lake in Fritton Country Park.
Flixton: Decoy farm and lake just south of the prison.
Friston: see below, p. 241.
Snape: Decoy farm and Decoy wood with a pond just north of Sailors Path.
Iken: The pond in an almost square wood half a mile south-east of the church was the decoy.
Chillesford: Decoy pond and wood south of the village.
Foxhall: Decoy pond still there on Purdis Heath golf course.

---

[2] Only the first below goes unmarked on 1766 map.

Parks around houses

Of the emparked houses on Saxton's *Suffolciae* map of 1575, only eight remain on Kirby's 1736 map: Henham, Heveningham, Huntingfield, Letheringham, Redgrave, Hintlesham, Tendryng and Ickworth.

Kirby, however, shows twenty-seven new parks at Bacton, Badley, Bealings, Benhall, Brettenham, Brightwell, Brockford, Brome (the park Saxton shows at Denham may have been this one), Christchurch (Ipswich), Combs, Culford, Dalham, Euston, Flixton, Haughley, Hawstead, Helmingham, Hengrave, Hoxne, Livermere parva, Melford Hall, Redisham, Rushbrooke, Somerleyton, Saxham parva, Thurlow parva and Woolverstone.

The twenty parks 'lost' since Saxton were Westwood, one to the south-west of Yoxford, Framlingham, Wingfield, Monk Soham, Debenham, Thwaite, Denham (see Brome above), Burgate, Westhorpe, Nettlestead, Smallbridge, Cavendish, Chilton, three near Lavenham and three between Stradishall and Hundon.

Racecourses

The courses at Ipswich and Snape, marked on the map at the bottom of the avenue of trees from Friston, are a reminder of the universal popularity of the sport of kings. Snape Race-Ground is omitted by Hodskinson. Had it fallen into disuse by 1783? Beccles racecourse, shown on Emerton's 1757 survey of Beccles Fen, is not marked on any Kirby map.

Other archaeological features

The Devil's Dyke.
The Seven Hills east of Ipswich are on the boundary of three parishes: Bucklesham, Foxhall, Nacton. Most are in Nacton and there are in fact fourteen mounds.
The Seven Hills north of Bury are on the boundary between Ingham and Little Livermere. Three mounds survive of more than seven there in Kirby's time, but seven were larger than the rest.
These seem to be Bronze Age round barrows or tumuli.[3]

---

[3] See A. J. Lawson, E. A. Martin and D. Priddy, 'The Barrows of East Anglia', *East Anglian Archaeology* 12, 1981, 8, 14, 80, 82, 84.

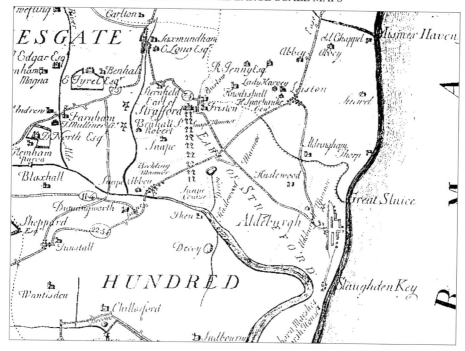

Fig. 5. Detail of the 1736 map from the Minsmere River to Slaughden Quay. (50% linear)

Notes on selected areas

Differences on the maps of 1736 and 1766 are probably accidental, but much that they show has changed in the last 250 years.

1. *The Lower Alde and Ore valley* (see Fig. 5)

This area is bounded on the north by the Minsmere River, its haven marked by Kirby. Further south he does not name the Hundred River or indicate Thorpeness Mere, which on Hodskinson extends from Thorpeness through the marshes as far south as the rising ground at Aldeburgh. Kirby marks the mouth of the Hundred River as Great Sluice where the Mere then flowed into the sea near the present Sluice Cottage. Kirby's eastern seaward margin allows for streets to the east of the Aldeburgh Moot Hall and a wider isthmus at Slaughden Quay on the Alde Estuary. Kirby's tracks crossing sandy heathland are now cut by new roads from Friday Street to Blackheath Corner (A1094) and the new road from Sternfield past Snape church to Snape Bridge. The original road from Snape to Leiston followed the line of Sandy Lane past the Golden Key Inn, and continues as a grassy track across fields to Blackheath Corner. Here the B1069 Snape road follows the line of Kirby's road to Leiston and the A1094 continues along Kirby's line to Aldeburgh. Kirby's road through Friston to Saxmundham survives as the B1121.

The area around Friston is confused on the 1736 map; the relative clarity on the 1766 map mainly reflects distinct omissions. A prime feature of the 1736 map is the avenue of trees running south from Friston Hall to 'Snape Course'. Though omitted (perhaps for clarity) on the 1766 map, it is marked by Hodskinson and survives today as a lime avenue. Kirby records Snape Race-Ground as he passes, 'leaving Friston decoy a little on the left, at 3m 3¼ furlongs, a view to Friston Hall. . . .At 4m. . . over Snape Race Ground . . .' He ignores the avenue which he had mapped, but the decoy, the remnants of whose pond may still be there in Decoy Wood next to Decoy Farm just north of the Sailors Path, is both mentioned and marked. Hodskinson has no race-course and there is no sign of it on modern maps. There is today, however, a wide flat field of rough grass south of the Sailors Path and north of New England Farm which is suitably positioned on heathland above the flood plain of the Alde. The positions of Snape Mannor (*sic*), Haslewood Mannor, Beckling Mannor, and Aldeburgh Mannor are all squeezed in on the 1736 map, but are pruned to just 'Snape' and 'Haslewood' by 1766. Only on the 1736 map does The earl of Strafford's name in capital letters stretches across the countryside from Friston to Aldeburgh. On the maps of 1766 and 1783 it appears reduced in size at Friston Hall. All that remains today of the Benedic-tine monastery described by Kirby in the *Traveller* is the fine Abbey Farm. Nearer Friston than Benhall on both Kirby maps is the surprising 'Benhall Sr Robert'. White's 1844 Directory has 'an estate [so named] forms a small manor', which Copinger[4] calls Benhall Sr Roberts, held in 1292 by Robert de Benhall, clerk, and by several generations of Benhalls until Sir Robert de Benhall died seized of it *c*.1400.

2. *Lowestoft and Lake Lothing*

Kirby records in the 1735 *Traveller* that he left Lowestoft by 'passing out at the South-end of the Town, between the Shore and lake Lothing'. In doing this he was crossing the sea bank which blocked the original outlet of the Waveney to the sea. By 1833 this channel had been reopened and the Island of Lothingland had been re-created by Act of Parliament. The Norwich and Lowestoft Navigation Channel was cut through the sea bank to create a direct route to the sea for vessels using the Yare and Waveney. Present-day travellers still cross the deep lock and cast-iron swing bridge as they leave Lowestoft.

---

[4] *Manors*, V, 106.

Appendix E

Maritime Craft Decorating the Maps

Hugh Moffat's tentative descriptions are given working from north to south on each map.

The 1736 one-inch map

Off Corton: probably a brig, a two-masted square-rigged vessel, widely used in the naval and merchant services.
Off Covehithe and Sizewell: probably warships with long commissioning pennants at the mainmast head. The one off Sizewell is a three-decker (80+ guns) with probably a vice-admiral's flag at her foremast head.
Off Slaughden: a ship-rigged merchantman (square-rigged on three masts). She could be a collier, or almost anything capable of ocean voyages.
Lower corner: certainly warships. The nearest flies a vice-admiral's flag at the foremast. The single-masted vessel may be an Admiralty yacht, as royal yachts were usually ketch-rigged with two masts by this date – unless the picture is out-of-date.

The 1737 half-inch map

Off Yarmouth: perhaps a small fishing boat working off the beach.
Off Corton: probably a small trading sloop.
Off Benacre: the men here may be working with crabpots, or perhaps tubs of smuggled liquor.
Off Southwold: perhaps a small fishing boat working off the beach.
Off Theberton: perhaps a ship's boat.
Off Aldeburgh: a merchant ship, perhaps a collier or Baltic trader. A West Indiaman would mount a few guns.
Lower corner: a warship of about 20–24 guns.

The 1764 quarter-inch map

Off Corton: perhaps a small trading sloop.
Lower down: all four vessels appear to be engaged in fishing (one for crabs and lobsters).

The 1766 one-inch map

Off Yarmouth: a warship.
Off Corton: a trading sloop.
Off Lowestoft: a small merchantman, but the foremast was usually the shorter of the two.
Off Covehithe: a warship.
Off Southwold: a warship, and, smaller, a yacht.
    Various small craft as on the earlier maps.
Off Orford: a merchantman

Appendix F

Estate Maps and Surveys by Kirby, Bacon and Emerton[1]

Each list for these surveyors is arranged in chronological order. Since most surveys are titled 'A plan of an estate lying in [parish] belonging to [owner], in the year A.D. [date]', just the date, parish and owner are here given before the reference. Most are on vellum; paper plans are so indicated.

John Kirby

Kirby's twenty-five known estate maps are generally less decorative than the work of earlier surveyors, even of his contemporary William Brasier.[2] One notable exception is the plan he made of Christchurch, Ipswich, for Thomas Fonnereau in 1735, which has a south elevation of the house, achievement of arms and an ungainly putto placing his dividers on a scale of perches. Another is the only known commission which took him west of Mendlesham. This is his 1737 plan of Beaumonts Hall Farm in Pakenham, Stowlangtoft and Norton. The client was the recently ordained Benjamin Lany, a junior cousin of the namesake who was twice master of Pembroke Hall and holder, successively, of three East Anglian bishoprics. This map's embellishments are charmingly naïve, particularly the antics of the 'LASCIVI PUERI'[3] surveying merrily on a plinth which is also a scale (Fig. 6). There is a similar scene on the 1736 map of Suffolk. However, since the miniscule ships on his plan of Hulver Marshes in Sudbourne are so unimpressive, those on his county maps must surely be the work of far finer draughtsmen, perhaps the engravers concerned.

1725: Melton, Daniel Vickers, Gent. (SROI HD80/1/1, fol. 27)
1726: Rumburgh and South Elmham St James, John Clayton, Gent. (SROL 742/H1/9)
1726: Mendlesham, Wetheringsett
1727: Bawdsey, Campsea Ash, Mendham
Book of 7 plats of several estates of John Sheppard, Esq. of Campsey Ash (SROI HA 30:50/22/26.1) [*Paper book of plans*]
1728: Great Bealings, John Pitt, Esq. (SROI HD 417/2)
1729: Rumburgh, Mr Manning (SROI HB 24/2)
1729: Great Bealings glebes (SROI HD 417/2)
1731: Friston and Knodishall, Benjamin Lea of the City of London, Gent. (SROI HA 15/B11/1)

[*From 1732 until 1734 or 1735 Kirby was surveying the county*]

1734: Martlesham, Mr William Leggat (SROI HA 119:562 [Box 8, bundle 4])

---

[1] It is well to remember that Kirby's association with Bacon ended in autumn 1733 and at the same time Emerton, at the outset of his career, joined Kirby as agent in south Norfolk, but only to recruit subscribers for the map.
[2] Brasier's survey of several Stour valley parishes in 1731 is SROI: FB 191/A8/1.
[3] Horace, *Satires*, 1, 3, 133.

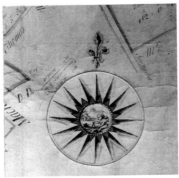

Fig. 6. Three details from John Kirby's plan of Beaumonts Hall Farm in 1737: the scale of perches with surveying putti, compass rose enclosing another of the 'lascivi pueri' and the armorial achievement of Lany.

1735: Bredfield, Samuel Thompson, Esq. (SROI HD 80/1/1, fol. 29)

1735: Christchurch Estate [*in Ipswich*], Thomas Fonnereau, Esq. (Ipswich Museums [*original framed and hanging in the Mansion*])

1736: Sudbourne, certain marsh lands. . . Hulver Marshes, Edward Hawker, Esq. (SROI HB10: 427/831) [*with small and nondescript drawings of ships moored at Slaughden Quay and others sailing in the Ore*]

1737: Beaumonts Hall Farm in Pakenham, Stowlangtoft and Norton, the Revd Mr Benjamin Lany (CUL Map Room MS Plans FR.x.1.)

1738: Loudham Hall in Pettistree, Charles Wood Esq. (SROI HB10: 50/20/41.1 (2)) [*includes a naïve south-east elevation of the Hall*]

1738: South Elmham St James, a certain common and ancient King's highway. . . from St James to Rumburgh. . . past the house late Stephen Elmy's to. . . Beccles. (SROL 192/1)

1740–41: Flixtow (*sic*), Walton, Trimley, the Lordships of Sir John Barker Bart. [*The original is lost, but* SROI HA 119/3/2/1/1/1 *is Isaac Johnson's version of the entire Orwell Park Estate made for George Nassau Esq. in 1784, and* SROI HD 1899/1 *is a copy made in 1872 by R.F.*] JK's written survey is SROI HB8/1/201

1741: Trimley St Martin and St Mary, parish perambulation (SROI HB 9:517/D5)

1741: North Glemham, Benhall and Sweffling, Mr Edmund Newson (SROI HA 43: T495/10)

1741: Glemham and Marlesford, William Tovell (NRO DS 413)

Not dated: Rendlesham, Eyke, Tunstall and Wantisden, various owners (SROI HD 427/1) [*Paper book of 5 plans*]

The Naunton Hall Farm survey in this last collection is a better than average example of Kirby's work (Fig. 7), showing as it does the house and outbuildings in some detail, and the avenue of trees then leading to the old road from Wilford bridge to Snape bridge. The short stretch of road from the old school to the gothic lodge perpetuates the line of the avenue. The [Campsey] Ash Road which passes near to the house is not marked, nor the church which lies south of the Farm and east of the same road. Few of the field boundaries and none of Kirby's names persist.

Nathaniel Bacon junior, fl.1733–50

There survive by this man four plain but well designed and lettered surveys of estates to the north of Ipswich. It was not surprising, therefore, to discover that he came from Tuddenham St Martin where Nathaniel Bacon senior was a yeoman farmer. When father died, he 'was carried to his grave by his own direction by his six sons & burried [*in Tuddenham churchyard*] November 30th 1743'.[4] Nathaniel junior was probably the eldest, and as his father was twice married (in 1684 and 1687), his mother Mary may have been a Keble or a Catchpool. In either case he was probably somewhat older than John Kirby. Still a bachelor and of Ipswich when in 1712 he married the widow Sarah Aylmore, also of Ipswich, the surveyor Nathaniel was buried at Tuddenham in 1750. It is quite likely that Bacon and Kirby divided the work of individual surveys between them, but Kirby realised that his whole-county survey could not be a co-operative venture. Bacon's 1733 plan of the Leathes estate at Walton is his most accomplished. That of 1736 for Mileson Edgar, Esq., at Tuddenham has a most

---

[4] Charles Beaumont, rector, wrote this unusual entry in the burial register. Bacon senior's will (SROI IC/AA1/172/68) mentions only his widow Mary and one of the sons, Phillip, named executor. Phillip was presumably taking over the farm.

Fig. 7. John Kirby's undated manuscript survey of Naunton Hall Farm, Rendlesham. (57% linear)

unusual feature. The plan, mounted on rollers, has worn decorative borders about two inches wide pasted around its edges with engraved scenes of surveyors at work and groups of their instruments (Fig. 8).

1733: Walton, Carteret Leathes, Esq. (SROI HA 403: T1039/13)
1733: Eccles town and manor, William Green Esq. (NRO MS 4527)
1736: Witnesham glebe lands, The Revd Mr Charles Beaumont, Rector (SROI HD 245/2) [*a nineteenth or early twentieth century copy*]
1736: Claydon, The Revd Mr George Drury, Rector (SROI HB 8/5/81) [*Two versions: one on paper*]
1736: Tuddenham St Martin, Mileson Edgar, Esq. (SROI HD 245/1)
1737: Culpho, Robert Edgar, Gent. (SROI HD 12:2750)

Fig. 8. Two details from printed borders of Nathaniel Bacon's survey of Mileson Edgar's estate in Tuddenham St Martin. The surveyor is using a spirit level with sights, which he would first level using the oversize thumbscrew. The seated putto, beside a surveyor's chain of 100 links totalling 66 feet, holds a simple theodolite without optics, which would always be used on a stand.

1744: Bond's, Freston, The Revd Mr Charles Beaumont, Rector of Witnesham (SROI HA 93/12/2)

1749: Grundisburgh, John Hurt, Gent. (HB10: 427/832)

Francis Emerton, fl.1733–61

The lands mapped by 'that curious Surveyor Francis Emerton at Gillingham', near Beccles, lie along the Waveney valley, and just one as far south as Huntingfield and Cratfield. Bacon and Kirby, whose 'curious' probably meant 'inquisitive', could have learnt from him. Emerton's careful work appears more accurate than theirs. A tiny perspective view of every building is drawn in ink and watercolour and his tables have dignified classical frames. The decoration and delicate colouring he adds to dividers and scales and to compass roses is delightful. If some of his lettering and his tables are overlarge, he nevertheless achieved legibility. As Kirby's agent in south-east Norfolk he was only involved in recruiting subscribers for the Suffolk map. Late in life Emerton moved to Flixton near Bungay, whence in January 1761 he wrote to Mr Moor, master of the Free School at Beccles: 'As I was lame in both my legs and one ancle at Xtmass and could not be at that time with you at Beccles. . . I was still very unfitt for so long a walk. . .'

1733: North Cove, Richard Manthorp (SROL 332/6/1)
    [This map has a triangular 'pediment' at the top containing the achievement of the Bakers Company to which Manthorp presumably belonged.]
1741: Haddiscoe and Thorpe next Haddiscoe, Elizabeth Castell (NRO MC 1785/1, 832 × 8)
1749: Ormesby 1749, copied 1833 (NRO LW 1560)
1752: South Elmham and Homersfield, John Boatwright, Gent. (SROL 741/HA 12/D4/10)
1753: Norton Subcourse Glebe Land (NRO BOL 3/78, 741 × 3)
1755: Needham, Robert Williams (NRO MEA3/639, 659 × 5) [*with view of house*]
1757: Beccles Fen (SROL Collection 1227, accession 1263)
    [A large and detailed survey including the Race Ground.]
1758: Huntingfield and Cratfield, Richard Aldous Clarke, Gent. (SROI HD 216/1)
1759: South Elmham St Margaret, James Denny (SROL 741/HA 12/D4/11)
1760: Bungay, Richard Nelson, Gent. (SROL 742/H1/2)
1760: Bungay Trinity, Thomas Sheriffe, Gent. (SROL 884/1)
Not dated: Ditchingham and Earsham, Zachariah Mayhew, Gent. (SROL 742/H1/24)

Index of Persons in the Introduction
and Appendices C to F

Index of Places in the Introduction
and Appendices

Parishes are in Suffolk unless otherwise indicated and modern spelling is adopted throughout.